SIR
SANDFORD FLEMING

~ *His Early Diaries, 1845–1853* ~

Sandford Fleming in 1845, age eighteen.

SIR
SANDFORD FLEMING

~ His Early Diaries, 1845–1853 ~

EDITED BY JEAN MURRAY COLE

NATURAL HERITAGE BOOKS
A MEMBER OF THE DUNDURN GROUP
TORONTO

Project Editor: Allison Hirst
Editor: Jane Gibson
Designer: Erin Mallory
Printed and bound in Canada by Friesens

Library and Archives Canada Cataloguing in Publication

Cole, Jean Murray, 1927-
  Sir Sandford Fleming : his early diaries, 1845-1853 / by Jean Murray Cole.

Includes bibliographical references and index.
ISBN 978-1-55488-450-6

  1. Fleming, Sandford, Sir, 1827-1915. 2. Fleming, Sandford, Sir, 1827-1915--
Diaries. 3. Railroad engineers--Canada--Biography. 4. Surveyors--Canada--
Biography. I. Title.

HE2808.2.F54C65 2009   625.10092   C2009-902459-4

1 2 3 4 5   13 12 11 10 09

We acknowledge the support of the **Canada Council for the Arts** and the **Ontario Arts Council** for our publishing program. We also acknowledge the financial support of the **Government of Canada** through the **Book Publishing Industry Development Program** and **The Association for the Export of Canadian Books**, and the **Government of Ontario** through the **Ontario Book Publishers Tax Credit** program, and the **Ontario Media Development Corporation**.

Care has been taken to trace the ownership of copyright material used in this book. The author and the publisher welcome any information enabling them to rectify any references or credits in subsequent editions.

J. Kirk Howard, President

www.dundurn.com
Published by Natural Heritage Books
A Member of The Dundurn Group

Dundurn Press	Gazelle Book Services Limited	Dundurn Press
3 Church Street, Suite 500	White Cross Mills	2250 Military Road
Toronto, Ontario, Canada	High Town, Lancaster, England	Tonawanda, NY
M5E 1M2	LA1 4XS	U.S.A. 14150

I have often thought how grateful I am for my birth into this marvellous world, and how anxious I have always been to justify it. I have dreamed my little dreams, I have planned my little plans, and begrudged no effort to bring about what I regarded as desirable results. I have always felt that the humblest among us has it in his power to do something for his country by doing his duty, and that there is no better inheritance to leave to his children than the knowledge that he has done the utmost of his ability.

It has been my great good fortune to have had my lot cast in this goodly land, and to have been associated with its educational and material prosperity. Nobody can deprive me of the satisfaction I feel in having had the opportunity and the will to strive for the advancement of Canada and the good of the Empire. I am profoundly thankful for the length of days, for active happy years, for friendships formed, and especially for the memory of those dear souls who have enriched my own life while they remained on this side.

> — Sandford Fleming (1827–1915), written late in his life. Quoted in *Sandford Fleming: Empire Builder* by L.J. Burpee.

CONTENTS

FOREWORD
by Michael Peterman

It is with great pleasure that I write this Foreword to *Sir Sandford Fleming: The Early Diaries*. As the Chair of the Publications Committee of the Peterborough Historical Society for the past fifteen years, I have shared with my fellow committee members a commitment to see this project shaped and realized. It began as an idea in the mid-1990s, spurred on by Jean Murray Cole, who had studied Fleming's life and admired his diaries in their home at Library and Archives Canada. We felt then that an annotated and accurate transcript of young Sandford's early diaries would make a useful and informative addition to the record of life in pre-Confederation Canada. It would provide a view of the colony through the eyes of a young and ambitious Scottish immigrant as he struggled to make a place for himself in a new land, to find satisfying work for his talents, and to develop his professional interests. Laconic and factual as the diary entries often are, they take us into the texture of Fleming's brave new world and alert us to the kind of community he had to deal with as he sought to make a career and place for himself. To him, Canada was "a marvellous world" and a "goodly land."

Sir Sandford Fleming has long been a major figure in the history of Peterborough, Ontario. He first came to Canada West as an eighteen-year-old and resided for his first two years with his father's cousin, Dr. John Hutchison and his wife Martha, in the stone house on Brock Street that has since become a living history museum. The house was built for Dr. Hutchison in the mid-1830s by dedicated members of the fledgling Peterborough community as a means of keeping the good doctor among them.

Though he was not long in exploring opportunities in places like Cobourg, Hamilton, and Toronto during 1845–46, his later accomplishments and fame made him a natural to be included among Peterborough's early celebrities. The city's Community College, begun in 1970, proudly bears his name. Hutchison House has designated a Fleming Room in his honour, which houses the sextant and other tools that he used in his surveying work. An immediate neighbour of the Hutchisons, Jeanie Hall, whom he met in 1845, would become his wife a decade later. It was also in Peterborough that he met Catharine Parr Traill who, in her early forties, continued to be a patient and friend of Dr. Hutchison. She was a kindly, supportive, and cheerful acquaintance, a model to young Sandford of the resilient immigrant in Canada. He admired her literary efforts and watched with interest as her books continued to appear decade after decade. Forty years later he would lead a campaign in Ottawa to commemorate her literary and botanical achievements on behalf of the government and his fellow Canadians. Many cities and communities like to claim Fleming for their own, but the fact is that he had his Canadian beginnings in Peterborough and he remained grateful for the strength of those roots.

Fleming's many contributions to Canadian engineering and society are a matter of fact and legend, but in these precisely written diaries we have the opportunity to see and meet the spirited young man at the outset of his extraordinary career, eager to get on despite many disappointments and setbacks, confident in his abilities, adept at socializing and professional networking, and always thinking ahead to future projects and possible inventions. His mind was never still and his energy was boundless. These diaries call for a wider audience of readers, for they tell us much about a colonial Canada we often struggle to know and understand.

Perhaps a few words about the Publications Committee will be worthwhile for the record. As the publications arm of the Peterborough Historical Society, the group — Jean Cole, Elwood Jones, Dale Standen, Enid Mallory, and myself — has edited and sometimes written the Occasional Papers that represent one of the Peterborough Historical Society's enduring contributions to local history. This year saw our twenty-ninth publication. One of the earliest was Jean Cole's essay, "Sandford Fleming: No Better Inheritance" (1990), which was Occasional Paper No. 11 in the series. Still, the Committee has had a desire to make some sort of larger contribution to local and national history beyond the scope of the yearly OPs. Hence, the Fleming diaries emerged in the mid-1990s as an idea for a book-length project. The problem then was to find the right person who had sufficient time available to undertake the work. As all the committee members are writers with an interest in history, we were well aware of the work that was involved and of our limited availability as individuals. With some initial financial support from Trent University's Frost Centre (for graduate work and research in Canadian Studies), we were able to engage a graduate student to begin the laborious task of transcription. Progress, however, was slow during this period; in fact, it was not until Jean Cole was able to free herself from the call of other projects that we were able to begin our work in earnest and to move the project toward completion.

As a committee we had in mind our own publication of the book and proceeded on that assumption for several years. We were thus delighted by the eagerness of Barry Penhale (Natural Heritage Books, a member of the Dundurn Group) to help us reach a larger reader-ship. In early December 2008, Jean Cole and I met with Barry, Jane Gibson, and Dundurn Press president, Kirk Howard, at their Toronto office. It proved a very congenial occasion; indeed, we were able to strike an agreement to publish the book. Our collective aim, spurred by Kirk Howard, was to release the volume in the fall of 2009 as part of the City of Toronto's 175th anniversary. Young Sandford had first arrived in the town some eleven years after Muddy York became Toronto, but he was there often during the years covered by this book and made numerous and important contributions to the life and look of the growing metropolis.

These diaries show the young man in action, eager to get on with projects, seldom wasting his time or an opportunity, and refusing to be daunted by negative advice or difficult situations. He offers a study in hard work, unflagging vision, and a strong sense of duty to his family and "the advancement of Canada." "I have," as he once wrote, "dreamed my little dreams, I have planned my little plans, and begrudged no effort to bring about what I regarded as desirable results." Few men in Canada have succeeded so well in their aspirations.

Michael Peterman,
Professor Emeritus, Trent University
March 31, 2009

INTRODUCTION

Canadians know the imposing figure standing by the right hand of
Donald A. Smith in the iconic photograph that records the driving of
the last spike of the Canadian Pacific Railway at Craigellachie, British
Columbia, symbolizing the linking of Canada coast to coast. Sandford
Fleming, as engineer-in-chief of the CPR from 1871, supervised the
survey of the western line, and mapped the route across the prairies
and mountains. He well deserved his position of prominence on that
memorable day in November 1885.

*Donald A. Smith, Lord Strathcona, driving the last spike on the Canadian
Pacific Railway at Craigellachie, British Columbia, November 7, 1885.
Sandford Fleming in top hat stands behind him.*

What many do not know is that he was also the chief engineer on the surveys of the Ontario, Simcoe and Lake Huron Railway (later Ontario Northern), and the Intercolonial Railway from Quebec to the Maritime provinces. Nor are they familiar with the many other accomplishments of this remarkable man. Later in life he was the creator and primary promoter of the worldwide system of Standard Time. He urged the building of the Pacific Cable uniting Australia by telegraph with the North American continent. He was a talented artist who designed Canada's first adhesive postage stamp — the Beaver — and many of his drawings and engravings survive. In January 1846, before Thomas Edison (1847–1931) was born, nineteen-year-old Sandford invented an "electrifying machine" as a new form of lighting, one of his numerous innovative experiments. In his early teens he even designed a version of today's popular rollerblades.

Young Sandford Fleming began his lifelong habit of journal-keeping in Scotland on January 1, 1845, just seven days before his eighteenth

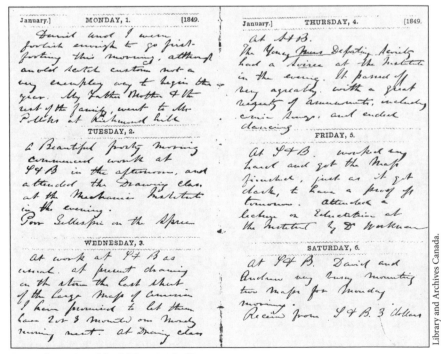

Page from Sandford Fleming's diary.

birthday. Plans were already afoot for Sandford and his older brother David, along with an older cousin Henry Fleming, to go to Canada to seek new ventures — *and* to look into the possibility of their parents and six younger siblings following after them. They had been encouraged by relatives already in Canada and hoped for greater opportunities in the expanding new world.

Sandford already had railway building experience in Scotland. Apprenticed to John Sang, a prominent Fifeshire surveyor, he had assisted in tracking the new lines between Edinburgh, Perth, and Dundee. With Canada just entering the railway era, the outlook was promising. His diary records the preparations for the journey (John Sang assisted in outfitting him with the tools he would require for the adventure), his farewells to family and friends, and graphic details of the Atlantic voyage, the journey to Canada West (now Ontario), and their first home in Peterborough. For the rest of his days, Fleming continued to chronicle both the daily happenings and the highlights of his life experience, often with hand-drawn illustrations. Only one year of his diaries (1847) has not survived.

This volume contains the early journals (1845–1853) which give a vivid picture of Fleming's development and maturing as he sought to make a place for himself in the competitive atmosphere of Canada West

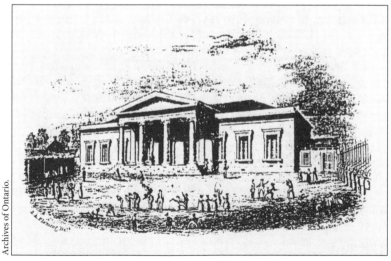

Archives of Ontario.

Kirkcaldy Burgh School. Engraving of a sketch by Sandford Fleming, age seventeen.

in the 1840s and 1850s. It was not an easy road, but he was energetic and resourceful, a handsome youth with a persistence and enthusiasm that got him past occasional rebuffs and disappointments.

When the two brothers arrived in Peterborough, their father's cousin, Dr. John Hutchison, welcomed them and promised to make introductions and assist them in getting established. David soon joined the work party building the new lock at Crook's Rapids (now Hastings) on the Trent Severn Waterway, but Sandford waited for the doctor to have time to go with him to Toronto to meet potential employers there. Meantime, he did a little work for Richard Birdsall, a local surveyor, and helped the Hutchisons on their property. On his own initiative he created a map of Peterborough (and later, produced and marketed one of Cobourg, and another of the Colborne District) which he lithographed himself and arranged to sell to bring in a little income.

He met with some discouragement when he first arrived in Toronto. He had a letter of reference to officials of the Canada Company, developers of the large Huron Tract, from Edward Ellice, their London governor, but the Toronto office indicated they had more or less wound up their survey work and there were no openings. Casimir Gzowski, the chief engineer for roads and harbours in York (Toronto), plainly advised him to go back to Scotland. But John G. Howard, the city engineer, assured him that he had been "ten times worse off" when he first arrived and urged him to stay, advising him to write his surveyor's licensing exams in Montreal.

After a brief foray into the Hamilton area, to see if there were opportunities there (there were not), and some time spent in Cobourg, Fleming settled in Toronto in 1847. He secured work with Scobie and Balfour Printers & Lithographers which gave him a basic income while he pursued survey work as it came up. In the fall of that same year, Andrew and Elizabeth Arnot Fleming arrived with their four younger sons and two daughters, Andrew, Henry, Alexander, John, Anne, and Jane. Sandford and David, who was by this time working at the Toronto furniture makers Jacques and Hay, joined the family in their rented quarters on James Street.

Sandford soon opened an office of his own and became part of the community of engineers, architects, and surveyors, both at work and socializing in the evening hours.

Preparation for his surveyor's exams in Montreal, in the spring of 1849, occupied much of his spare time that winter, but he was also busy broadening his circle of friends and colleagues. In May of 1849, he was apprenticed (half time) for six months to the Weston surveyor, J. Stoughton Dennis, a move that brought him in contact with many of the prominent engineers and architects in Toronto, and set him on the road to future success. Other well known architects with whom he worked closely included John Howard, Kivas Tully, Thomas Ridout, Collingwood Schreiber, and Frederic Cumberland.

His major projects in the city included surveys of the new Garrison and Military Reserve, the Toronto Harbour, the Queen's Wharf at the government docks at the foot of Bathurst Street, the railway terminal, and numerous private projects. During the same period, his work at Scobie and Balfour ranged from lithographing his own drawings of important sites such as St. James Cathedral, to the months-long chore of mapping and lithographing the large-scale plan of Toronto; he began working on it in mid-1848 and was still correcting it in June 1851.

A time-consuming preoccupation during Fleming's early years in Toronto was the creation of the Canadian Institute (now the Royal Canadian Institute), and subsequently its offshoot the *Canadian Journal*. By November of 1848, Sandford was giving evening classes on drawing, geometry, and arithmetic at

John G. Howard, prominent Toronto architect who encouraged Fleming when he first arrived in the city.

the Mechanics' Institute, forerunner of the public library system, which operated then with a board chaired by Frederic Cumberland, with Henry Youle Hind as vice-president. Fleming saw the need for a collegial organization that would bring professional colleagues together to meet regularly to exchange ideas, give papers — and eventually to publish some of them. In June 1849, a group of young engineers met in Kivas Tully's office and agreed to convene a larger meeting. The organization soon broadened its membership to include all the arts, and a wide range of topics were discussed by experts in their fields. After a slow start, the Institute became an important fixture on the Toronto scene. By May 1851, when the group held its first Conversazione, the gala affair drew about eighty of the most prominent academics and professional men of the community. Plans were already in the works to found the *Canadian Journal*, which by 1852 became another of Sandford Fleming's projects, both as editor and an author. More than thirty of his articles appeared in the *Journal* over the years.

Fleming's association with John Howard, Frederic Cumberland, Kivas Tully, and others in the Canadian Institute circle brought numerous commissions, and it was Cumberland, as chief engineer for the Northern Railway, who appointed him assistant engineer in August 1852. From that time railways became his career. Fleming took up the task immediately. The Toronto to Barrie route was well in hand, although he was responsible for many final details before the first trains ran to Barrie on May 16, 1853. In October 1852 he was investigating the Penetanguishene area and his crew made their way from Barrie to Collingwood and Nottawasaga Harbour. By June 1853 the survey party was working up the Bruce Peninsula to Tobermory Harbour and Manitoulin Island.

Fleming was back and forth to Toronto frequently, finishing off jobs there, attending to Canadian Institute affairs, and continuing his active social life. He remained with the Northern Railway, promoted to succeed Cumberland as chief engineer in 1855. In 1863 he was named chief engineer of the Intercolonial Railway from Quebec to the Maritime provinces and Halifax. In 1871 he was appointed engineer-in-chief of the Canadian Pacific Railway. In his later years he was closely associated with Queen's University, Kingston, serving as chancellor from 1880 until his death in 1915. Among his many honours, he was created a Companion of the Order of St. Michael and St. George in 1877, and knighted K.C.M.G.

(Knight Commander of St. Michael and St. George) by Queen Victoria in 1897, her jubilee year.

The diaries contained in this volume conclude with the year 1853, with Fleming firmly established as a railway builder and a prominent figure on the Toronto scene. The last few months of the year mark the beginning of his courtship of his Peterborough friend Jeanie Hall, which culminated in their marriage in January 1855. His growth from the ambitious eighteen-year-old Scottish lad who landed on Canada's shores in 1845 to a figure of substance in those eight years set the pace for his future life.

Sandford Fleming was a man with a great appetite for life and the energy, enthusiasm, and capability to accomplish whatever he set out to do. His inventive mind was always at work and he had the resourcefulness and determination to follow through. In his personal life, he was an attentive and devoted son, brother, husband, father, and grandfather. In his professional life, he was an achiever, with a vitality and loyalty that attracted friends and colleagues alike.

All this is revealed in the pages ahead.

CHAPTER ONE
Kirkcaldy to Canada 1845

Sandford Fleming and his older brother David were the advance party when they set off from Glasgow for Canada. Their father, Andrew Greig Fleming, had heard glowing reports from friends and relatives who had emigrated, but before making his final decision to move his family to the New World, he sent out his two eldest boys to see for themselves what the opportunities might be. Sandford, at eighteen, had been apprenticed to a prominent Kirkcaldy surveyor for four years and had already had some experience working on railways between Edinburgh, Perth, and Dundee, which would prepare him for the rapidly developing railway expansion in Canada. David, age twenty, was a skilled woodcarver who learned his trade in his father's small furniture manufacturing business. There were six younger siblings in the family, four boys and two girls, and their futures were much on the father's mind.

Preparations for the departure were well under way at the beginning of the year. With the sense of occasion that was inherent in his character, on New Year's Day 1845, young Sandford made his first entry in the diaries he would keep for the rest of his long life. This was to be an eventful year and he knew there would be no shortage of interesting things to record. In the months before the final leave-taking there were many farewell visits to friends and relatives in nearby villages, among them a trip to Balbirnie with his father to see Edward Ellice, deputy-governor in London of the Canada Company and an influential Hudson's Bay Company governor. Ellice provided him with a letter of reference to Toronto officials of the Canada Company, who were then developing the huge Huron Tract of land in the Goderich area.It was hoped they might have work for a young surveyor. John Sang helped his young protégée make a collection of surveying tools to take with him and presented him with a pocket sextant as a parting gift (now in the collection at Hutchison House Museum).

New Year's Day was a festive occasion in Scotland and less than two weeks later came Handsel Monday, another day of visiting, gift-giving, and dancing. Later, on the first day of April, came Huntigowk, when the morning was spent in tricks and foolishness. Knowing that these might be his last celebrations of these old traditions, Fleming describes them in fond detail. Regular Sunday church services were a ritual. So, too, the many evenings spent with his chess club, often just for a few games before going on later to other pursuits. Chess was an important pastime throughout his long life and the core of many friendships.

The time passed quickly. On April 21, a few days before sailing, the two youths went down to Kennaway to say goodbye to relatives there. Souvenirs were exchanged and "My Grandmother was a little affected and with tears in her eyes she said, 'In danger we can no help ye anyway but I can pray for ye.'"

Andrew Fleming and several friends ran out to the end of the dock cheering his boys (and their older cousin Henry Fleming who was crossing with them) as their ship *Brilliant* sailed out the Clyde. Soon Glasgow faded in the distance and they were admiring the beautiful scenery along the river and the Mull of Kintyre. All that changed when they came to the rain and wind in the stormy Atlantic Ocean. "The trunks in the hold are all tye & jambel … pots & pans slide from one side of the cabin to the other," Fleming wrote. The rough passage to Quebec City took six weeks, with only a few fine days of relative calm, but Sandford made the most of it, getting acquainted with the captain and crew, impressing them with his sextant and the compass given to him by his uncle, and learning all he could about the workings of the ship. Drawings of ships at sea, and, as they neared their destination, of icebergs and rocky cliffs and sea birds, adorn the diary pages. The ship paused near Grosse Isle, the quarantine station, and a doctor came on to inspect the passengers, but almost all stayed on board and went on to Quebec.

The Flemings left the *Brilliant* at Quebec City, where they boarded a steamer to Montreal. From Lachine they travelled via Lake of Two Mountains, the Ottawa River, Bytown (Ottawa), and the Rideau Canal, encountering along the way several of their father's friends from Scotland, all of them demonstrating their comfortable circumstances in their new homes. From Kingston they went along Lake Ontario to Cobourg where they left the Toronto-bound steamer and made their way up to Peterborough, to be welcomed by their father's cousin Dr. John Hutchison. This was to be their headquarters until they could find suitable work.

It took longer than they had hoped, especially for Sandford. David was placed briefly on the new Trent-Severn Waterway locks being built at Crook's Rapids (Hastings) but found the work uncongenial and soon moved on to a furniture maker in Toronto. Sandford did a little surveying for the most prominent Peterborough practitioner, Richard Birdsall, but it was sporadic and he decided to augment his income by creating and selling his own original maps of the area, still hoping to get employment in Toronto that would lead eventually to his establishment in his profession. Railways were to be his future but the path to that end was not an easy one.

Early attempts to find employment in surveying circles in Toronto were discouraging. A "city" of about 20,000 population, it was the centre of commercial activity in the province, but breaking into the inner circle took some influence — and perseverance. On his first visit there in August, Sandford attempted to present his reference to Edward Ellice's colleague, Thomas Mercer Jones, commissioner of the Canada Company, only to learn that Jones was in Goderich supervising the work being done at the Huron Tract. Casimir Gzowski, chief engineer for Roads and Harbours, gave him a very cool reception, and advised him to return to Scotland. John G. Howard, the city engineer, felt that Gzowski was wrong, and told him that *he* had been far worse off when he first arrived. Howard advised him to write his surveyor's exams in Montreal and establish his Canadian credentials.

A side trip to Hamilton where Andrew Fleming had connections also proved to be fruitless, so Sandford went on to the Caledonia area where his cousin Henry Fleming had settled near his in-laws, the Bethunes. Several weeks of helping with odd jobs there only confirmed that he should return to Peterborough. There he worked for a time as a clerk in the general store of Dr. Hutchison's friend and neighbour, James Hall MPP, who several years later was to become Sandford's father-in-law. Hall became a true friend and was one of Fleming's most helpful supporters. It was he who, as a member of the Legislative Assembly's railway committee, was able to provide Fleming's first introductions among the railway builders.

January 1845

Wednesday, 1st day of January, 1845: I went to bed for the last time in the year 1844 at 11 oclock, and rose at ½ past 7 on new years day. Almost everyone you met said "good new year to ye" &c. Happy to say I saw noone drunk except a carter boy who I believed pretended more than anything else. I finished a sketch of 'Ravenscraig Castle' in the morning which Mr Crawford was to make arrangements with Mr Lizars about the engraving of it. Began in the evening to draw on stone Kirkcaldy harbour to be lithographed by Mr Bryson. My present wish is to write a sort of diary so that I can put down anything particular that happens or is of utility to recollect.

Thursday, 2nd: Drawing Kirkcaldy harbour until 3 oclock this morning. Rose up at ½ hour past nine, at Burntisland all day. Mr Bryson had the misfortune to break the stone with my drawing on it.

Friday, 3rd: Went to bed the night before at 11 o'clock and rose at ½ past eight. Out all day gathering accounts with my father, home again at 6 o'clock visited Mrs Wemyss (late Flora Sang) for the first time after her marriage. Went to the "Divan" (a chess club which I joined three weeks ago under the above title) where I took two games from Charles Lockhart, and left a third one unfinished. Went to bed at ½ hour before twelve.

Saturday, 4th: Rose up at 7 oclock at Burntisland surveying till 4 oclock, drew Kirkcaldy harbour over again, and saw Mr Bryson. Transferred it correctly to the stone. Got my hair cut at Barber Muirs. Went to bed at 11 oclock.

Sunday, 5th: Rose at 9 oclock. At church forenoon and afternoon. To bed at 10.

Monday, 6th: Rose at 6 oclock. Burntisland all day. At Miss Sangs at tea. Played two games and finished an old one with Chas Lockhart. He took the unfinished one and one of the others. To bed at ½ hour to twelve.

Tuesday, 7th: Rose at 8. Went up with Father to Balbirnie to see Mr [Edward] Ellice [governor of both the Canada Company and of the Hudson's Bay Company] about going to Canada, he wanted him to write before the time with my description, age, character &c. We also went to Strathendry that day. This is my Birthday and I am now 18 years of age. Went to bed at ½ hour to eleven.

Wednesday, 8th: Up at seven. At Burntisland all day. Made a paper chess board for the Divan. Went to bed at 11 oclock.

Thursday, 9th: Rose at seven, at Burntisland all day. Tea with Mr Barclay. Went to bed at ½ hour past eleven.

Friday, 10th: Rose at seven, at Burntisland till the six o'clock omnibus. Got the survey completed. I saw Mr Ferguson for the first time after he came home from America, he being out with us all day. At the Divan, played with Charles Lockhart. We took a game each, and Mr Forrester tried his chess for three playing at once for the first time. Went to bed at ½ hour past eleven.

Saturday, 11th: Rose at 9 o'clock. At Mr [John] Sangs [surveyor] all day. My Father and all the others went up to Kennoway (Monday being Handsel Monday [traditional day of New Year gift-giving and celebration]) except David, Mother, Archy & me. Got Ravenscraig Castle engravings from Mr Crawford which he got engraved by Lizars, Edinburgh. He wanted them done this week for the chance of them selling on Handsel Monday, the Castle being open to the public on that day. Went to bed at ½ hour past eleven.

Sunday, 12th: Rose at 8 and set off for Kennoway with David and Andrew, at Mr Stewart's church all day. Went to bed at ½ hour to eleven.

Monday, 13th: Handsel Monday. Rose at nine, the young country lads running about with guns. Went down to Dura Vale with David & Uncle William to see Miss Simson's picture of the Slave market at Constantinople it is one of the finest paintings I ever saw. The Slave dealers selling the beautiful women for slaves, tearing the child from the mother and the wife from the husband never to see one another again. Called at Miss Beaton at Balcunvia with David and then came to Haugh mill. Let me suppose I entered the kitchen at 6 oclock AM, here is Uncle at the fire heating the meal, Aunt at the boiler stirring and boiling the head of a fat ox. At a long row of tables is placed large wooden cogs which is now filled with oatmeal, they are mixed with the water with which the head was boiled. The Plowmen with their wives and children comes in, amounting to upwards of forty on some occasions. A noise of endless "fine days," "merrie Handsel Monday to ye" occurs, along with the shaking of hands &c. They are now seated on forms, chairs, & planks of wood. Silence now reigns (after the blessing is asked) except the noise occasioned by the horn spoons & the sloustering and snoring of the company, what a scene of happiness scarcely to be intimated by the immortal pencil of Wilkie. But this is not all; the best is now commenced upon and crowned by the introduction of Bacchus. The farmer begins "heres a' yer healths an many a Handsel Monday may we see," the bottle passes round along with cheese and bread and the dejeuner is never closed without the whole may well say they are "foin." The plowmen now set out to see their friends and the farmers sons and relations get the guns ready for field sports. They course at a field well known as the most proper to begin at. Those that have guns are spread at regular distances across the field intermixed with boys and others that have no guns. After schowsing the fields until 2 or 3 o'clock they come in to a hearty dinner intermixed with whiskey & toddy and a general talk of the adventures of the day. Tea & toddy follows in succession, songs, scotch, proverbs, cards, dice, recitation and divers games. The amusements are carried on to a pretty late hour when once more Handsel Monday ends. To bed at 12 o'clock.

Tuesday, 14th: Up at 9 — got breakfast. Shot at a target in the haugh. Went a shooting with Sandy Robert & David for hares, only saw one. After dinner went up to the Rifle at Windygates where Robert Irwin touched the Bullseye and got the prize, then came home and were at Kirkcaldy about ½ past six, to bed at ten.

Wednesday, 15th: Up at ½ hour past eight. At Mr Sangs all day. Went to bed at 11.

Thursday, 16th: Up at ½ past eight at Mr Sangs. Made at night wooden moulds for a pair compasses. Went to bed 11 oclock.

Friday, 17th: Up at 7. At Burntisland forenoon. Dined with Mr Barclay, Kinghorn. Got Miss Barclays album home to draw in it. At the Divan, Joe Crichton took 3 games from me in a very short time and I the last one. Went to bed at 12.

Saturday, 18th: Up at ½ hour past 8 making a pair of compasses at Mr Sangs. Played chess at Joe Crichtons, 1 game each. Bed at ½ past twelve.

Sunday, 19th: At Church, rose at nine to bed at ten.

Monday, 20th: Up at 6. Making compasses and calculating at Mr Sangs. To bed ½ past 11.

Tuesday, 21st: Up at ½ past eight. Tuesday at Mr Sangs and making out accounts to my Father. To bed at ½ past 11.

Wednesday, 22nd: Up at six making compasses till 9. Writing to my father all day. To bed ½ hour past eleven.

Thursday, 23rd: Up at nine assisting my father in the forenoon, finishing my writing Desk in the afternoon & evening. To bed ½ past eleven.

Friday, 24th: Up at six finishing writing Desk. At the Divan got two games from Mr Stark and left one unfinished. To bed at 12. This is Davids birthday.

Saturday, 25th: Up at ½ hour before 9 at Mr Sangs. 2 games of chess at night, took one from C Lockhart & lost one with John Black. To bed ½ past twelve.

Sunday, 26th: Up at ½ past 8. At church 3 times. To bed ½ past 10.

Monday, 27th: Up at 6 at Mr Sangs all day. To bed at 11.

Tuesday, 28th: Up at 8 at Mr Sangs. The ground is covered with snow 4 inches up both yesterday & today. Still snowing. To bed at ½ past 11.

Wednesday, 29th: Up at ½ past 8. The snow 6 inches deep on cow byre. Making compasses all day. Got a pocket sextant [now at the Hutchison House Museum, Peterborough] as a present from Mr Sang on the thoughts of going to America. Bought tape for to make lines of and Mrs Sang promised to divide them to me. Went to bed at twelve.

Thursday, 30th: Up at seven oiling tape lines. Doing some things for my father. Ordered Mr Russels man to make 6 brass scales to divide at my leisure. To bed at 11.

Friday, 31st: Up at seven. Went away to Strathendry with my father to get the extra work settled. The snow very deep & excessively cold, the thermometer was at 12½ [degrees] at Strathendry. At the Divan where it was proposed to compete for the Caliphate next evening. To bed at 12 along with David & Sandford Imrie. Very cold.

Courtesy Hutchison House Museum.

Pocket sextant presented to Sandford Fleming as a farewell gift by his employer John Sang, now in the collection of Hutchison House Museum.

February 1845

Saturday, 1st: Up at ½ past 8. Making compasses &c. At the west mill pond in the afternoon skating. Very good tea. To bed at 11 oclock.

Sunday, 2nd: Up at nine. Took some medicine & at home all day. To bed at ½ past ten.

Monday, 3rd: Up at 7. Making scales all day. Played at chess in the back ware room with some of the Divan folks. To bed ½ past 11.

Tuesday, 4th: Up at ½ past seven. Making scales. At the Quarterly meeting of the Divan where accounts were settled and other business. Mr Forrester had refreshments prepared in a little Barrel. 1st we were all served with coffee flavoured with cinnamon which came out of a small cock that shut & opened. He then ordered the barrel to give us sherbet which without altering the barrel any way came out of the same cock. After a while he ordered wine, when we were served with cinnamon water in the same manner. It was exceedingly neat. He must have 3 cells & valves in the inside some way. To bed at ½ hour past eleven.

Wednesday, 5th: Up at 8. The snow entirely away except some small patches. It has been fresh since last Sunday. At compasses. Away to Lochone for my Uncle. Very cold & hard frost at night. To bed at ten.

Thursday, 6th: Up at 8. At compasses forenoon. Making plan of Stable afternoon. Very hard frost. Bed at 12.

Friday, 7th: Up at 7. Giving my uncle a ride to Lochone in the forenoon. At scales in afternoon. At the Divan evening, played for the Caliphate. I was fixed my lot against David, Black against Lockhart. The one that got the best of three games played with one another by lot & then the last victor was to play with the Caliph. I got the 1st of our three games from David. To bed at 11.

Saturday, 8th: Up at 8. At scales forenoon & drawing afternoon. Played at chess at night in the ware room. Took two games from Mr Stark. To bed ½ past eleven.

Sunday, 9th: Up at 9. Slept 3 in bed with Uncle Hutchison last night. At church all day. To bed ½ past ten.

Monday, 10th: Up at 6. Marking two tape lines, one into links & the other into tenths of feet & inches. To bed at 11.

Tuesday, 11th: Up at ½ past 7. Make tape lines & finished them. Got Mr Sangs dividing machine (a loan) for scales. To bed 11.

Thursday, 13th: Up at 7. Drawing forenoon. Making a machine for taking portraits. To bed ½ past eleven.

Friday, 14th: Friday. Up at 8. Drawing &c. To bed at one oclock. Took another game from David which made the best of three & began a game with Black.

Saturday, 15th: Up at ½ past seven. Got 2 pieces of brass to make parallel rulers of. To bed at 12.

Sunday, 16th: Up at ½ to 9. At church 3 times. To bed at ½ past ten.

Monday, 17th: Up at ½ past 6. Filing parallel rulers. To bed ½ past eleven.

Tuesday, 18th: Up at 8. At rulers. Played 3 games with Stark. He had 2. To bed at 11.

Wednesday, 19th: Up at 6 making parallel rulers. Got this problem: White to move mates in 5. Black to — from black Q to 1 (K takes Q) check with B by moving C to 2 — (K to 3) check C to 4 (K takes C) take Kt with C5 check (K to 6) Kt to Y & mate [problem sketched in diary]. To bed at 11.

Thursday, 20th: Up at ½ past seven. Got axles with steel waked on each end from Bogie the smith for parallel rulers. Got them all centred & the ends turned. To bed at 11.

Friday, 21st: Up at ½ past seven. Making moulds for wheels & bushes and got them cast for rulers. At the Divan & Mr Black took the game we left unfinished. The Divan book was balloted for what came to my lot. To bed 12.

Saturday, 22nd: Up at seven. Turning axles parallel rulers &c. Drew a small chess board for lithographing. To bed 11.

Sunday, 23rd: Up at 8. At church twice. To bed ½ past ten.

Monday, 24th: Up at seven. Got brass wheels soldered on axles in the morning at Dysart. Forenoon measuring for railway, turning wheels &c. To bed at one.

Tuesday, 25th: Up at eight. At parallel rulers. Had the misfortune to let fall one of the brass plates over the window three stories high. It was on the chair and in pulling up the window it fell down between the glass. Although it was very much spoiled I was very happy it did hurt no one. To bed at 11.

Wednesday, 26th: Up at ½ past 7. At parallel rulers & divided the first of my scales at night. To bed at 11.

Thursday, 27th: Up at seven. Away to Nevety measuring the house with my father. Went to Parsons mill and saw the saw mill, he has a little gas work the iron of the retort is about 1 inch thick & 2 ft long the pipe passes through 3 boxes first with water line, & ashes and then goes to the gas meter a short iron thing in a barrel of water about 2 ft dia but by far too little. To bed at 11.

Friday, 28th: Up at seven drawing furniture for David. At miller got the teeth cut in two of the wheels. At the Divan and took two games from John Black which settled I was to play with the Caliph next night. To bed ½ past eleven.

March 1845

Saturday, 1st: Up at ½ past seven. At rulers &c. To bed 10.

Sunday, 2nd: In bed nearly all day with the cold.

Monday, 3rd: Up at 9. At rulers & divided a scale at night. To bed 11.

Tuesday, 4th: Up at ½ past 7. Snow on the ground. At rulers, divided a scale at night. To bed at 12. My fathers away to Glasgow.

Wednesday, 5th: Up at 8. Got the wheels & axles fitted on one of the rulers & divided a scale at night. To bed at 11.

Thursday, 6th: Up at 6. Reading *Herchells Astronomy*. At second ruler. To bed at 11.

Friday, 7th: Up at 7. At rulers &c. Play at chess with Forrester for the Caliphate, he took the first game and left the second unfinished. To bed at 12.

Saturday, 8th: Up at ½ past 7. Went to Lochone for an acct to my father. To bed at ½ past eleven.

Sunday, 9th: Up at 8. At church twice. To bed at 10.

Monday, 10th: Up at seven. At rulers, got 12 zinc scales from the plumber to divide. To bed at 12. David ill with the cold.

Tuesday, 11th: Up at seven. Make a bargain with Roger the plumber to get a brass casting from him for parallel rulers & he to get the old one (sheet brass) divided into inches &c. To bed at 11.

Wednesday, 12th: Up at 7. Filing casting &c dividing Rogers scale. To bed 11.

Thursday, 13th: Up at 8. Cutting out a groove in plate for axle & filing edges straight. At Rogers scale. To bed ½ past ten.

Friday, 14th: Friday. Up at 8. Grinding & polishing edges and sole of brass plate. Fitted up a machine for taking profiles which did very well. At Divan left the game unfinished which was left last night. To bed at 12.

Saturday, 15th: Up at 8. Snow very thick. Making seals for letters. To bed ½ past 11.

Sunday, 16th: At church twice. To bed ½ past ten.

Monday, 17th: Up at seven. At parallel rulers. To bed at 12.

Tuesday, 18th: Up at 6. Making machine for taking portraits. At rulers. Took my father, mother &c portraits, very like. To bed 11.

Wednesday, 19th: Up at ½ past 7. At rulers. To bed ½ to 12.

Thursday, 20th: Up at ½ past 7. At rulers. To bed at 12.

Friday, 21st: Up at ½ past 7. At rulers. At the Divan evening. I took the game left & Forrester took other two which made him again the Caliph. To bed ½ past 11.

Saturday, 22nd: At rulers. To bed ½ past ten.

Sunday, 23rd: Up ½ past 8. At church twice. To bed 11.

Monday, 24th: Up at 7. At rulers. To bed 12.

Tuesday, 25th–Thursday, 27th: At rulers.

Thursday, 27th: Went up to S Wilson, Haugh mill with a letter for some money. He said he would answer by post. To bed 11.

Friday, 28th–Saturday, 29th: At rulers.

Sunday, 30th: At church twice.

Monday, 31st: Up at 7. At rulers. To bed 11.

April 1845

Tuesday, 1st: Up 7 (hunt the gowk) [April 1 is Huntigowk — Scot tradition was to spend the morning playing tricks and passing them on, making others look foolish; "gowk" means "cuckoo."]

Wednesday, 2nd: At rulers.

Thursday, 3rd: Got rulers so far finished & began to draw specimens. Uncle Hutchison came down to work.

Friday, 4th: Drawing &c.

Saturday, 5th: Drawing. Got a silver watch from my father.

Sunday, 6th: At church twice.

Monday, 7th: Cut a white coat for Henry Fleming suit and one for David & I.

Tuesday, 8th–Saturday, 12th: &c. Got 6 specimens finished.

Sunday, 13th–Saturday, 19th: Getting scales &c prepared.

Sunday, 20th: At church twice expecting it to be the last time in Scotland. Went up & took farewell of Mr Law, Mrs Fleming &c.

Monday, 21st: Went to Kinghorn in the morning with book of plans of Kinghorn town house and Maggie Barclay album. Mr Barclay promised to send some letters through to Glasgow. David & I up about Kennoway taking farewell of our friends & waiting for Wilson, Milspinen [at Haugh Mill] to get some money from him. My Grandmother was a little affected & with tears in her eyes she said "in danger we no can help ye onyway But I can pray for ye." We waited for Wilson till 8 PM when he came home & he told us he had settled with my father (to whom he had given £20). Robert & Sandford Imrie came along to a crossroad near the Milton & when parting they dropt a letter into our hand saying "just to put it into our pocket it might be of use to us afterwards." It was addressed to S & D Fleming enclosing 2 pounds & 2 crown pieces. It certainly showed an uncommonly kind and feeling heart and is ranking among the incidents of my life which I will never forget. On coming home our Kirkcaldy friends were at supper & the workmen were drinking Davids health with some money he gave. Rodger Black gave a present to David "Gems from American Poets" & I got from my Uncle Alex a pocket compass which also answers as a sun dial.

Tuesday, 22nd: Up at 6. Getting things prepared to go away and after taking farewells of our Friends, Mother, Brothers & Sisters. David & I accompanied by my Father to Glasgow, left Kirkcaldy perhaps forever. (I got a watch chain from Mr Sang). We saw Mr Arnot, Edinburgh, and I bought a camera lucida. We went with the 5 o'clock train to Glasgow. Stopped with Mr Kirving all night.

Wednesday, 23rd: Getting provisions prepared for the journey. Received a letter from Mr Barclay enclosing 4 letters to people in Canada, also a letter from someone in Edinburgh to him in a mistake which I sent back. Saw his son Robt and had supper with him. I intend to write to the following:

> Father J Sang Jas Patterson
> Mother Chas Irwin John or Jane Hutchison
> Sister T Martin Robert Blyth
> C Lockhart R Black S Grainger
> E Sang R Imrie

Thursday, 24th: Bought a pair portable compasses for 20/ and several other articles necessary for the voyage. The vessel cleared out from the

Issued by **ALEX. G. GILKISON**, 98, Miller Street, Glasgow, Licensed Passenger Broker.

SCHEDULE (B.)

REFERRED TO IN THE 19TH SECTION OF THE PASSENGERS' ACT.

PASSENGERS' CONTRACT TICKET.

N.B.—*Any one receiving money from, or in respect of, any Passenger about leaving the United Kingdom for any place in North America, without using this Form, and correctly filling up the blanks therein, and signing it with his name in full, will be liable to a penalty not exceeding £10 for each such Passenger.*

SHIP *Brilliant* of *Greenock* 428 tons register burthen,

to sail from *Glasgow* for *Quebec*

on the *24* day of *April* 18*45*

I engage that the parties herein named shall be provided with a *2d Cabin* passage to *Quebec* in the Ship *Brilliant* with not less than Ten cubic feet for luggage, for each statute adult for the sum of £ *13.10.0* including head-money, if any; at the place of landing, and every other charge; and *I* hereby acknowledge to have received the sum of £*13.10* in *full* payment.

Names.	Ages.	Equal to Statute Adults.
Henry Fleming	32	
David Fleming	24	3
Sandford Fleming	28	

Passengers to be forwarded from Quebec to Montreal by Steamer free of expense

Water and provisions, according to the annexed Scale, will be supplied by the Ship, as required by law, and also fires and suitable hearths for cooking

Utensils for eating and drinking will be provided by *Passengers*

Bedding will be provided by *Passengers*

Sig. *pro Alex. G. Gilkison*
William Orr

on behalf of *Owners*

Date *Glasgow 23 April 1845*

Deposit £ *13.10.6*

Balance £ *11 11 6* to be paid at _____

Total £ *13.10.0*

* Fill up these blanks by stating, in each case, whether the articles are to be supplied by the Ship or by the Passenger
† If signed by a Broker or Agent, state on whose behalf.

[At the end of this Contract insert the Victualling Scale, which must in no case be less than required under the provisions of the Passengers' Act.]

SCALE OF WATER AND PROVISIONS REFERRED TO.

A supply of Water daily, at the rate of *three* quarts for each Passenger, and at convenient times, not less often than *2* times a-week; a supply of Provisions after the rate of *seven* pounds of Bread, Biscuit, Flour, Oatmeal, or Rice, per week *One half* at least of the supply shall consist of Bread or Biscuit, and that Potatoes may be employed (at Master's option) to the extent of the remaining *half* of the supply, five pounds of the Potatoes being computed as equal to one pound of the other articles above enumerated; and that such issues, as aforesaid, shall be made throughout the whole Voyage, including the time of detention, if any, at any Port or Place before the end of such Voyage.

Sold by **Robert Jackson**. Wholesale and Retail Stationer and Bookseller, **5, St Enoch Square**, Argyll Street, Glasgow.

Passenger list of the ship Brilliant, *April 21, 1845.*

wharf about ½ past 1 P.M. It was tugged down the river by a steamer & we took farewell of my Father who followed her to the end of the wharf & gave us three cheers along with Robt Barclay & a Mr Dick who came with Mr Arthurs people. It was a fine spring day. The sun was high in the heavens & the scenery along the banks of the Clyde was truly beautiful. We left Glasgow in the distance amongst the mist & windings of the Clyde. A bold promontory comes into view, on which is built an obelisk with the inscription "to Henry Bell". On passing this we see Dunbarton Castle & the town of Dunbarton behind. The Clyde is a complete thoroughfare of steamers & vessels of every description & one is struck how so narrow a river can be so deep in proportion as to carry up so large vessels. We now arrive at Greenock where we lay for some time. The Captain went on shore, I suppose to get a new pilot for the Firth of Clyde. The scenery here is far from being inferior to any we yet passed, the hills & valleys and the entrances to Loch Long &c make a beautiful landscape. And while admiring the beauties of nature one is apt to forget they are leaving all behind, perhaps never to be seen again. Night comes on & the Pilot guides us safely to the Irish Sea by the lighthouses studded along the shore. We go to bed for the first time on the Deep & the steamer leaves us next morning at about 3 o'clock.

Friday, 25th: Up at 5. The only land that we see is Ailsa Craig due south amongst the mist a steep sided Island & apparently very rocky. In a short time an island to the north makes its appearance and about 11 A.M. the Mull of Kintyre due north and in about an hour the last of Scotland disappears. About 3 P.M. the north coast of Ireland lyes towards the south. The female part of the passengers through the day are beginning to get sick and the trunks in the hold are all tye & jambel as preparations for the pitching which in a short time we see the necessity. Towards evening it gets very rainy & windy. The pots & pans slide from one side of the cabin to the other & one has altogether a disagreeable sensation. I slept well through the night however.

Saturday, 26th: Very sick & throwing. The women are very ill. The vessel is sailing at about 8 miles an hour. In bed most part of the day & eat very little. David & I eat a fine biscuit to supper & two figs which relished very well.

Sunday, 27th: Very sick forenoon but quite well all the rest of the day. Potatoes & red herring to dinner. A frying pan which was hung to the roof amongst the tin things fell during the night on a jar of treacle & broke it all to pieces and dirten a great many things. Towards afternoon the wind gradually turned to the west & the vessel sailed S.W. We had tea in the evening & a pot of jelly of H. Fleming which had been broke in the packing. In the evening the wind died away and we had a pleasant sail with the vessel rocking majestically, altho before we got through it was going down. We read a chapter each in the evening & went to bed about ten.

Monday, 28th: Up about 8. Had brose [porridge] & coffee to breakfast. The vessel turned around & tacked N.W. The women all being in bed yet we set too & scrubbed & washed the floor it being very dirty & disagreeable. The most of the passengers are now begging to appear on deck & the fire is in great demand. We made potato soup to dinner. It was very fine & some of the Miss Aitkens got up after dinner. The wind got stronger towards night.

Tuesday, 29th: Rain & wind. Cooper to breakfast. I brought out my pocket sextant & the compass I got from my uncle. The Captain & mates thought very much of them. We were beginning to think the Aitkens were lazy. They got up [this] afternoon which was good although the sea heaved a little. Towards evening rain came on & wind from west.

Wednesday, 30th: Slept little or none all night & we thought sometimes we were like to be pitched out of bed. It was H. Fleming, another man & my turn to kindle the fire. Up at ½ past 5. Could not walk very well along the deck. Could not get a light from the cook for an hour. Got angry & would not wait any longer, one of the sailors did it. Came down to the cabin wet. We were sitting on the trunks & provision chests. In a short time the vessel took a great heave, the weight of the boxes burst the nails that nailed them to the floor. They all slid to the opposite side of the cabin, some on their side & others topsie turvie, then came back with the ship & went to & fro, some of us betwixt them & others on the top. The scene which ensued cannot be described, the boxes thumping & jambing the beds on the floor which were filled with Mr Aitkens family. David had been sitting on the box containing 2 doz porter, 2 doz ale, 2 bottles whisky, 2 bottles pickles. His feet & legs were wet with porter &c &c the floor was swimming. The laughing was abundant, here is the charm of emigration cries one. Again they cross the floor & breaks a piece of the foot of the ladder which comes crash down amongst the Pots & tins which are also dancing. We were all surprised to pick out 2½ doz whole bottles which had been saved by the straw. They were handed into the beds. Come for water cries a sailor on deck, which must be attended to or we shall want.

The trunks were secured with great difficulty owing to the floor being wet. The water comes & secured, but whilst securing the bottles the ropes slip & a large pitcher of water sweeps the floor. In comes Mr Lilleave, a neighbour passenger saying the trunks in the hold are broken loose & one of his through the middle. We all went down & got them secured between the ports. The cracking there & noise was really fearful. We came up & went to bed after clearing the floor a little from the broken bottles, eggs & cakes &c. In the afternoon we were called to the trunks again. The sea by this time was very rough. It has not the appearance of waves but rather like rough hilly ground. The greatest distance between the heights & hollows appears to be about 40 or 49 feet. The ship being going N.W. turned & sailed sometimes nearly due south. At 3 P.M. it had only one small sail up. As the evening advanced the storm grew worse, the sea sometimes washed across the deck & I never expected to see daylight again. When a great wave swept above our heads it had a sound as if the sea was closing over us. We slept none all night, the timbers were cracking terribly, the bottles & tins rattling from one side of the floor to the other & pity the poor sailors on deck all night.

May 1845

Thursday, 1st: The weather rather better towards the morning when we had some short sleeps & dreams (about drifted on the rocks &c). We were all happy to get up. The ships galley had been very upset during the night. In the afternoon the wind fell a good deal & I sent a letter to my father away in a bottle. The wind turned to the north west & we got more sails up. The Aitkens were up in the afternoon. We slept well.

Friday, 2nd: Made porridge & treacle for the first time. Nothing extraordinary happened during the day. We looked at some French books & Wilcocks Arithmetic &c.

Saturday, 3rd: Up at 6 getting water brought up from the hold. The wind has fallen & a beautiful day with considerable swell. The 2nd mate gave me two charts of the Atlantic which will amuse me a little. It was a beautiful evening & I stayed up with the mate till 12. To be ½ past 1 Glasgow time.

Sunday, 4th: Very little swell on the sea & a smart breeze from the N.W. All the principal sails were up & we sailed at about 6 miles an hour. Broth & beef to dinner & pancakes. Reading chapters &c.

Monday, 5th: Got a Navigation book from the mate Arch Hutchison by Nathanial Bonditch, an American author. The vessel turned round to the north and we sailed W by N at 8 & 9 miles an hour. An Irish man Arthur McInnis came down to our cabin and gave us some nice fun, and we were in steerage singing in the evening.

Tuesday, 6th: Up at day, our day to kindle the fire & supply coals & water. The wind had fallen a good deal & we had 14 sails up. Saw a schooner to the north

Fleming's sketch of the ship Brilliant's *second mate.*

about 8 A.M. homeward. Sat a game of chess forenoon. David won. Got the Longitudes & Latitudes of the preceding days from the mate. Singing & dancing to a flute in the evening. The water immediately around the ship both last night & tonight was illuminated by brilliant sparks of light. Some appeared to be considerable distance below the surface. It was very beautiful. The sea was very calm.

Wednesday, 7th: The sea very calm morning but the wind from the west. We sailed N.W. by N. & N.N.W. about 8 oclock A.M. & schooner sailed past. When out very near us her name was *Tyfus* or *Tixus* and we saw the upper part of the masts of a bark to the W. Pricked off the track of the *Brilliant* up to this date on the mates chart. The weather rather foggy in the evening.

Thursday, 8th: A Brig quite close to us on the north side about 7 A.M. & it keeps up with us all day, the name is *Weir*. It appears that it was bound for Quebec as they fell in with it the last voyage. It was a good N ward in the forenoon but fell away towards the evening when it was quite calm. We had singing & dancing on the deck.

Friday, 9th: Strong west wind & foggy weather. The Brig still in sight but gradually disappeared in the fog. The Latitude today was 47° 53 &

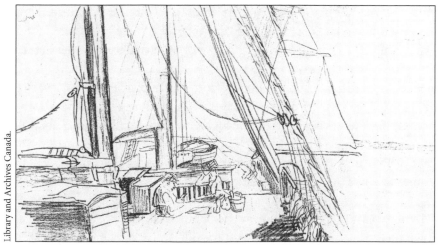

Scene on board deck of the Brilliant *from Fleming's diary, May 10, 1845.*

Longitude 26° 12. We got some of the chests better nailed expecting a storm but the weather got no worse after bedtime.

Saturday, 10th: A beautiful morning with a good breeze. The Brig again in sight. The females employ their time in working little shawls for the neck. David & I have 2 games chess a day generally, as well the two cabin passengers who play at chess. It is very pleasant to sit on the deck in a sunny day & read while the vessel is flying through the water. Another vessel a three master appears in the afternoon to the north, apparently homeward bound and we see the top mast of another immediately in front. The wind still blows from W. By N.

Sunday, 11th: Longitude at noon 28° 51', Latitude 46° 49'. We were tacking N.W. & S.W. turn about with a pretty good breeze from the west. All the passengers wash themselves today, get on clean shirts & appear decent on deck. My chest being down in the hold it was my dressing room. The weather was a little hazy through the day but cleared up towards night. Saw a seaweed floating along which the mate supposed to come from the Gulf of Mexico by the effects of the Gulf Stream. We read sermons & religious books through the course of the day. The wind having completely died away the vessel remained stationary in the midst of a calm sea with a little swell. A shoal of porpoises of about 30 perhaps swam along by our side of the ship & across her Bow. They were large unshapely monsters, some might be one ton weight. They amused us a little, rolling about & splashing in the water at intervals. We saw 2 or 3 whales blowing near the horizon. The water appeared to go rather higher than the masts of a vessel which was about the same place. About 8 P.M. a whale appeared at about 300 yards from the ship side blowing away in fine style. The noise occasioned by the water falling again in the sea was something like a little waterfall. We also saw a few small nautilus floating about. They appeared like a large mouse but none came within 10 or 20 feet of the ship. There was a great quantity of red things in the water, something like the linty stuff that grows on the stones of running burns.

Monday, 12th: Fine breeze from the south west. A large Bark came in sight on the horizon sailing before the wind. It passed us and disappeared in a short time. We were sailing about 6½ miles an hour. It looked very

Ship at sea, sketched by Sandford Fleming.

majestic & I took a sketch of it. It was our day to kindle the fire & serve out the water. The sailors & some of the passengers were at Gymnastic Exercises in the evening.

Tuesday, 13th: I went on deck at ½ past 2 A.M. The mate told me a vessel had just passed very close to ours. He spoke to her with a speaking trumpet. Someone answered but could not make out what they said. It was probable they heard him through the trumpet & would report to Scotland. We had a fine south breeze all day & were happy to learn at midday that we were more than halfway between land & land. The strong wind raises a swell on the sea & the ship pitched considerably. We slept very little all night.

Wednesday, 14th: The vessel had been going all night & just now about 8 miles an hour. It was very difficult to cook at the fire. The spray was going across the ship & we got ourselves wet. The pump for serving out fresh water had broke & we tried to solder it with a spoon & bolt which one of the passengers had & tartaric acid. The ship was labouring very hard. We had no sleep. It took nearly all we could do to stick to the bed. The trunks broke loose about 2 oclock A.M.

Thursday, 15th: [continued] & were sliding back & forward on the floor which was in a horrid state with nuisance, the chamber pots having upset & the tins. Spoons, teapots &c were flying from underneath one bed to another. (Some of the females had fallen & slid on the floor last night & dirtied their clothes very much, the smell was unpleasant.) We got up & got a light & got temporarily fastened. We then sat down on the top of them along with the mate & refreshed on ale & currant loaf. We were scarcely in bed when we had to be at them again. We had even to tye the pillows to the bed for they rolled into the west floor. So much for that. It was not at all pleasant (even though we washed them well) to eat out of the tins next day. The reason of all this was said to be onto the ballast (pig iron) being too low in the hold with the wind blowing right at the stern. However the wind gradually wore round to the North & we went through the water nobly. We passed a Brig which I sketched. We were also fast taking in another which was now on the horizon. We were making a lemonade drink down stairs when a cry of "a ship wreck" was heard. We all flew on deck & saw what we thought a vessel lying on her broadside right before us. With anxious looks the Captain got the spy glass, and were all agreeably surprised to find out that it was an ice berg about the same place as the ship. When we came up to it, it had a pure snow white appearance, shining like glass & the spray flying over it. It would perhaps be 200 ft dia. & 20 or 40 feet out of water. Before night came on we had the pleasure to pass this other vessel also.

Friday, 16th: Slept very sound the past night & I may say that we were very happy when going to bed. The moon was shining in the heavens & the silver water sparkled under its rays while the ship glided through the water at 7 & 8 miles an hour, and at this rate we were assured of reaching the Banks of Newfoundland in 2 days. In the morning, however, the wind was scarcely favourable. The days pass away very agreeably & we must certainly grow fat as we have little else to do but eat. Brother David tried the flour bannock baking in the afternoon. He certainly deserved great credit for the first time, being composed of currants, soda & sugar they relished exceedingly along with jelly we got from our aunt to our tea. In the evening we passed to the leeward of an ice berg which caused the air to be very cold, but after we had passed a short time it got warmer.

Saturday, 17th: Up at 4. Saw the sun rising. It had a most magnificent appearance, being intermixed with clouds on the horizon. The sea was very calm, but a breeze sprang up in the afternoon, though not altogether favourable. About 6 P.M. an iceberg or island made it[s] appearance on the horizon in N.W. It seemed to be very extensive but the haze prevented it from being very visible.

Sunday, 18th: Up at 5 kindling the fire & serving out water. A very pleasant day of fair wind. A good many flocks of sea birds are seen flying about. Not having seen any previous except a few canaries & Mother Carries chickens. Saw the top mast of a Brig to the north & an ice berg to the south horizon. About 5 P.M. we passed about a ship length from a large conical ice berg. We supposed it to be about 40 ft high x 100 visible above water. There were a great many sea fowls sitting & flying about it. We had a nice view of it. It was all worn into fissures on the surface by the spray, but at no place could a boat have landed on it. A little to the leeward were a great many small blocks of ice with whales or bottle noses blowing amongst them & in other directions.

Monday, 19th: Sailing to the North West with a strong breeze right astern, we are now on the Great Bank of Newfoundland sailing at about 10 miles an hour. There are a great many fishing schooners with little boats flying about, a few fish blowing. Towards evening it gets very hazy & when sitting down [in] the cabin we hear a great crying on deck. It is a large schooner right ahead having been obscured in the fog until about 2 ship lengths from us. We would have struck her amid ships if our course had not been altered. The night is very wet & a stiff breeze. A man rings the bell continually & one or 2 looking out. We got 2 lbs of flour each from the ship instead of biscuit which we liked very well having plenty of biscuit. If we had struck the schooner she would have been divided in two by the speed we were going at & the mate thought we would [have] sunk in half an hour by the damage we would have received, her bows would have been stove in & at least some of her sails stripped off.

Tuesday, 20th: Still hazy & wet. Some of the passengers had used precautions the past night for the vessel sinking such as sleeping with their clothes on & pocketing their money &c and having a bag of biscuits ready to throw into the small boats. The weather cleared up in the afternoon & we saw two vessels at the horizon. We are now across the banks. The night passes with an intermediate fog & clear moonlight.

Wednesday, 21st: The weather still foggy. Latitude now 45° 36' & Long. 56 ° 16'. The sun having made its appearance for a short time exactly at midday which was of great advantage for the true reckoning. One fishing schooner in sight throughout the day. Since we came on the Banks the weather has been rather cold.

Thursday, 22nd: It is now 4 weeks today since we left Glasgow & I must say it has gone away very quickly. We began to wash a few handkerchiefs &c when a Betsy a female passenger kindly offered to do them. I was just appearing on deck to put out some to dry when agreeably surprised I was to see hills on the horizon. They had been hid before by the mist. Immediately on deck came everyone, some nearly dancing with joy. I took a sketch of it as they appeared. This was the south coast of Newfoundland, the first I have seen of the New World, the first of our adopted country. We were at noon in Latitude 47° 28' & Long. 58° 4'. We tacked N. By W. 20 miles, when we were then only about 2 miles from land. The hills were covered partly with snow & looked very rocky & cold like. The wind being right against us we then tacked S.W. Before we saw land & throughout the day a few beautiful land birds were seen flying about the vessel & one or two leaped about the deck picking up crumbs for a long time. When near land we saw a beautiful gold yellow fish about the size of a haddock floating dead on the water, as well as a considerable quantity of seaweed & sometimes pieces of wood.

Friday, 23rd: We sailed a little in the morning but during the remainder of the day we were quite becalmed. Some of the passengers were trying to fish but caught none, the water being too deep at that place. The day was uncommonly pleasant, the sky clear, & although 50 or 60 miles from land we saw it all day. The sunset was most beautiful, scarcely a cloud was to be seen & about 6 vessels scattered round the horizon. After the sun disappeared on deck I went up the riggings & saw it for a few minutes longer.

Saturday, 24th: We had a slight breeze during the night but it died away in the forenoon. Exchanged signals with a London vessel named *Glenlyon* which seemed to be bound in the same direction as we were. Caught on board a beautiful little land bird which had been fatigued flying so far. In a ship becalmed at sea one tires very soon, although the two finest days during the passage. I never felt tired so much of it as today & yesterday (excepting the dangerous weather). A pig was killed on board which was something to look at. Towards night we had a slight breeze going about 6 miles an hour. Saw land of Cape Breton & Newfoundland, but St Pauls Island is not visible at 7 P.M. The lighthouse was seen at 11 oclock.

Sunday, 25th: Called up at 4 to see St Pauls Island, we had a good breeze & are now entering into the Gulf of St Lawrence. In the forenoon we saw the Bird Isles, a group of steep rocks, two only of which we saw in the distance. There were a good many birds flying across to them large & white with the tip of their wings black & some black altogether. It is said that swans is to be found on these rocks, a thing not improbable. In a short time we came in sight of the Brion Island, having come up behind the Bird & Brion Island. None of them we saw very distinctly owing to the wet weather which continued all day & changed into half snow or sleet towards night

Monday, 26th: A fine morning & good breeze. The Captain had given the steerage people & us a bottle of brandy last night. They got very merry but ours was reserved as it was Sunday. Laughable affair happened through the night. Mr and Mrs Aitken having suspected the 2nd mate [of] troubling their daughter Isobel through the night. Mr Aitken lay down where she used to be. The 2nd mate comes down in the middle watch & lift off the cloth, he felt it was a man. He was completely puzzled after find out to be her father & no doubt unlikely escape. Cape Gaspe appeared in sight through the day & at night we had Amherst Island on our side & the mainland well seen on the other. Anticosti was apparently a very low lying island, but Cape Gaspe & the mainland had some picturesque hills above it but was not very distinct. I commenced to copy the log book today. About bed time we found that preparations were making for Mrs Lilleave having a child. A screen was put across the room but we, Henry Fleming, David & I determined not to go to bed. The poor woman commenced to cry & continued in great trouble all night. The Captain allowed us to go down to the cabin after all & the two passengers were in bed. We had coffee through the night & I got into the mates bed at 12 when it was his watch on deck & David & I got in the 2nd mates from 4, it being a large one. We had our porridge on deck & a little after that she was delivered of a daughter.

Tuesday, 27th: We were rather in an awkward condition by the past nights work. Went to bed for an hour or so in the forenoon. The vessel not making much progress the wind being right against. We tacked between Island of Anticosti & the mainland. The island was entirely covered with short fir wood, very thick. The mainland here & up the Gaspe channel is pretty high, perhaps 1,000 feet some places, above the sea covered chiefly with trees interspersed with fine bold promontories. The weather is still coldish yet & some snow is visible on the land.

Wednesday, 28th: We had sailed very well the past night. The forenoon is very warm & we felt it more so having on our thick clothes. The wind rises very quick here & dies away as quick. We were becalmed several times through the day & sailed quick at others. We feel no disadvantage from the water being so ill tasted. It was a little the second week but that was owing to the water being in spirit casks which were made use of first. What we were now using is as good as one day or so old, it being nice & cold by being kept in the hold.

Thursday, 29th: The past night had been very disagreeable for the sailors having had very little sleep & snowed all night, very dark & rather dangerous not seeing far before the vessel. We were looking out for the pilot boat but noone in sight. We tacked very close to the main coast. It was very rugged & where no rocks covered by stunted like trees except in the hollows. There are a great many vessels in sight tacking up against the wind like ourselves. About sunset we were becalmed for a little & a light breeze sprung up right up the river which gradually grew stronger & continued all night.

Friday, 30th: Sailed very quick all [night] with the advantage of the tide and we were up as far as Green Island by two o'clock. The south side of the river is now covered with huts, small villages with their allotments of ground adjoining but the other side is very rugged, some places having much the appearance of highland scenery. The tide being down we only made up to the Island nearly opposite to the Brandy Pot where we were becalmed & cast anchor. The wind now changed & blew right down the river, where we began tacking, where the tide flowed, having now the safety of a Pilot who came on board in the afternoon.

Saturday, 31st: Awakened in the morning about 10 miles further into the river. The wind was right against us & we tacked to the best advantage till midday when we again anchored. The river here is about 12 or 14 miles broad. The land on both sides is very hilly & woody interspersed by a few green spots with islands & a few rocks along the shore. The scenery is rather better than we have yet passed.

Entrance to the Saguenay River, sketched by Fleming on board ship in the St. Lawrence River.

June 1845

Sunday, 1st: Heaved anchor about 10 & tacked up the river till about 2 oclock P.M. We made very little of it, not being above 10 or 12 miles further up. Began to sail at 10 o'clock being floodtide. I stopped up with the sailors all night till about ½ past 4 A.M. doing a little with the ropes.

Monday, 2nd: Rose about 10 A.M., the ship tacking again up the river. The land on the north side is pretty high & covered with trees except where cleared. We see great fires up & down the riverside, likely to be the settlers burning trees. There are some little bits of snow on the hills here & there yet. We have had a good stiff breeze today, having made up above the light ship where we came to anchor.

Tuesday, 3rd: Sailed again next day about 11 & made up past the Pillars lighthouse to about 12 miles below Grosse Island in the evening where we came to anchor. There are a great many white houses on the shore south. It is just like a village continued all the way up. The ground is level for a good many miles on each side of the shore & high hills rise up in the background.

Wednesday, 4th: Lying at anchor opposite Grosse Island the quarantine land. The passengers were all dressed for the doctor coming on board, which he did about 9 oclock. He made us all pass him twice to see us & count the number. We got off without washing clothes or required to throw our clothes &c overboard owing to our clean appearance. The Captain went ashore with 2 cabin, 2 intermediate or steerage passengers, had not the good luck to get David & Henry Fleming from our cabin. I was rather disappointed. I wished to take a sketch of the place. They brought on board bread &c that was baked on the island for the supply of sick emigrants who by [bide] there for some time till they get better;

Grosse Isle, the quarantine station sketched by Fleming, June 3, 1845.

80 sick persons were there at this time confined by measles &c. They also brought flowers & plants which were found on the island. A common dandelion was one of them. The numerous rocky islands covered with fir trees are most beautiful with high hills in the background. We lay at anchor the same evening opposite Orleans Island, the land there & the country on the other side is apparently good & interspersed with trees is really beautiful, as it appears on a warm calm sunny night. The day was very warm & we donned our white clothes. It has gradually become so as we came up the river.

Thursday, 5th: Came up on deck to see Quebec about 5 or 6 A.M. just there opposite a waterfall. The river at Quebec was immensely crowded with vessels & pilot boats flying about in every direction. The roofs of houses & the spires were shining with the suns rays, they being almost all covered with tin which stands without rusting. After coming to anchor the Harbourmaster & doctors &c came aboard, looked down to the several places & went away. We packed up all our beds &c in hopes of getting away with the 5 oclock steamer to Montreal. Went on shore some of us in a boat to see the town in the forenoon. Everything seemed strange., the steamers especially. Some were driven by horses walking on deck, but the Montreal ones were splendid. Very happy to get our feet on terra firma once more. We set off to see the ruins of the great fire which had taken place one or two days before. It had an awful appearance. More than 20 acres of houses were burnt to the ground, nothing left but a forest of blackened chimneys, the houses being chiefly built of wood. The pavement of the streets being made of wood was also burnt. It was really a melancholy catastrophe. The inhabitants thus made homeless were lodged in churches & other large buildings & subscriptions were raised in every quarter for their support. Our pilot's house was burnt, & a Mr Dennys which I had a letter from Kirkcaldy to. The people here are almost all french & have of course a very foreign appearance. I bought a chip hat for the warmer weather for less than 2/ of our money. After going about for some time we came on board to be in line for the steamer, but found we could not get till next day as the customs house officer had not come on board. The bed being all packed & sewed up we laid there on the floor & made the best of the night we could.

Friday, 6th: The vessel weighed anchor & came to a wharf. We went thro the town all forenoon, saw the inside of a Roman Catholic Chapel. It was really splendid & elaborately finished. Saw the spot where General Wolfe was killed & broke a piece off the monument. Had fresh fish & potatoes to dinner & got the luggage put on board the steamer *Queen* in the afternoon. The customs officer only opened one chest & was very reasonable. We left the *Brilliant* & crew with a little sorrow, having made up a pleasant society amongst them notwithstanding the hard nose of the Captain. The river St Lawrence for 2 or 2½ miles above Quebec is a complete forest of vessels taking on cargoes of wood. The scenery along the river is good, some places rocky on the shore & others fertile, but all covered with green trees except where cut down by the farmers who are not so numerous as below Quebec. The vessel was a little crowded but a magnificent steamer. We passed the night the best we could on the top of chests, beds &c. The vessel was pretty well filled with Canadians — queer looking fellows.

Saturday, 7th: A beautiful morning & the river as smooth as glass. The country is very beautiful about 30 miles below Montreal, the shore indented with capes & islands covered partly with trees forming a very picturesque appearance. We landed about 8 oclock. Henry Fleming went in search of his brother in law Mr Bethune. Was told that He & his family had that day started for Hamilton, a very unexpected thing but during his absence Mr Bethune & wife came to the steamer & said they were to start about noon. We made up our minds to go with him & got the luggage driven to the barge & left the box with two chairs with Mr Laverock to sell. Took farewell of the other passengers & left the canal basin about 3 P.M. with Mr Aitkens family & Lilleave. The country is most fertile & beautiful. The farmers have beautiful cottages & steadings. We got milk &c at some of the locks as we passed. Our barge very deep laden stuck in the mud a little below Lachine & we lay there all night. It rained very heavy but we slept under oil cloth on deck, the hold having been filled up before we got our passage.

Sunday, 8th: Our barge was taken up as far as the locks but it being against the law to pass on Sunday some went to Scotch church in town. The minister was very kind, gave us books & conversed with us about

Scotland before preaching. We got through the locks after the churches were out & got up into the wharfs at the river. Got plenty milk here. Something being wrong with the steamer we lay all night at Lachine.

Monday, 9th: Started early in the morning with a new steamer. Got up as far as St Annes where the steamer left us to go for some more barges. There is a lock here on account of strong rapids. The people are all French. The river is very beautiful having a great many islands covered with high trees. We went out shooting through the day in the bush. I got a few fine birds, some of them very pretty.

Tuesday, 10th: Still at St Annes, the steamer being under repair. We got a small boat & sailed round some of the islands scattered through the river. They were really pretty along the shore but marshy. Sent a letter & newspaper home to my father & Mr Bethune. Mr Aitken & Mr Fleming went away to see Mr Crighton from Kennoway, and to get up the St Lawrence to Kingston we started from St Annes about 4 P.M. & sailed up the Lake of Two Mountains to the Grand River. The banks are very level & covered with trees, but hills appear in the distance. Further up the Ottawa River saw miscatoes for the first time. Got several bites on my hand. They are very itchy. If you do not scratch them they soon go away, but if you do they swell very much. Some people they do not sting, or at least they never feel them. About 12 [at] night the steamer stuck & did not get her off till next morning.

Wednesday, 11th: The Ottawa is really a good river swelling into lakes indented by capes & studded with islands. At several places the shores are hilly, but generally very level all covered with hard wood of different kinds. The steamer stops once or twice a day to get in wood where we get fine sweet milk but about twice as dear as at Scotland or at least 2/3d. Came to Conan about 8 P.M., a very pretty clean place, where we went through 3 locks to get into the canal, there being a great rapids there extending up to Grenville about 7 miles.

Thursday, 12th: Pulled up at Grenville by horse, where we lay all day waiting on the steamer. The inhabitants here are principally Scotch & Irish. The ground round about the wharf is very marshy. Went out to the woods & contrary to expectations heard the birds singing nearly as well as at home. Heard the bullfrogs in the evening. They have a very hoarse cry. A steamer came from Bytown for some barges lying here & Mr Aitkens family went away with it, not having paid their passage here & this being so slow. We would all have gone if our passage had not been paid. The steamer did not come this evening.

Friday, 13th: The steamer came up this morning but could not get through the locks being too broad. They had to cut the paddles. We were all very angry being hindered so much & the owner got us stored on board another companies barge & we left Grenville about 12. Pretty well acquainted with the country here. The country we passed through before dark was barren & hilly. The barge being crowded with luggage & we had no little amusement taking tea on the top of the luggage. The hold was cleared out & we got some beds spread out at one end, the other being possessed by passengers having the itch. To have no communication we built up a wall of trunks. There was 15 persons in each bed to the side, the females together & the males & children. Before going to bed we had bread & lemon syrup mixed with water, a large jar containing the syrup placed beside the candle & us all sitting round it drinking out of a pint stoup looked tinkle enough like. We spent the night very well & arrived at Bytown at 6 A.M.

Ottawa in 1845. From Sandford Fleming Empire Builder *by L. J. Burpee.*

Saturday, 14th: The shores of the river Ottawa here are very steep. We enter the Rideau canal in a series of locks, then passing through a bridge which connects the upper and lower towns of Bytown together. The whole buildings forming a grand work of art & even a beautiful landscape being bounded by 2 woody hills on each side. This is a growing little town, fine wide streets with good stone houses rising up. The Bytown falls are a grand sight from the Barracks, a beautiful chain bridge extends across the river immediately below them, forming the first connection between the two sides of the river. Above this the river spreads out into a lake with many islands. In this town we met with an old acquaintance of my father Robert Blyth & his family who left Kennoway 1 year ago. They are now in good worldly circumstances & very comfortable tho poor enough before. David & I got a nice dinner in his son Johns house. Here separated from (the last but one of our *Brilliant* passengers) Mr Lilleave wife & sister in law who went up with a Mr Whellman, a builder in town. Left Bytown about 1 P.M. by the Rideau Canal, came to a double lock about 4 miles up. The country here is partly cleared. It has a bare appearance with so many long naked stumps here & there & the branches &c being burned off the left trees when removing the cut wood. About a mile further up we have another fall where the canal spreads out in a sort of narrow lake — the spill water falls over a rock forming a pretty little waterfalls. The rock behind, sandstone, splits into flags all having the rippled appearance of the sand on a seashore. Robert Blyth says a miller is a very fine trade here, especially a flour miller, oats not being so much used. They get good wages & plenty of trade for them. We were at the Black Rapids about 6 P.M. exactly 10 miles from Bytown. There is only a single lock here. The canal is now formed by damming up the water & allowing the water to flow over the country above it. The river & the course forming locks at the rapids. Where the embankment is formed where the banks of the river have been high the canal is very beautiful. Where the country is level, the water having flowed amongst the trees around, has now rotted there leaving long bare & rotten stumps along the edge in some places dangerous. Very difficult there. We have left several rafts of wood by the way on this canal in the Grand river. Came to Long Island locks in the evening. They are 3 in number, a few houses here & store.[Continued in new book]

The locks at Bytown (Ottawa), sketched by Fleming, June 14, 1845.

[Notebook continued: Voyage to Upper Canada]

Sunday, June 15th, 1845: Awakened at Merrickville Locks after sleeping very well through the night as usual. Since going to bed we have passed 3 different lock stations. At this place there is a nice little town. We then passed Maitland locks & another one before coming to Ley Rapids where I had a letter to Alex Kinmouth, Lockmaster, from his nephew the baker in Kirkcaldy. He was very kind to us & asked about his friends at home. It had been 30 years since he left Kirkcaldy and although the ague was common in this part of the country he had not yet taken it, nor his wife. Every house bakes its own bread there & I can say it is as good as any I have ever tasted. I walked up the river side about 1 mile to Smith Falls, the name of the locks & village. There are several fan & other mills here. The vessels are raised by 3 locks into a basin answering as a dam for the Mills & there by another lock to the canal again.

Monday, 16th: Up at 6 to see St Johns Locks. This is a very pretty place not at all like what we have passed on this canal. It is hilly & rocky & all covered here and there with trees. The second lock after Smith Falls is the last rising one. The first is Parliamentary Locks entering into Lake Rideau & the next Lara Lock from that lake to the highest part of the canal between Bytown & Kingston. During the night we passed 2 lock stations more before coming to St John which consisted of 6 locks. The river along here takes a very circuitous route amongst the rocks which are very prominent along the banks. We then pass the Bruce Mill Locks, 2 stations of locks each & about a mile between them. The country around is now alternately consists of immense marshes & long rotten stumps of trees sticking in them & fallen down in the winds &c, &c, banks rocky & covered with green trees. Heron & birds of that kind are very common here. We now pass through Kingston mill locks, they are 5 in number & very substantially got up. The country around there is high & rocky & very picturesque. From the top of these rocks Kingston is at right. Between this & Kingston the land is level & marshy but some good farms are seen here & there. Kingston is a pretty considerable town, wide streets & well laid out. There are some good public buildings, more especially the market house which is extensive & splendid in the form of T with colonnade & pillars in front supporting a dome & clock tower, with the roof covered with tin. There are some good churches, a new Gothic catholic one building & a large plain college. The country in the suburbs is level with good villas here & there with a few trees left around them. Sailed in the *Princess Royal* steamer up the Lake on time at 7 P.M. along with Mr Bethune, Henry Fleming & the Aitkens who had come up before us. The steamer, chiefly Irish, some supposed there would be 500 on board. Got no sleep all the night. The lake was a little rough & some of the passengers were sick.

Tuesday, 17th: Landed at the town of Cobourg at about 8 A.M. Took goodbye of our friends who were going up with the steamer to Toronto & then to Hamilton & spent the time very pleasantly in the Bourg with Mr Bethune & Mr Gowans familys. They are very kind obliging people, far different from the Arthurs. They are away up to the Bush in Chippewa. Cobourg is a nice healthy little town apparently thriving very well being on the banks of Lake Ontario it is just like a seaport town there being nothing to be seen but the lake on one side of the horizon. Being too late to catch the steamer at Rice Lake to Peterboro, on account of a strong headwind keeping back the Toronto steamer, we got a returning farmers cart on the wharf to take David & I & luggage for 3½ dollars, being anxious to see the inland country. There are good comfortable farms round this town with good houses. The road is a little rough for about 5 miles, they being just in their original state, but we have about 4 miles of a new metaled road (which is a little better), being the one from Port Hope to Rice Lake. I drove the waggon here & when leaving this for another road one of the wheels went into a rut in the road, thru me off the waggon. Did not get upset it was a wonder some of the chests did not come off above me. The farmer of course now took the reins. He being better accustomed to the corduroy roads as they are called. They are indeed rough enough especially where they pass over marshy places of which we had 3 or two, perhaps 7 miles altogether. The trees are cut in lengths & thrown across close to one another & filled up on the top with earth or stones but when one goes even, the wheel goes in with a jerk but the waggons will scarcely upset being on 4 wheels. The country we passed through was at first good soil with gradually rising banks but opposite Rice Lake it was very sandy although good pines grow upon it. The road in some places was steep & in some places marshy between the hills. The roads are all straight being between the farms & continue so for a great length. We saw some large pines by the way & when on a height on the road it looked strange to see nothing but woods around from horizon to horizon. Arrived in Peterboro about sun down, it looked rather a poor like place where we entered, the stumps of trees still in the middle of the streets, a wood house here & there with a few good villas with verandahs around in the suburbs. Drove up to Dr Hutchisons, a two-storey little house. He was not at home but Mrs told us to bring in our chest & was kind to us. Saw James who has grown a good deal & quite altered in features. After seeing the Dr & talking a little we went to bed being tired having slept little the last two nights, it rained heavy in the Barge & not getting the bed laid down for the wet coming in.

Wednesday, 18th: Up at 11. Being well rested got our clothes aired & arranged our trunks before dinner. The trunks were worn as much by knocking about yesterday as all the rest of the passage. Went out with the Dr to see the town. There are some good shops & stores in it and a large court house & cells which we were through. There was one debtor, a man & wife for burning a house & a Lunatic, now being the prison for the whole district of Colborne. The place looks very well down about the river — it is more than ½ the size of the Clyde at Glasgow. A small steamer plies between this town & Rice Lake. A part of the town is on the other side of the river which is crossed by a wooden bridge. It consists of about 2 thousand inhabitants.

Thursday, 19th: It has been cool the last 2 or 3 days there being a good breeze today. It is very warm, the thermometer standing in the shade at 85 degrees. It was a little fatiguing when working outdoors but not so much uncomfortable as one would think. I was doing a little in the Dr's garden. Took a stroll about the town. Saw Mr [John] Halls flour mills a little above the town, they are very well fitted up & good machinery. There is also a saw mill beside them, it is a rather primitive concern. The water wheels in these mill are driven by the pressure of water from the bottom of a large tank which is constantly supplied from the river by a canal from above the rapids. The water power is great. The owner is just advertising to let part for any purpose.

Friday, 20th: David & I went with Dr Hutchison in a spring waggon up as far as Mud Lake a distance of 8 miles, calling at several farmers houses where he had patients along the way. About ½ this distance out from Peterboro is covered with good farms partly cleared. The houses are not fine but the farmers appear well off. Mud Lake is about 12 miles long, about 1½ miles shallows & woody banks & an Indian village on the opposite side, Peter Nogey, chief. We brought home a fat lamb & some eggs for provisions which was killed in the evening. I have always a good appetite but very tired & drowsy at night & sometimes through the day, I suppose with the heat.

Saturday, 21st: Very warm, the thermometer steady at 85 in the shade. Sent away the letters we brought out & wrote home to my father with more newspapers to him & Robert Imrie.

Sunday, 22nd: Sunday at Episcopal Church where the Doctor has a pew, the Scotch church minister was from home.

Monday, 23rd: Copied the letter to Scotland. Went out to fish in the afternoon & got a Bathe in the river. It was very pleasant.

Tuesday, 24th: Finding the levels of the ground at the back of Dr Hutchisons home for a stable & assisting to cut the foundation posts &c.

Wednesday, 25th: Reading & fishing. The Dr has not yet had time to go to Toronto, he being very busy.

Thursday, 26th: Took a stroll up the brook [Jackson Creek] that passes through the town, it comes through a pretty good sort of a glen with limestone quarries on the banks with some organic remains in them. This week being the longest days, they are not so long as in Scotland ending about 8 P.M., but the winter days (nights) are longer.

Friday, 27th: Went down in the steamer with Dr Hutchison to Rice Lake where there is an Indian village. Got some stone arrowheads from a Miss Anderson, a half Indian, her father [Charles Anderson] a large proprietor having married a squaw. These arrows along with many other things were found in hillocks on their farm where the Indians have a tradition of a great battle being fought. There are a great many of these mounds [Serpent Mounds] all containing the bones of grown up men, no women nor children, which identifies the fact. The Indians are a very dark & languid-like people having no energy nor skill about them except for baskets & trifles of that kind which they ornament very tastefully. Government is very kind to them having built good houses, cleared land for them (which they now almost neglect) and gives them clothing & money every year, a Doctor to attend and give them medicine & a school house, but notwithstanding all that they are idle and hence miserable in the wintertime. They are dying away every year and it is supposed their race will soon be extinct. We missed the steamer and set off on foot for Peterboro about 12 miles. It being so warm the Dr took us into a friends to rest, he had been an old military officer and was very frank to us, got our dinner there. Set off again about 8 P.M. but the Dr took rather unwell so he and I stopped in an inn 8 or 9 miles below Peterboro and David went on to send down a waggon next morning. He had a dark walk through the woods & was like to lose the road sometimes.

Saturday, 28th: Morning rainy. Came up to Peterboro in the forenoon with the waggon. Day spent as usual doing a little in the garden.

Monday, 30th: Intended to go to Toronto this morning but Dr Hutchison thought it better to stop another day and he would get some information, letters &c. Working in the garden.

July 1845

Tuesday, 1st: Could not get away, same excuse as last day.

Wednesday, 2nd: Spent the day the same as yesterday doing little jobs. We are waiting on the Dr who wished to do us as much good as possible & wishes to write 2 or 3 letters to friends in Toronto but cannot find time, he being much out.

Thursday, 3rd: The Dr came home this morning at 5 oclock & went to bed so we could not get away this morning. He got a letter from Capt McDonald to Sir Allan MacNab in Hamilton as a recommendation for me. David turned a little bench for Mr McDonald out of a piece of the *Royal George* which he gave him.

Friday, 4th: This is the great day of the Yankees throughout all the United States. It is also Mrs Hutchisons birthday. She had a nice party in the evening of young ladies & gentlemen, daughters of wealthy farmers & millowners hence it passed off very pleasantly.

Saturday, 5th: The Dr is always very busy looking out for an opening for us. He got Mr Wilson, superintendent for the Board of Works, to take David to work at the construction of Locks, bridges, &c on the Trent River. He gets 6/6 a day at first. It is likely he may get in to get the management of some work from Mr Wilson & he says he will require someone for that who can draw &c. We had a walk in the country a little bit tonight and saw a snake for the first time. It was about 2 feet long an inch diameter & a beautiful skin. They bite but are not venomous.

Sunday, 6th: At the Scotch church morning where there was a collection for the fire sufferers at Quebec, the news of the second fire has just come to hand. At the English church evening.

Monday, 7th: David left this morning with Mr Wilson and some others for the Trent River. Dr Hutchison went down to Rice Lake village with them. It is very warm today, everyone saying it was the warmest we've had.

Tuesday, 8th: Got a sail in a boat & sketched the English church.

Wednesday, 9th–Friday, 11th: Very much alike. Out 4 or 5 miles in the country.

Saturday, 12th: This is the great day for the Orange Men of Ireland, being the anniversary of 1690 the day they gained the great battle over the Catholics. They had an Orange walk here but rather a poor turnout, altho as Dr Hutchison said providence gave them a warm reception, the thermometer standing at 93 in the shade.

Sunday, 13th: Still warm standing at 96 degrees. Someone says his stands at 102 degrees but I suspect it must be hung on a warm wall &c. It is clear moonlight & very sultry.

Monday, 14th, Tuesday, 15th: Very warm but beginning not to feel it so much. I have seen several people who never felt it so warm in their life before, although 6 years & upwards in the country. The air is getting very smokey on account of great fires in the woods round.

Wednesday, 16th: Still warm & no rain although it looked like it every night this week. There is very great necessity for it. The grass is withering away & the crop drying up, all except the Indian corn which looks very fresh. It is supposed that if this weather continues 5 days longer almost everything will be dried up.

Thursday, 17th: Good showers through last night which has cooled the air very much. Dr Hutchison got a letter from David today. He complains very much of the heat, scarcely very able to stand it. I go to bathe every day in the river which is very refreshing.

Friday, 18th: A good breeze & cool. I have been drawing the English chapel of this town these last two days with a flowered border & butterflies, bees &c colored which looks very well. Gave it to Miss Benson as a philapine last night. She & her sister came up to thank me for it.

Saturday, 19th: Got a Berlin wool watch pocket as a philapine [philapine — a forfeit collected the day after a party where two shared a double-kernel nut] from Miss Hall. In the country a little bit with the Dr.

Sunday, 20th: At church as usual. Fine thunder showers. David came here from Crooks Rapids in the evening, quite tired of that place & not going back.

Monday, 21st: Making a dam on the creek opposite the house.

Tuesday, 22nd: Digging a water course through the garden. Saw the Scotch Giant & Tom Thumb who have visited this town.

Wednesday, 23rd: Digging drain.

Library and Archives Canada.

Sketch of St. John's Anglican Church, Peterborough, from Fleming's diary.

Thursday, 24th, Friday, 25th: Sundries.

Saturday, 26th: Had a sail on the little lake & crossed the river on 3 planks laid together.

Sunday, 27th: Went with Mr Armstrong to his fathers place Millbrook, Cavan 16 miles off. At church afternoon.

Monday, 28th: Came back to Peterboro along with him. Down at the Halls in the evening to talk about picnic proposed to be tomorrow. Saw a field of wheat ripe & cut down at Cavan on Sunday last as well as several small patches.

Tuesday, 29th: The morning very rainy. We were to start for Mud Lake at nine oclock but did not till eleven when the weather looked a little better. The party consisted of 5 buggies or double wheeled gigs & a 2 horse waggon, Put up the horses at a house near the lake. Went on a boat, sailed & fished for some time. Landed on an island which we christened picnic island. Went on shore again, made a table & forms under a tree with board. Kindled a fire, made coffee & set to eating & drinking. Tried to get up some amusements but the grass being so wet, it did not go off well, it being what may be called a Scotch mist all day. We set off home again & were met by a very heavy thunder shower half way which finished the days wetting. We all went to tea at the Halls where we finished the picnic by dancing &c. Things were suffering for want of rain before today.

Wednesday, 30th: Spent the day as usual with catching & losing philapines.

Thursday, 31st: Went a fishing up the river with Mr Harvey & the Drs sons, caught a few small bass. Kindled a fire, roasted & ate one. Got tea at Mr Harveys fathers about 3 miles up & as many raspberries & currants as we could eat. Raspberries growing wild.

August 1845

Sunday, 3rd: At church.

Monday, 4th–Friday, 8th: As usual working in the garden &c. Mr [John] Butler, Priest of the Catholic Church, wants a plan for completing the spire of the church. Up on Friday looking at it.

Saturday, 9th: Drawing out a design for the spire.

Sunday, 10th: At church twice.

Monday, 11th: The Priest was well pleased with the Plan as well as Mr McDonald.

Tuesday, 12th: Sundries. Preparing to go to Toronto.

Wednesday, 13th: Left Peterboro with the stage to Port Hope. The driver was a Scotch man with whom we were highly amused. Some strong thunder & lightning on the road.

Thursday, 14th: Port Hope is a nice thriving little town situated between two hills which are covered with trees & beautiful cottages, with a considerable stream running through the town which has good falls for the mills situated here. This place may be said to be like a Scotch town but the houses being painted white & some of them tastefully built it looks even much better. The shingles in course of time have the same colours & appearance as slates which looks very well. We left this place by the *City of Toronto* steamer for that city. It is not so handsomely fitted as the *Princess Royal* but a very kind obliging Captain, Mr Dick. Sailed about 7 A.M. Called at several intermediate ports on the way up & arrived at Toronto 1 P.M. Got the luggage put in a store & went in search of Mr [George]Holland, Mrs Hutchisons brother. We did not find him till night & when walking up George st at 6 P.M. He pointed out David, Dr Hutchisons brother, who has not had any correspondence with any of his family for two or three years. He was glad to see us & asked all about his friends. He will not write before them (they are certainly a strange family). We were in his house & saw his wife & a nice family of 6. He is well paid but drinks & his house has that appearance. His body is like his brother Williams & his head betwixt that & Johns. We slept in the Edinburgh Castle tavern all night.

Friday, 15th: David has just got work from Mr Wilson, cabinet maker, to commence Monday first. We got a nice private boarding house @ 2½ $ each a week. Mrs Buchan, east Queen, but really a very nice place, and we were very happy to get away from tavern. Mr Jones [Thomas Mercer Jones, Canada Company commissioner] is in Goderich & will not be home before Sept. The McGlashens are not at home, one in the states & the other not returned from Scotland yet. We saw Mr Albro when the Niagara steamer landed. On the road to Peterboro on the Kingston Steamer.

Saturday, 16th: Learned in the evening that Sir Allan MacNab had been in town but left for Hamilton at 3 P.M. & intends to leave with his Lady in a short time for England.

Sunday, 17th: At Scotch church morning & free church evening.

Monday, 18th: Mr Holland knows of no situation for me as yet but is to try what he can to get me in as a clerk &c.

Tuesday, 19th: Tried my camera lucida on a stand I made yesterday. It did not do so well as I would wish. Saw Mr James McGlashen who thinks I have every chance of success & said he thinks it is the best business in this country (civil engineer). I am to call frequently as I pass.

Wednesday, 20th: No Employment for me yet. I wrote to Henry Fleming by Thos Anderson to Hamilton who is to forward the letter.

Thursday, 21st: Wrote to Dr Hutchison. The English mail came in today. I called on Mr [John] Howard, Architect & Engineer here, but he does not require anyone. Tells me how to get License by surveying in the Bush &c.

Friday, 22nd: Friday. The Canada Companys surveys are all completed & so not requiring anyone. Also called at the Board of Works office but the gent was not at home. Saw Sir Allan MacNab in the evening who says he'll give me a letter to an engineer in Hamilton, not knowing anyone here.

Saturday, 23rd: Called twice at Judge Jones where Sir Allan stopped but did not see him. Called again in the evening but he had gone to Hamilton and left no letter for me. I also called at the Board of Works office but Mr Souskie [Casimir Gzowski] was not home yet. Intending to go to Hamilton on Monday if I do not succeed.

Sunday, 24th: At English church morning and left Mrs Buchans prayer book there. At David Hutchisons in the evening.

Monday, 25th: Saw a large party leave this in a steamer to see the falls of Niagara. The cost was 10 shillings to return & dinner. Called again at Mr Gzowskis but he was engaged, again after dinner but he knew of nothing in the province. The great works were nearly finished and the funds were exhausted and they would require to pay off several of the assistants in a short time. In fact he thought it a very bad country for professional men and would advise me as the most profitable for myself to return to Scotland. However this may be but I did not like the idea of returning so soon. I called a short time afterwards to see if I might have a chance in the Geological Survey but he told me it only required two persons, one for the upper province and another for the lower who travelled the country. So I went to Mr Howard the architect to see what he thought. I showed him my book of specimens which pleased him very much & did not at all like the idea of returning home again. He thinks Mr Gzowski and others wish to monopolize & frighten all young men out of the country. Mr Howard says he was ten times worse than I am at first, lived in a garret for half a year and was very badly off, but he has not had rest since, and he believes Mr Gzowski the Pole was as bad himself at first and had now 6 or 7 hundred a year. This was after I discovered Sir Allan had been in town but had left by the Kingston steamer for England and had left no letter for me. Mr Howard would advise me if my finances would allow to go to Goderich, make a plan of the town, and take my letter to

Colborne Lodge, the home built by John G. Howard on 165 acres of land in west Toronto, later donated to the city to become High Park. From Landmarks, Volume 1 *by J.R. Robertson.*

Mr Jones [Canada Company]. Before tonight I felt rather dull, but now I am relieved for after these difficulties it will be the more honour to me when I succeed.

Tuesday, 26th: Tuesday. Left Toronto by steamer for Hamilton in the morning. David was likely to commence carving for Mr Wilson today. After calling at 2 or 3 places we arrived at Burlington Bay which is separated from the lake by a narrow slip of land & joined by a canal about 60 feet wide. The appearance of Hamilton from here is very good, a range of high ground in the back (where they get free stone) being the continuation of the Niagara Falls & Allegheny Mountains. Hamilton is a nice thriving town with the principle part almost all stone & brick houses. The free stone is beautiful & white & is here used for columns &c. Hamilton is doomed to be a great city one day. It is the centre of a rich & extensive agricultural district, communicated by water with Toronto, Kingston & the cities on both sides of Lake Ontario and in a short time with Montreal, Quebec & the Atlantic. Its free stone & and limestone rocks appear immediately in the suburbs and the shipping of them alone will likely be considerable. I called on Mr [James] Merrilees with whom I stopped all night, and he went to some engineers with me but they were out.

Wednesday, 27th: Could get no employment here as a surveyor or engineer but Mr Merrilees inquired at a foundry about a clerk they want, the present one not pleasing them. They were to think a day to see if I would answer. In trying to find out anything about our ship friends, I called on Rev Mr Sale who said he saw Mr Bethune in town today, but thought he had gone by the stage. Sent me to Mr Walker who might know about the Gowans family, and Mr Mitchell about Mr Bethune. He said that he met Mr Bethune on the street and gave his brother in law a letter that was left with him by Mr Anderson. I now sought out Mr Gowans, his daughters have a dressmaking shop on John street. I opened the door and saw Mr Bethune, Henry Fleming and them all, we were very glad to see one another. I had tea there and spent the night very happily and intend to set off next morning to Mr Bethunes. Mr Aitken has taken a farm up at Galt.

Thursday, 28th: Stopped the night as before at Mr Merrilees and set off next morning with the stage with Mr Bethune & Henry. Mr Merrilees promised to write to me if anything cast up for me to do. We went along the Port Dover road, which is planked to that place a distance of 36 miles. We passed the village of Caledonia on the Grand river at 12 miles from Hamilton. There is a steamer passes this place from Lake Erie (Port Maitland) to Brantford & also a good many flour and saw mills. We rolled along this smooth road almost like a floor, halting at several taverns & other places until we came to Mr Secords Tavern 24 miles from Hamilton, and then we walked about 2 miles through the Bush when we came to Mr Bethunes clearance. They were all very happy to see us. He has about 15 acres cleared with a shanty of two rooms in the middle. I chopped down one or two trees until I got my hands blistered until bedtime. Stirred & heaped up the fires that were burning around.

Friday, 29th: Set off to Simcoe along with a Mr Buck & Henry Fleming who was going to pay first instalment of a Lot of land he has bought adjoining Mr Bethunes. In the neighbourhood of Simcoe the land is very sandy but bears pretty good crops & betwixt that & Port Dover one is surprised to see what grows on nothing else apparently but sand. It is a good place for fruit trees & every farm has large orchards as we go along. It is old settled at this place and many fields are even without a single stump, the sandy soil being one advantage of course. Port Dover is a small village where the plank road from Hamilton ends. Here I saw Lake Erie for the first time. They are making a pier by driving oak logs in the ground by piling machines. We got a new waggon here (cost 60$) for Mr Bethune along with some other things and drove home along the plank road. The lightning was very great & rain came on before getting to the Bush road so we put up at Secords Tavern.

Saturday, 30th: The thunder, rain & lightning had been very great thru the night. We set off to the clearing to breakfast & commenced work driving stones in a sleigh by oxen all day.

Sunday, 31st: Mr Bethune had a sermon in forenoon in his shanty when some of the neighbours met & I walked through Henrys Lot in the afternoon along with him.

September 1845

Monday, 1st: Went with Henry Fleming to see a Lot for sale about 4 miles distant. We had great difficulty in finding our way through the Bush but made it out. One part was wet but the rest was good (cost 2¼ $ per acre of 200). Everyone thought it was very cheap and I proposed to borrow the money from him & commence to farm for my father.

Tuesday, 2nd: Making a sleigh to drive stone all day.

Wednesday, 3rd, Thursday, 4th: Driving oxen & working the clearance as usual.

Friday, 5th: Went along with Henry Fleming to see a farm for sale about 3 miles distant. It consists of 200 acres good rolling land with a creek (15 or 20 ft under the general surface) running through one end of it, about 60 or 70 acres cleared for 6 or 7 years. The stumps are almost all loose (except a few pines), could be taken out with oxen very easy. The soil is clay & black earth on the top, not at all run out, it having been hay except the first or second year, with the exception of a few acres. There is a good well but the houses bad, all $1300, considered by everyone very cheap & about the same distance from towns as Mr Bethunes. We had dinner at Mr Jacksons but the son is in Seaforth, and tea with John Wilkie who has 100 acres & 35 cleared. Had great difficulty coming thru the Bush at night.

Saturday, 6th: Working as usual.

Sunday, 7th: Home of Mr Bethune. People had been up almost all night. Watch the house in case the log piles would set fire to the house, the wind being very strong. Heard a Methodist preaching in a neighbours house where the farmers &c around were gathered together.

Monday, 8th, Tuesday, 9th: As usual working about the clearance.

Wednesday, 10th: Henry Fleming left for Hamilton & Dunnville on business concerning his new farm.

Thursday, 11th: As usual.

Friday, 12th: Henry returned who told me he saw Mr Merrilees. There is nothing for me to do in Hamilton but Mr Merrilees saw Davids master from Toronto who said David had written me about something to do about Peterboro. I wrote immediately & Alex Bethune took the letter this night. To go to Port Dover for provisions tomorrow.

Saturday, 13th: Very heavy rains all day. Got wet to the skin first shower, little doing.

Sunday, 14th: Owing to the heavy rains yesterday & last night the ground has entirely flooded and the whole is a miserable appearance. I got Davids letter back today, I having forgot the post. Mr Bethune had sermon.

Monday, 15th: Henry Fleming went to Simcoe but forgot to take Davids letter as proposed. I made up my mind to go to Toronto, being rather short of cash & not liking to ask Mr Bethune. I expected him to offer some for my services. I felt myself in a very aroused state. I took good morning of them all & left for the stage, having about 1½ miles to walk I did not hurry much and I saw both stages pass when about 4 minutes walk from the plank road. I returned & made up my mind several times through the day to ask for some, but I failed. At last about sundown I managed to get up courage (while chopping alone with Mr Bethune) to say that I would require to seek a lend of 3 dollars or so before I went off tomorrow. He in a moment said he would do it with pleasure. I skinned a large groundhog in the evening which had been caught through the day & stretched the skin for the purpose of making a fur cap in winter.

Tuesday, 16th: Got 3 dollars from Mr Bethune (as a lend). I thought he would have given me more & I started for the plank road to catch the sage. I met Henry F on the way who had been at Simcoe. We rattled away along this fine road, arrived at Hamilton about one P.M. Went to Mr Merrilees who was in bed with a cold. Told me what he told Henry F last Wed. No Prospects in Hamilton for me. I then saw Mr Webster who was out but there had been a letter for me at his house about a fortnight. I went there & found one from Dr Hutchison dated 24 August enclosing one from C. Lockhart, Kirkcaldy. Took goodbye of Mrs Webster & Henry Webster & hurried down to the steamer reading the letter. Sailed for Toronto at 2 oclock on board the *Queen Victoria*. Landed at Toronto - 7 evening. David was very glad to see me, he was very much taken up about me owing to my not writing. The second day after I left it appeared Mr [William] Thomas, Architect, wanted a draughtsman.

Wednesday, 17th: Went to Mr McGlashen, Holland, &c but nothing as yet has cast up. I enquired about Mr Thomas but he had got someone before they had mentioned me to him. Mr Jones is not yet come to town but is expected tomorrow.

Thursday, 18th: Very tired of this place having nothing to do & intended to go to Hamilton in the afternoon boat, but Mr Wilson, Davids master, wanted a plan of the Methodist Church made for letting the seats which I began in the afternoon.

Friday, 19th: Finished the plans. Mr Jones is not yet come.

Saturday, 20th: Took home the plans for which I am to get 10/.

Sunday, 21st: Heard Dr Burns in the forenoon & Mr McLeod in the evening.

Monday, 22nd: Mr Jones is not come & it is doubtful when he may. No appearance of anything to do. I make up my mind to go to Hamilton tomorrow & see if anything can be done in the Architect way, if not to go to Mr Bethunes again. Wrote to Dr Hutchison & David to Montreal about the chairs.

Tuesday, 23rd: Left Toronto by the *Queen* steamer, the weather very stormy. The lake very rough & the steamer laboured very much. We only called at one intermediate port owing to the above. Called on Mr Webster & Mr Merrilees & stopped at Mr Gowans all night. Mr Merrilees went along with meet to the two principle builders in town. They both thought I might succeed very well as architect.

Wednesday, 24th: Intended to go along with the stage to Mr Bethunes. I took out my seat, the driver said he would be back to the tavern in 10 minutes but having got the coach filled I as well as another passenger was disappointed, not being able to get another conveyance. I had just to wait till next day. I met Henry Fleming at Mr Gowans in the afternoon. He is going next day to Niagara & Chippewa about the title deed of his farm.

Thursday, 25th: Went down to the wharf intending to go to the falls with Henry but the boat having not come in owing to the weather I came up again & caught the stage for Port Dover. Got to Mr Bethunes for 4 dollars.

Friday, 26th: Up at 5, came to Shermans 5½ miles off for a letter & working on the clearance.

Saturday, 27th: ditto.

Sunday, 28th: Henry Fleming came home today.

Monday, 29th, Tuesday, 30th: As usual (very rainy).

October 1845

Wednesday, 1st: Up at 5 & set off for Guelph with Mr Jackson & Henry Fleming. We travelled along the plank road till about 5 miles beyond Caledonia. From thence across the country to Ancaster, then to Dundas along a first rate Macadamized road winding down the hill. The scenery here & on the other side of Dundas is really very pretty, having much the appearance of some parts of Scotland. We see Hamilton and far down Lake Ontario from the hills on each side. We then went through Flamborough along the Gore road to Guelph. There is a great deal of prime land on the road. We came to Guelph about 9 and was made comfortable before a wood fire after the journey of about 60 or 70 miles. Here we saw Jacksons, some more that was in Kirkcaldy. He is partner in a store & has a good business.

Thursday, 2nd: Went out to David Andersons place about 6 miles from Guelph. He has two daughters married very well. We like his wife. Saw other 3 Kennoway people the names of Orme & Tom.

Friday, 3rd: Saw Thomas Anderson. He has 100 acres, 90 cleared & a Bush lot & is apparently very cozy and comfortable.

Saturday, 4th: About Guelph & a few miles to the north the land is in general pretty good, but the Ormes could not have chosen a worse place as theirs is very hilly & rocky.

Sunday, 5th: Mr Jackson & Henry Fleming left in the waggon for Walpole by Hamilton & I went to see Mr Aitken along by Preston & Galt, through the township of Waterloo which is chiefly settled by Dutch. Galt is situated on the Grand river about 3 miles from Preston. It has plenty of water privilege & high ground along the banks of the river. Between this town & Mr Aitkens the ground is very uneven, consisting of grand knolls. Mr Aitken has 100 acres, 90 cleared, good soil about 5 miles east from Paris on the high ground which surrounds Dumfries plains. They were all very happy to see me & went over ship stories.

Monday, 6th: At Mr Aitkens all day and at a singing school on the Plains in the evening where they were teaching singing to the melodeon.

Tuesday, 7th: Left for Hamilton with the mare & colt which I brought from Guelph belonging to Mr Jackson. The town of Paris is really well situated on the Grand river. I think it is amongst the best I have seen in this country. The river runs rapidly & the ground around is high & uneven. I came down the Governors road to Dundas and I must say the land in Flamborough West is [the] most picturesque I have yet seen on this side the Atlantic; arrived at Hamilton at 6 P.M. Got the mare put up then saw Mr Merrilees & Mr Webster. There is nothing for me yet in this town. Mr Merrilees has got a letter from my father. Stopped at Mr Gowans all night.

Wednesday, 8th: Left for Mr Bethune but did not make the length for rain & the mare very tired. Stopped at a Mr McBrides 4½ miles beyond Caledonia.

Thursday, 9th: Went off at 6 A.M. & got home about ten. Putting shingles on the house all day.

Friday, 10th: Chopping down trees & making a brush fence.

Saturday, 11th: Making a pump to draw the water from the foundations of the house to get them finished.

Sunday, 12th: at home.

Monday 13th–Saturday, 18th: Shingling the house, building stone &c.

Sunday, 19th: At stage road chapel. Mr Bethune preaching.

Monday, 20th: Away for a fat cow along with Henry & the two boys.

Tuesday, 21st: Assisting to kill the cow.

Wednesday 22nd–Friday 24th: As usual (putting up a log oxen house). Mr Bethune cut his ankle with an axe when chopping.

Saturday, 25th: Went to Dunnville 28 miles down the river below Caledonia with Mr Bethune & Henry Fleming, Fleming to get his land registered & Mr Bethune to preach for the first time in that place, he being chosen as a missionary by the Presbytery for the district around here.

Sunday, 26th: At sermon forenoon & English church after. Mr Bethune away about 12 miles further down for the evening. Having heard that Mr Thomson, a great mill owner & store keeper wanted a clerk we called but he had someone else in view, but I would have answered if I had been accustomed with the business. I got yesterday at Caledonia post 3 letters & two from Dr Hutchison. Surveyors are much wanted at home. The doctor advises me to come to Mr Birdsall at Kingston.

Monday, 27th: Came up again to Mr Bethune. Very dull & low spirited Henry having spoken to Mr Bethune about wages to me but he says his money is all spent & unable to give any.

Tuesday, 28th: Went down with Henry to his farm & agreed with him to take the stumps that are loose & chop down the old girdled trees for 3½ dollars an acre, having the assistance of Mr Bethune &c.

Wednesday, 29th: Working about the oxen house. Henry away to the Plank road for Mr Bethune.

Thursday, 30th: Intended to go to work this morning but Mr Bethune required the oxen on Saturday first. He was very much against me going to chop & advised me strongly to go to Kingston. I thought it the best way myself but had no money & did not like to borrow. Henry said he would give me what I wanted.

Friday, 31st: Not having altogether fixed I did not leave this morning but went along with Henry Fleming who was going to his farm. After stopping all forenoon, Mr Clark who is stopping there at present asked us in to get a little dinner. We were scarcely begun when in comes one of Mr Secords sons & another man. He said he came up in a buggy for Sandford Fleming. He had a letter but had left it in his greatcoat at the tavern. All we could learn was a man had come up in the steam boat from Toronto to Hamilton, had taken suddenly ill in Press's Hotel and was not expected to live & Mr Webster the druggist had sent up for me as his nearest relation. How unexpected this bad news came and it could be no one else but brother David on his way up to see us. We hurried away to Mr Bethunes through the woods 3 miles off. Got myself changed & set off by Secords with all haste. Made my mind up for the worst. I thought I might bear up myself, but how was I to communicate the news to father and mother. I concoct the letter, but how painful. Hundreds of thoughts passed in my mind while we dashed through the woods without scarcely a word being spoken until we came to the tavern, got the letter and read thereby the following: "Dr Hutchison has taken suddenly ill at Press's Hotel so that his life is despaired of. He expressed a wish to see you and please return with the bearer. We have written for his family to come in haste. Yours &c C.H. Webster." You may be supposed my feelings were changed to a different course. I got 16 dollars from Henry Fleming & set off for Hamilton, arriving a little after seven, being scarcely 3 hours on the way. I called at Mr Websters shop where the shopman said the Dr had been conveyed to Mr Websters house. I went there and saw Mr Webster before I entered. The Dr had been almost gone in the morning but was much better now & considered out of danger if a 3rd fit of apoplexy did not attack him. I got instructions not to talk much to him. He knew me at first sight. Sat up all night along with Dr Grainger & Mr Hubbard who came up in the afternoon boat. The Dr was delirious all night.

November 1845

Saturday, 1st: Mr [Alexander] MacPhail [Peterborough druggist] having left yesterday for Mrs Hutchison & James, I started for Cobourg to meet them and tell of the Dr getting better. I saw her at the Globe Hotel with James & MacPhail. They had just come in about ten minutes before me. She was very much affected & in a mistake thought I said the Dr was dead, but were all much relieved when they knew the true case.

Monday, 3rd: Continued the journey to Hamilton, David also with us. We arrived there between 11 & 12 oclock. Mrs Hutchison almost fainted at the sight of the Dr, he was so pale & his eyes sunk. On Saturday after I left he would not stay in the house, he had another attack on the street more severe than ever & was carried to the house. This is the first day he has been in his senses.

Tuesday, 4th: David & I stopped in the room beside him last night. The Dr slept well. David left for Mr Bethunes place.

Wednesday, 5th: Dr still continuing better & walks out a little every day. Henry Fleming & David came in by the stage. We all three slept at Mr Gowans.

Thursday, 6th: Dr continuing better. David went down to Toronto in the afternoon. At Mr Gowans.

Friday, 7th: Henry Fleming went out to the Bush again today.

Saturday, 8th: Bought a carpet bag & pair trousers 2 dollars each. The Dr still keeping better and left along with Martha Webster & us for Toronto in the afternoon. Brought James, stopped with David & I. Dr wrote to Mr Birdsall concerning me.

Sunday, 9th: Commenced a letter in the forenoon to my father. At Mr Hollands along with David to dinner & tea.

Monday, 10th: Monday. Called to the Canada Company office with the Dr. Mr Jones to be all winter at Goderich but sent up Mr [Edward] Ellices letter. Left Toronto for Port Hope.

Tuesday, 11th: The English mail went off early this morning so I lost it. Set out for Peterboro. The roads are very rough. The Peterboro folks are all enquiring for the Dr and very glad to see him it having been said he was dead.

Wednesday, 12th–Saturday, 15th: In Peterboro. The Dr wrote off again to Mr Birdsall having found out he was in that quarter. Writing a long letter to my father & drawing the Court House for Mrs Hutchison.

Sunday, 16th: At English church.

Monday, 17th, Tuesday, 18th: Working about the Drs stable &c. Went in to see Mr Albro at Mr [James] Halls in the evening. He asked me to come by Mr Halls store in forenoon. I said I would & bade me see Mr Hall next day. When sitting in MacPhails who came in but Joseph Armstrong. I was really glad to see him and we went together to Miss Halls.

Wednesday, 19th: Mr Armstrong left today. I saw Mr Hall and made arrangements to come next morning to his store as I could not do much at first he could not fix a salary until he saw.

Thursday, 20th: At the store. First time behind a counter in my life with scissors in my pocket. Rather awkward. Boarding at Mr Halls & sleep at the Dr.

Friday, 21st: At store. Sent off a long letter to my father enclosing two muscetos & a flower I got at St Anne in the passage from Montreal.

Saturday, 22nd: At the store.

Sunday, 23rd: The English mail is expected any day. At English church.

Monday, 24th, Tuesday, 25th: Hard frost. Thermometer 13° above zero.

Wednesday, 26th–Saturday, 29th: Frost & snow. Thermometer two mornings from 3 to 6 below zero. I have felt it colder in Kirkcaldy.

Sunday, 30: At Scotch church morning. Had my first sleigh ride 6 miles up the river. James & I to meet the Dr. Road rather rough yet.

December 1845

Monday, 1st: English mail arrived this evening. One Glasgow paper to the Dr. Wrote to David.

Tuesday, 2nd–Friday, 5th: At store. More frost & snow. The sleighing getting better. Bought a fox skin to make a cap from Perry at 6/3. Got cloth from Mr Hall, & Haffey to make a vest at 5/ Cloth 13/9d.

Saturday, 6th: Received a letter from David enclosing a letter from father and one from Grainger concerning me. Surveyors getting 3, 5 & 7 guineas a day when the letter left date 27 Oct.

Sunday, 7th: Wrote home to mother.

Tuesday, 9th–Saturday, 13th: At store.

Sunday, 14th: Port Hope Harbour meeting.

Monday, 15th–Saturday, 20th: At store. Received a letter enclosing one from Mr Merrilees concerning a situation for me at Dunnville. Wrote Mr Bethune at Dunnville enclosed to David at Toronto.

Tuesday, 23rd: Fair Day. Very busy in the store.

Wednesday, 24th: At store.

Thursday, 25th: Christmas. Out sleighing. Good dinner at the Drs.

Sunday, 28th: Scotch church (wrote my father by the 24th mail).

Monday, 29th: Making a fur skin cap for myself in the evening & drawing the English church & courthouse on fine enameled paper for Mr MacPhail for the bazaar.

Tuesday, 30th, Wednesday, 31st: 1845 is finished and I am in Canada at Dr Hutchisons fire side.

CHAPTER TWO
Finding a Footing 1846

Sandford Fleming was still behind the counter in James Hall's store in Peterborough on his nineteenth birthday, January 7, 1846. At mid-month he left Hall's to go to work for Richard Birdsall at his home on Rice Lake. For a few weeks he spent his days there drawing a plan of Birdsall's proposed road from Kingston to Ottawa, and the evenings teaching Birdsall's young sons to draw. Unfortunately that did not last long so Fleming decided to take the initiative and do some work on his own. He borrowed Birdsall's compass and chain, hired a chain-bearer to assist him and set out to map Peterborough, taking advance orders for copies of his proposed plan to bring in some income. David felt more secure, working for a cabinet maker in Toronto, with the hope of soon moving on to the city's biggest furniture factory, Jacques and Hay.

February is not the choicest month to be surveying outdoors in Canada, especially in a winter of record-breaking severity, but Sandford outfitted himself with high boots and a coat "made for surveying men ... Beaver on one side and strong Canadian blue cloth on the other" and got on with his task. By early April he was able to return Birdsall's instruments and go in to Toronto to arrange to produce the plan himself on the newly-acquired large press at the Scobie and Balfour Lithographing Company. While he waited for the arrival of Scobie's new press he engraved on stone and sold a hundred copies of a sketch he drew of St James Cathedral.

A highlight of that summer, recorded in his diary in vivid detail, was a trip he and David made to Niagara Falls and Buffalo with new-found Toronto friends George B Holland (Martha Hutchison's brother) and his wife and her parents (Mr and Mrs Alexander Cowan). They left the city by ship on a lovely afternoon in late June, making their way to Queenston, with a brief stop at Lewiston "where we were for the first time on

American soil & off British ground on boards." The next day, with Mrs Cowan — "a firm loyal pious old Scotch woman" — they climbed to the top of Brock's monument, and then went by railway to the Falls seven miles away. The party viewed the wonder from all angles, from the top of the Pavilion Hotel and from the ledge of the Table Rock overhanging the Falls. George Holland and the two boys decided to "go under the sheet of water." Directed by their guide to remove all their clothes and don waterproof garments that were provided, "We descended a long flight of circular steps with our loose oilskin clothes dangling around us. We ... follow the guide along a narrow path with the massive rocks projecting far over our heads & steep bank of shale & broken fragments of rocks rising from our own feet into the milk white water." They did not stay long "as the place is not altogether free from danger (from pieces of falling rock &c) ... but none of us would have lost the sight for anything." He noted the many amusements around them "museums, camera obscuras &c — but who could look on them when Niagara is before our eyes ... there is only one Niagara."

The Niagara excursion was a happy diversion, but work was still uppermost on Fleming's mind. He did a few private surveying jobs in Peterborough, and some copying for the Canada Company, but there were no serious prospects. When he met with Thomas Mercer Jones and Frederick Widder, co-commissioners of the Canada Company, he was disappointed to learn that they had no openings. They promised to do what they could to help him make contacts with the railway companies.

By summer Sandford was working at Hugh Scobie's and his diary entries dwindle to nothing. In September he went to Hamilton to see [James] Merrilees, a family acquaintance, "about my father coming out," though it would be a year before his parents and siblings arrived. The other noteworthy event recorded that year was the production of 235 lithographed maps of Peterborough, "my first attempt ... the largest and perhaps best work of its kind ever done in Canada." It was a big achievement and brought him many compliments, but although his experience at Scobie's would stand him in good stead for years to come, the sparseness of the diary entries indicates that he had higher ambitions.

January 1846

Wednesday, 1st: It is now 365 days since I commenced to write a journal and it is as long since met with all my friends in my fathers house, instead of looking at the smoking turkeys on Dr Hutchisons table. We skated almost all day. Got two fine clear glass bottles from the Dr to make a electrifying machine to present to the Bazaar.

Sunday, 5th, Monday, 6th: At the machine in the evening.

Tuesday, 7th: It is now 19 years since I came into this world.

Wednesday, 8th: Set off with Dr Hutchison to Asphodel to see Mr Birdsall. Got down about 8 miles when we were obliged to stop at a coroners inquest upon the body of a lumberman who died in a shanty this morning, about the first dead man I have seen. Returned to Peterboro.

Thursday, 9th–Friday, 10th: At Mr Halls store.

Monday, 12th: Left Mr Hall intending to go to Mr Birdsall. Got pair of mitts from Thomson & Harvey @ 1/6.

Tuesday, 13th: Finished machine & took it to the Bazaar. It was bought in the evening at the auction by Dr Hutchison for

Dr. John Hutchison, cousin of Fleming, who welcomed Sandford and his brother David into his home in Peterborough on their arrival from Scotland.

15/. Sorry I did not give it to him at first. This Bazaar went very well, reports say they drew £150.

Wednesday, 14th: Got 5/ from James Hall. Got my trousers from the tailor & drew his portrait which I think will balance. Saw Mr Birdsall at MacPhails. He wanted me to go down with him (the Dr intended to go down with me today but he was called out and had not yet come back). I left in the afternoon with Mr Birdsall.

Thursday, 15th: Drawing with Mr Birdsall a plan of a road from Kingston toward the Ottawa.

Friday, 16th: As yesterday.

Saturday, 17th: As yesterday.

Sunday, 18th: Went to Peterboro with Mr Birdsall & family. Posted a letter to David, enclosing a letter to Anna for the first mail. Left Peterboro after church.

Monday, 19th: Drawing & teaching Mr Birdsalls two boys to draw in the evening.

Tuesday, 20th, Wednesday, 21st: As before. Dr Hutchison came with Mr Albro, brought a letter from David enclosing one from father dated 30 November.

Thursday, 22nd: Sent off a letter to Anna & mother enclosing one from David to father. Dr Hutchison went off to some place in the neighborhood. Came back in the evening.

Friday, 23rd: Dr Hutchison left. Drawing as before.

Saturday, 24th: As before.

Sunday, 25th: Reading.

Monday, 26th, Tuesday, 27th: Writing specifications & estimates of road.

Wednesday, 28th–Saturday, 31st: As before.

February 1846

Monday, 2nd–Thursday, 5th: As before making out reports &c.

Friday, 6th: Left Mr Birdsalls. Got some home cloth to make a pair of trousers for teaching the boys to draw and $5 note. Came up to Peterboro along with Mrs Birdsall & him. Got the use of his compass and chain intending to make a plan of Peterborough.

Saturday, 7th: Got things prepared to commence the survey on Monday.

Sunday, 8th: At church.

Monday, 9th: Commenced the survey with Donald Haggard chain bearer at 2/6 a day. The snow about 2 feet deep some places. Me drawing. Wrote David to send down things & clothes.

Tuesday, 10th: Out surveying. The thermometer 4 degrees below. Fine in the morning, very snowy in the afternoon.

Wednesday, 11th: Very stormy. Not out.

Thursday, 12th: At survey. The snow drifted. Got 2¼ yards cloth at James Halls and 4½ home cloth at Nichols at 6/3. Got Slater to make a coat for me. Got two flannel shirts which Miss Divine has made at 1/ each.

Friday, 13th: At survey.

Saturday, 14th: At survey. Got letters from my father which had been sent down to Mr Birdsalls before I came up. He enclosed the copy of a letter from a Postmaster in Devonshire about a bottle found enclosing a letter from me found in the Atlantic Ocean 630 miles out from Glasgow.

Sunday, 15th: At church.

Monday, 16th: Surveying. 16 degrees above zero. Snow in the afternoon.

Tuesday, 17th: Snow & stormy. Not out.

Wednesday, 18th: Surveying. Received a box from David with Instruments and clothes.

Thursday, 19th: Surveying. Very tired. Snow deep.

Friday, 20th: Not out. Plotting the survey. Sent off a letter to Father.

Saturday, 21st: Plotting survey.

Sunday, 22nd: At church.

Monday, 23rd: Ordered a pair long boots at Keele & Wright. Price 7 dollars.

Tuesday, 24th: Got a wood cutter and cutted a great deal for the Drs house.

Wednesday, 25th: Received letters from home dated 31 January.

Thursday, 26th: Plotting survey. Got the long boots and a new coat Mr Slater has made, price of making 25/. The coat is from Beaver on one side and strong Canadian blue cloth on the other and made for surveying men.

Friday, 27th: Plotting survey.

Saturday, 28th: Went up with the Dr, Mr Carnegie and James to Mr Carnegies house and to Mr Sawers in Douro. Went up a creek at Mr

Sawers to a little lake about 2 miles up. Mr Sawers wants me to survey this creek when the snow is not to deep.

March 1846

Monday, 1st–Saturday, 6th: Plotting and occasionally out alone, inserting houses, &c in the plan. Measured the bearing along the river above the bridge, they agreed pretty well. Snow very deep. Priest [John] Butler called and wanted me to make plans & specifications for finishing the Roman Catholic Church. Received a letter from David & answered it.

Sunday, 7th: At church. Heard W. Burns who I had heard before in Kirkcaldy.

Monday, 8th, Tuesday, 9th: Drawing spire.

Wednesday, 10th: Went over with Dr Hutchison to Captain Brays, an old naval officer who fought alongside of Nelson at Trafalgar. He died while we were there, and as no one but his sons & daughter were there, we had along with another man to arrange his body.

Thursday, 11th: Out with the Dr.

Friday, 12th: It rained all day or rather a Scotch mist which made very splashy roads.

Saturday, 13th: Drawing plans.

Sunday, 14th: At church. About 4 inches more of snow which makes a little sleighing again.

Monday, 15th–Wednesday, 17th: At plans. My name appeared in the paper as an advertisement as Architect & Civil Engineer.

Thursday, 18th: Went up with Dr Hutchison to Mr Carnegies.

Friday, 19th, Saturday, 20th: Measuring his land. Got a pair snow shoes from him with which I walked very well.

Sunday, 21st: At church.

Monday, 22nd–Wednesday, 24th: At spire plans.

Thursday, 25th–Saturday, 27th: Making fence & working in the Drs garden.

Sunday, 28th: Sunday & church.

Monday, 29th, Tuesday, 30th: Finished plans & specifications. There is an advertisement in the Chronicle for tenders. Got a letter last night from Kirkcaldy, 2½ or three sheets. Sent it off to David.

Wednesday, 31st: Went up to Carnegies in the moonlight, the sale having taken place today.

April 1846

Thursday, 1st–Saturday, 3rd: Occasionally surveying in different parts of the town. Received a letter from Mr Jones acknowledging the receipt of mine.

Sunday, 4th: At church.

Monday, 5th, Tuesday, 6th: At plan.

Wednesday, 8th: Went up to Carnegies in the evening. His sale took place today.

Thursday, 9th: Got Carnegies horse & went down to Mr Birdsalls with his surveying instruments.

Friday, 10th: Went out to run some lines with him. Dined in a lumber shanty.

Saturday, 11th: Set off again for Peterboro. Got some plans from Mr Birdsall to paste on cloth &c. When I came to the Scotch village the bridge was broken. Was obliged to leave the horse & cross in a canoe. Got a letter from David enclosing an order on Mr Ridley for £5/5.

Sunday, 12th: Had to take home Mr Carnegies horse 8 miles. Came down as far as S Cunninghams where I stopped the night.

Monday, 13th: Stopped. Dinner. Writing out accounts of Carnegies sale. Came down along with Cunningham to Peterborough. Paid for my boots $7 making cost $5 & slippers 11/3.

Tuesday, 14th–Wednesday, 15th: Working in the Drs garden.

Thursday, 16th: Wrote to David to see if he would come down to take the building of the Catholic spire.

Friday, 17th: Surveying the Scotch village.

Saturday, 18th: Working in Drs garden.

Sunday, 19th: Went up with James to meet the Dr. He had taken sick up the river. He is now better but weak having been bled. The Drs dog went mad today.

Monday, 20th: In garden.

Tuesday, 21st–Saturday, 25th: In garden & sundries.

Sunday, 26th: At church.

Monday, 27th–Thursday, 30th: In garden trenching & making flower garden. Received a letter from John Sang dated March 16.

May 1846

Friday, 1st–Saturday, 2nd: Garden.

Sunday, 3rd: At church.

Monday, 4th: Surveyed a lot for Mr Wear 12/6 & 1 for Mr Moffat 7/6.

Tuesday, 5th: Gardening.

Wednesday, 6th, Thursday, 7th: Drawing plan of a house for Mr Haggard, the Tailor about 7 dollars.

Friday, 8th, Saturday, 9th: Gardening. Wrote home to Mr Sang and Father.

Sunday, 10th: At church. Commenced Sunday School.

Monday, 11th: At plan of Peterboro.

Tuesday, 12th: Plan & sundries to 21st. Received a letter from David enclosing one from Father of 28 March.

Friday, 22nd–Sunday, 31st: At plan. Commenced a finished copy. Received by this English mail a letter from Father & Andrew with date 29 April with a view of Kirkcaldy from Pathead.

June 1846

Monday, 1st: Received a letter from David. He is leaving Wilsons & going to Jacques & Hay but he intends to come down next week on a visit. Sent in Mr Butler his account for spire plan £6/5. He came today & thought it by far too much.

Tuesday, 2nd–Thursday, 4th: Got the plan for Peterboro finished. Had a notice in the *Chronicle* for subscribers.

Friday, 5th–Saturday, 6th: Going about the stores & public places of the town getting subscribers.

Sunday, 7th: At church.

Monday, 8th: Getting subscribers. Plain lithographed plans @ 3 dollars & coloured @ 6 dollars. In all they amounted to 45 copies & 204 dollars.

Tuesday, 9th: Partly as yesterday. David came from Toronto tonight.

Wednesday, 10th: Went up to the Court House & got statistical table of the District. David commenced copying it.

Thursday, 11th: Making out report of the Colborne District for the Canada Company. At the Stewarts in the evening.

Friday, 12th: As yesterday. Did not get it finished as I expected the Dr was from home.

Saturday, 13th: David left this morning, he being anxious to go up to his new work.

Sunday, 14th: At church.

Monday, 15th: Writing report.

Tuesday, 16th, Wednesday, 17th: Slept at [Alexander] MacPhails house, he being away to get married & no one but an old housekeeper being there.

Thursday, 18th: Left for Toronto to get my plan printed. Dr gave me a letter to Mr Whitchurch, Port Hope. He was not at home. Left my card.

Friday, 19th: Came up to Toronto & [Hugh] Scobie is getting a large press from New York. Expects it in about a week.

Saturday, 20th: Copying papers for Canada Company.

Sunday, 21st: Rain heavy.

Monday, 22nd: Copying papers.

Tuesday, 23rd: Called on Mr Jones. He was pleased with the plan & paper, but told me to call next day & see Mr [Frederick] Widder [Canada Company director].

Wednesday, 24th: Called at Canada Company office. Mr Jones introduced me to Mr Widder. Told all he knew about me. They desired me to put my name to the papers. They knew of no situation just now but would not fail to let me know if they knew anything and when the railways commence they would use all the influence they had.

Thursday, 25th: Drawing on stone a view of St James Cathedral & King street to fill up the time until Scobie gets his press.

Friday, 26th: Same as yesterday. Wrote the Dr & sent 3 pineapples to Mrs Hutchison.

Saturday, 27th: Got a proof of the drawing today. Left on the afternoon boat for Niagara along with David, Mr & Mrs Holland [Martha Hutchison's brother and sister-in-law] and her Father & Mother. We had a very heavy shower in crossing the lake but it cleared the atmosphere. We had a delightful sail up the river with the British ground on the right hand & the American on the left. We arrived at Queenston, crossed over to Lewiston where we were for the first time on American soil & off British ground on boards. We crossed the river again after dark in a small boat & put up at Queenston.

Sunday, 28th: After breakfast Mrs Cowan (Mrs Holland's mother) a firm loyal pious old Scotch woman, with David & I went up to the top of Queenston Heights to see Brocks monument. Did not stop long but came down & started in the railroad cars for the Falls about 7 miles off. The Railroad goes first in a westerly direction along the face of the hill

Fleming climbed Brock's Monument when he visited Niagara Falls, June 28, 1845. From Landmarks, Volume 2 *(1896) by J.R. Robertson.*

(being a continuation of Queenston Heights) until it reaches the permanent level then it crosses a beautiful partly cultivated country in a direct course to the falls. As we occasionally stop at the different stations we hear the falls like distant thunder. At last when stopping at the Pavilion Hotel we see the white spray rising from behind the trees a little bit to our left. We first went up to the top of the Pavilion Hotel where we had a fine view of the rapids & river above the falls & just saw the whole falling down amongst the spray. We descended the steep bank of the River & landed a little above the falls & walked down by the side of the rushing waters. We are now on the Table Rock, the immense waterfall before our eyes & eternity under our feet. The ledge of rock is only about 1 foot or 15 inches in thickness & projects several yards beyond its support & points towards the river like Conder Cape or promontory. We gaze on here but who could hurry away from it, or who in gazing does not feel their nothingness. My brother, Mr Holland & I having made up our minds to go under the sheet of water, we got a guide who recommended us to take off all our clothes & put on others which he supplied. We descended a long flight of circular steps with our loose oilskin clothes dangling around us. We reach the bottom at last, and follow the guide along a narrow path with the massive rocks projecting far over our heads & a steep bank of shale & broken fragments of rocks rising from our own feet into the milk white water. When entering under the sheet of water a strong current of wind rushes out & dashing the spray in our faces. This is soon over & everything is hid from our view except the ponderous falling water which before reaching the bottom is altogether formed into white spray owing to the tremendous descent. As the place is not altogether free from danger (from pieces of falling rock &c) it is advisable not to stop long, but none of us would have lost the sight for anything. In coming out we take another look all around us. With the awful grandeur of the scenery & the immense quantity of water falling before our eyes, the noise of which sounds like thunder in our ears, who would not be struck dumb with amazement, or who could attempt the shadow of a description. There are many other places of amusement about the neighborhood such as museums, camera obscura &c but who could look at them while Niagara is before our eyes. These can be seen at many places but on this Globe there is only one Niagara.

We crossed in the ferry boat a little bit below the falls & landed on the American side where we again had to ascend the high bank, which is accomplished by a long straight flight of steps or by a waggon which is drawn up by machinery while another one comes down an inclined plane. This side of the river there are some splendid hotels. In one of them we dined but never before did I eat with so many individuals from all parts of America & I may say the world who have come to see the falls. We took the train after dinner for Buffalo. The passenger cars are very well got up but the rails are very mean. The railway goes right up the middle of the street & stops opposite the Western Hotel where we put up for the night.

The town of Buffalo is about as large as Toronto but the streets not so well laid out & it has no good public buildings, not a spire to be seen in the whole town, only a few small domes on the Hotels. We were taken through the town by the Toronto steam boat agent, and also through the fine steam boats. They are really fine & large. The cabin is on the deck & all the length of the vessel. They are filled with splendid furniture. The sleeping apartments are in the shape of little rooms along each side of the cabin with which they are connected by a stained glass door, the under panel being wood with fine landscapes painted on them.

Monday, 29th: Left Buffalo at nine in the morning by steamer down the River Niagara, Chipaway about 2 or 3 miles above the falls. When we enter the harbour the current of the river is very rapid & a few hundred yards below this the Rapids commence which continue rushing & foaming to the brink of the falls. We took the railroad from the town to Queenston by the falls where we had another hour to stop. We enjoyed this hour very much. I went down the stairs again & to the edge of the sheet of water where I took a rough sketch of the landscape. We arrived at Queenston in time for the afternoon boat to Toronto.

Tuesday, 30th: Told Scobie to print off 100 copies of the [St James] Cathedral.

July 1846

Wednesday 1st–Saturday, 4th: Coloring maps of Canada for Scobie amounting to 53/ altogether.

Sunday, 5th: Heavy rain & thunder.

Monday, 6th: Went to show the Bishop [John Strachan] the view of the Cathedral. I was asked into his room where he was very polite & talked to me a good deal. He took one & gave me a dollar (the price was 1/6). I went along King calling at the stores till tea time.

Tuesday, 7th: Peddling about the views the same as yesterday, sold in all 45/ worth.

Wednesday, 8th–Saturday, 11th: Drawing apothecary labels on stone for Scobie. His press has not come yet, expects it every day.

Sunday, 12th: This is the day the Orangemen walk.

Monday 13th–Saturday, 18th: Drawing labels &c. The press came on Thursday but no stones, just as bad as ever. Sent off 3 views to Peterboro.

Fleming's engraving of his sketch of St. James Cathedral, Toronto, 1846. From Sandford Fleming: Empire Builder *by L.J. Burpee.*

Sunday, 19th: At church.

[The diary resumes on the same page on September 19]

September 19th: Nearly two months have passed away. The lithograph stones came at last. I commenced drawing on them & to make a long story short, got 235 maps of Peterboro printed off, rather with considerable difficulty, it being the first long job for the press & stones & the first attempt of this of my own. However they are no disgrace to me considering everything & they are without boasting the largest & perhaps best

Sandford Fleming's Map of Peterborough 1846, which he lithographed at Scobie & Balfour's printing plant in Toronto.

work of the kind ever done in Canada. I about 12 days ago went up to Hamilton with David to see Mr Merrilees about my father coming out. I went as far as Mr Bethunes & Henry Flemings. I have got about 2 doz put on rollers & varnished & about 1 doz more on cloth but not varnished. I went up to Hamilton again to see about getting subscribers for the plan of that town & yesterday I sent up printed prospectuses to Mr Merrilees who kindly consented to get subscribers. My debts in Toronto are with Lee 7/6 — J Laidlaw 40/ — Scobie & Balfour acct £14/10/3, David about 35 dollars or 30. Scobie however owes me my contra acct, Canada Company 7 dollars & Mr Lewis 7 dollars which he was to pay to Scobie. I left 5 5-dollar ones, 1 at 6 dollars & 2 @ 7 dollars and Holland, Page Milroy & Scobie have cathedral views. I am now sitting in the steamer *Forester* on my way up to Peterboro.

[End of 1846 diary]

CHAPTER THREE
The Missing Diary 1847

Fleming neglected his diary in the latter months of 1846 when he was in Toronto, working at Scobie and Balfour's printing company. On September 19, two months after his previous note, he made a catchup entry on matters of business, mentioning his work on the Peterborough map and a map of Canada for Balfour, as well as a humdrum order of apothecary labels. He was busy, but obviously it was a far cry from his hoped-for occupation. No diary at all has been located for the year 1847. It is possible that he may not have kept a journal during this period. He may have felt there was not much worth recording, although this was the year that his parents and siblings came to Canada and a collection of letters is preserved at Hutchison House Museum recording preparations for the move.

Sandford and David wrote fully and frequently to their parents after their departure from Scotland, giving the details of the ship's passage and their arrival in Canada, and, finally, at the Hutchisons in Peterborough. As the months passed, there were practical suggestions about the best route to take, what supplies to bring, what to leave behind. It is evident from this correspondence that the boys had been sent out to test the waters and report back to their father what they thought about the idea of the rest of the family (including four younger brothers and two sisters) following them to Canada, telling them what they might expect.

Dr John Hutchison had visited Kirkcaldy when he returned to Scotland with his two eldest sons for the winter of 1842–43 and had obviously painted an attractive picture of the potential for success in the new land. Andrew Fleming had a small furniture business in Kirkcaldy, but he had a large family and his concern for his children's future was no doubt a deciding factor in his ultimate decision to leave his life there. The boys

Andrew Fleming, father of Sandford and David, who brought the rest of his family to Canada two years after Sandford and David arrived.

encouraged him. About a year after their arrival, in June of 1846, Sandford wrote to his father, "The Dr, David and I all think it a good move for you to come out this fall," and giving a list of things they should bring with them, but Andrew was still wavering. On November 8, 1846, Sandford wrote to his sister Annie that "Father has almost made up his mind to leave."

As it turned out, it wasn't until the following summer that they made their move. Andrew wrote to the boys on July 15, telling of the difficulties he had in getting passage. Elizabeth Fleming was becoming a little impatient. She wrote to David that she was "anxious to be off," complaining that they had been living with their clothes in their trunks since April. Illness on board immigrant ships and the quarantine at Grosse Isle led Dr. Hutchison to write recommending that they come by New York rather than the St. Lawrence River.

In the same letter the doctor reported that Sandford was now the "second engineer" on the Peterborough–Port Hope Railway, although no further details of this appointment are known. This railway line did not materialize, but it is likely that Sandford did play a role in planning the plank road from Cobourg to Peterborough, which was built in 1847–48. It is known that he spent a large share of his time in the Cobourg area at this time, creating a map of Cobourg and another of the Newcastle District, which he sold to subscribers. He also did

Courtesy Hutchison House Museum.

Elizabeth Arnot Fleming, mother of Sandford and David, who immigrated to Canada with her husband and six younger children in 1847.

several engravings, including one of St. Peter's Church, Cobourg, and one of Victoria College, which found a market. Cobourg's first Town Hall design was another of his assignments.

Sadly, Dr. Hutchison was not there to greet the Flemings when they finally arrived in the fall of 1847. A new wave of Irish immigrants had arrived in Peterborough that summer, many of them ill and suffering. They were detained in the immigrant sheds at "Hospital Point" on Little Lake, just south of the town, to be nursed back to health. Dr. Hutchison died in August after contacting typhus from the patients he tended. Mrs. Hall (who would become Sandford's mother-in-law some years later) wrote from Peterborough to her daughters visiting friends in Toronto that Mrs. Hutchison had moved from the stone house (now Hutchison House Museum) to "the cottage" (owned by the Halls).

The Fleming family learned of Dr. Hutchison's death when they arrived in Montreal, so they bypassed Peterborough and went on to Toronto. A letter survives from Andrew Fleming, written December 23, 1847, from their temporary home at 16 James Street, apologizing to Martha Hutchison for not yet having come to see her and thanking her for her "kindness to my sons." Sandford kept up his close Peterborough connections all his life, visiting frequently and undertaking projects there during the years he was becoming established in Toronto.

Hutchison House Museum today.

Photo by Dale Standen.

CHAPTER FOUR
Move to the City 1848

Life was still unsettled for Sandford Fleming as he approached his twenty-first birthday in January 1848. He had no regular employment and filled his time following up on connections he had made in Cobourg, working on a design for their Town Hall. He completed an engraving of St. Peter's Church, Cobourg, and on January 10 went back to work at Scobie and Balfour's lithographing firm, doing odd jobs for them and filling his idle hours on a large map of the Newcastle and Colborne districts, making several trips to Cobourg and Peterborough to sell his works of art. In Peterborough, he also spent time helping Dr. Hutchison's widow sort out the doctor's account books.

His parents and younger siblings were now in temporary quarters on James Street in Toronto, anxious to find an opportunity to establish a business somewhere nearby. On the nineteenth, he went out with his father to see the Humber Mills, a saw- and gristmill operation that was available for lease; but no decision was made until mid-March when Andrew wrote to his son in Peterborough telling him he had decided to sign the contract. David provided his savings as a down payment and gave up his job at Jacques and Hay to help his father run the mills, but the project did not go smoothly. Money Andrew counted on from Edinburgh failed to appear, and Mr. Keating, the mill owner, stalled. It was finally settled that Andrew would take over the sawmill in April, but was to wait another year to get the gristmill. The family moved out to the Humber in the spring and Sandford was back and forth regularly, spending much of his time helping with getting the mill running and planting extensive gardens. Andrew was still waiting for funds to arrive from Scotland.

Sandford continued to work at Scobie and Balfour, but on May 1 he was engaged to join the well known architect J. Stoughton Dennis for six months, working half-time at Dennis's Weston office while preparing to write his surveyor's exams in Montreal. Dennis soon put him to work at Brampton "superintending" the work in progress on the Hurontario plank road. Two weeks later he took his new apprentice to the office of architect John G. Howard to see the large rough city plan which Sandford was asked to reduce for engraving. It was the beginning of a task that hung over him for months and years to come.

Sandford began copying the map in Dennis's Weston office on May 19, then moved to space in Upper Canada College, and finally to the Scobie and Balfour plant. The plan was rough, drawn to a small scale, and full of inaccuracies and omissions — a difficult undertaking — and frequently Sandford himself went out to re-survey uncertain sections. Dennis brought in two of his apprentices who had worked on the plan to assure him that they had completed the survey "except for the Garrison and some other little things," but Fleming knew that he had much to do besides merely copying the map to scale and engraving it on stone. Finally he became so "disgusted" that he stopped work on it altogether. He still had responsibilities on the Hurontario plank road, whose directors were not happy with Dennis's progress there.

Out at Humber Mills things were not going well either. Andrew had to purchase a fresh team of oxen to replace the tired and worn animals that came with the mill to do the heavy work. Frequent breakdowns on the dam caused holdups, sometimes resulting in no water to keep the mill running, and Mr. Keating proved to be a manipulative and unhelpful landlord. By August, Dennis had convinced Sandford to get back to work on the city plan, but he took it out to the Humber to work on it there while his father and David struggled with their problems at the mill. In September he moved back to the city. Andrew and David decided that the Humber Mills project was hopeless and by the end of the month they left it behind them. The family moved back to Toronto and temporary quarters at the corner of Richmond and Victoria streets, where they turned the garden into a lumber yard.

Toward the end of 1848, Sandford's diary entries become infrequent, though it is clear that he was spending much time on the city plan, both at the drawing board at Scobie and Balfour, and in the field surveying. The Garrison survey took his attention. At the same time, John Balfour engaged him to do a large plan of America for the Company.

He also became associated with the Mechanics' Institute, where he met with congenial friends and professional colleagues, and in November, began giving classes there in geometry, arithmetic, and drawing. He had Christmas dinner at the Hutchisons, with young James home from his pharmacy job in Hamilton. At year end, Sandford was fully occupied at work and in his leisure hours.

January 1848

How strange it sounds, but it will soon be familiar to us. Poor 1847 is dead, is now numbered with the past, and all our deeds and actions, evil or good are sealed. Yes sealed with the great seal of time. Let us form a good resolution to live the lives of honest men, let us learn the way to do good, and walk upright. If it should be for no other purpose than to honour our Father and Mother dear, to comfort them in their old age. Surely we could not see their grey hair go with sorrow to the grave.

Saturday, 1st: Last night David, Ann & I were at a wedding. The party were very merry, finished about 3 A.M. and most of us went to finish at another party. It is enough to say we got to bed about 7 oclock and got up about eleven. David and I called upon several friends during the day, being the usual custom.

Monday, 3rd: At work again, engraving a view of St Peters Church, Cobourg. It is very tedious work. Would rather be in the country chopping. It may be so but one is never content with their present condition.

Tuesday, 4th: Again at St Peters in the forenoon, but think it as well to give it up, in the mean time, as it is not likely that I shall make a good job of it when my mind does not go along with it.

Wednesday, 5th: Today I have commenced to design a Town Hall for the Town of Cobourg, as I promised when I was down last. It may never be of any pecuniary advantage to me but it is practice and they may probably take my unsold plans of Cobourg, as a sort of remuneration for me.

Thursday, 6th: In the forenoon today I have been engaged sketching out a plan for the Town Hall at Cobourg. Afternoon I volunteered my services to take out two voters to the Township of Scott about 50 miles from Toronto. We started about 5 oclock P.M. and slept in Buffalo robes at the village of Stouffville 30 miles out.

Friday, 7th: Pretty cold this morning but we must get the carriage repaired, which broke down last night about 12 oclock. Managed to get to the polling place about an hour and half before it closed. This is my birthday, it is now 21 years since I came into this world. "Adieu to my youth —"

Saturday, 8th: Winter morning — snowing. Started for Toronto, our ride was through the bush, only one house for about 10 miles. Arrived at Newmarket where the Hon Robert Baldwin is here with his party, they having defeated our friend Mr. Scobie by 260 majority. Went up to Sharon and saw David Willson & Temple.

Monday, 10th: Sunday is omitted in this Diary. It being near one before getting home I did not get up till near church time. Poor Mr. Russell confectioner was burnt out yesterday morning at 4 oclock. Lost all but the lives of his family. Today I have commenced at Scobie & Balfour again.

Tuesday, 11th: The balance of the lst Quarters rent is due today amounting to £3.10. £1.10 being paid on taking the house. Recd 10/ from Scobie & Balfour to make up the balance. Mr. Holland promised to give me 4 dollars for making a plan for Mr Bethune.

Wednesday, 12th: Little Mr Buchan, Scobie & Balfour engraver had been drunk last night and cant work today. Silly fellow to spend his time and money, and breaking his constitution. Can it be possible that I shall be a drunkard; surely not. Paid the Jew £3/10 the Quarter rent.

Thursday, 13th: At work as usual. Nothing much of importance going on. Electioneering is about an end. The reform party are likely to have a considerable majority. I am glad of it, little good can be done unless some side have it.

Friday, 14th: The weather is unusually mild, it rained almost all day. In the evening a fire broke out in Yonge Street in a wooden house, but owing to the rain and the plentiful supply of water in the ditches, the fire was prevented from going farther.

Saturday, 15th: Last evening I saw along with Cochrane the sculptor, some plaster casts that have just been brought to town for the Society of Arts. There is some good things among them. Went over to John Buchan's last night, he was just getting better from being drunk poor fellow. He has kept sober a long time now.

Monday, 17th: Today is Handsel Monday, if all is well there will be great merry makings at Haugh Mills. Recd from Scobie & Balfour £2/10 paid Father £2/5. Last Wednesday I got from David 7 dollars to help pay the rent which with the other two makes 9 dollars I gave my Father that time & owe David $7. Engaged at Scobies just now making a title to the Newcastle & Colborne map. There is a vast deal of work at it, but shall try to make a good job.

Wednesday, 19th: In the afternoon today my Father, David, Mr Pollock & I went out to the Humber Mills about 16 miles out, to see them, they are to let or sell. It is a pretty place, a flour mill with two runs of stones just finished and a good saw mill with plenty of pine.

Thursday, 20th: At work as usual. The Humber Mills would make a fine place for us to enter, if we could only manage to lease them. Poor Mr Gillespie has got his head broken and has not come to work.

Friday, 21st: Nothing extra going on. The same old jog trot. I have some difficulty in filling this space as I really forget what happened, particularly today.

Saturday, 22nd: Recd from Scobie & Balfour 5 dollars, gave Father 3. This is a strange winter, some days as mild as spring, really it is not unlike the winters in Scotland. Getting pretty well on with the work at Scobies, but it will be some time before we finish.

Monday, 24th: I half promised to make a design for a Town Hall and other buildings for the Town of Cobourg. I must see and get on with it. I may not derive any immediate benefit, yet it is practice and may be of use at a future period.

Wednesday, 26th: I have been thinking for some time that, the charcoal light of the magnetic battery might be brought to some practical use. I only require one experiment, but it would be an expensive one for me unless I could meet with a powerful battery, but I dont think there is one in Canada. It is to try if more than one light can be formed with one set of wires by masking the connection and interposing charcoal points. If this is the case, we have a good and cheap substitute for Gas, would give a much better light, and at least could be easily adapted to lighting streets or churches just by having a wire like the Telegraph ones, with a charcoal apparatus here & there. Worth trying.

Saturday, 29th: Recd from Scobie & Balfour $5 dollars paid my Father $6½. We paid the taxes for the house today the Jew would not pay his half & we must keep it off his Quarters rent at the end.

Engraving of Victoria College, Cobourg, by Sandford Fleming.

February 1848

Monday, 7th: As usual at work at the Newcastle & Colborne map, will soon get a proof of it now, got one of the first stone in the afternoon. Got an order from Scobie & Balfour on MacFarlane for £2/12/8 being 79 yds cotton @ 8 c.

Tuesday, 8th: Got a proof of the second stone today. They look pretty well together. Got 24 copies home with me in the afternoon and commenced coloring and putting them on the board in the evening.

Wednesday, 9th: The Statistical Tables having yet to be engraved on the stone, we commenced to do that today. I thought it as well to get a few thrown off to get on with the mounting and we can paste on the Tables afterwards.

Thursday, 10th: Got one of the maps put on rollers today and taken down, everyone is very well pleased with it. At work getting some additions put on the stone. Mr Balfour being from home for the last three weeks came home, is well pleased.

Friday, 11th: Today finishing the second stone of the District map which was begun to print in the afternoon. Got home with me 26 copies. The map indeed looks pretty well now.

Saturday, 12th: Recd order from Scobie & Balfour on Keeshan & Co for £2, got from them 18/ of goods & to get the balance afterwards; also from Scobie & B. 5 dollars cash. Mr Balfour has ordered me to get a machine for ruling wavy and straight lines for him (price probably 50 or 60 dollars).

Monday, 14th: Left in the morning for the Humber with Father & David to see the property to let. Walked over the farm and the lots adjoining to see about the Pine. Mr Keating to be in Town on Wednesday.

Saturday, 19th: At design for Cobourg Town Hall.

Tuesday, 22nd: Delivered a plan of Cobourg to Mr Sinclair, Hotel keeper, also two maps of the District mounted on linen which cost 3/ for each, the one will cost 7/6 & the other 5/.

Wednesday, 23rd: Selling maps of the Newcastle & Colborne District through the city, one to the Board of Works to be paid afterwards. Making preparations to leave for Cobourg tomorrow. Got from Henderson & Laidlaw cotton to the amount of about £2/12 to be paid afterwards.

Thursday, 24th: Left for Cobourg at 11 oclock today by the stage, left with Scobie & Balfours 14 maps colored & mounted with a few quarter dollars in my pocket. Roads very rough. Broke down. Wheel came off, had to wait till the Driver went back for another coach.

Friday, 25th: Rolling away on the rough road, arrived a Cobourg a little before 4 in the morning, got to bed & slept till a little after nine. Got breakfast and sallied out to see the Folks, terrible dull times, no money in the town.

Saturday, 26th: It snows & rains a little today, not doing much, just feeling the pulses of the people here, found out that a perfect screw can be made at the Woollen Factory. They have a fine Lathe. Ordered one for Scobie & Balfours ruling machine.

Monday, 28th: Left with Mr Milne 36 Dr Chalmers Mr Brodie one. The Traveller for Blackie & Sons 3 colored mounted @ 20/, 6 sheets 10/ allowance 20 per cent. Also with Mr House 12 Dan O'Connoll & Mr Corrigal 10 McFee 20 — 2 @17/6 & 12 @ 10/. Mr Dingman Plan of Cobourg 20/3 board 15/ 3 each 5/.

Tuesday, 29th: Left for Port Hope, sleigh 2/6 dinner etc 1/6. Went with a farmer (Mr. Lightfoot) for Monaghan. The sleighing is good but bitter cold. Just now sitting in Grahams Tavern halfway to Peterboro & about going to bed. Had 7 meals and was 2 nights at Mr Pratts.

March 1848

Wednesday, 1st: I owe Mr Graham about 3/6. Left a 20/ map with him. Left in a chance sleigh for Palmers about 10 miles farther on, and got there to Peterboro in another team.

Thursday, 2nd: Not doing much more today than seeing the good folks and getting the maps untied, they are not much worse for coming up. Sleighing is very good and Peterboro is quite stirring.

Friday, 3rd: Today I have commenced posting poor Dr Hutchisons books. [Dr Hutchison died August 1847] Gave a 10/ map each to the Despatch, Gazette & Mr [Walter] Sheridan [Peterborough County Clerk], everyone is well pleased with the map.

Saturday, 4th: It is very stormy & snowing today. Received a letter from Mr [Thomas Mercer] Jones (Canada Company) disputing my account for the map of Peterboro. I should say it is very shabby of him. When I showed it to them he said (the company) would be glad to take one when published.

Monday, 6th: Today I have been at the Court House receiving orders for the District map. Got a loan of "London's Rural Architecture" from [Alexander] MacPhail, he proposed to part with it, the price is £4/7/6.

Tuesday, 7th: This is the Peterborough Fair. I left with Mr Ryan 12 [maps], Dan O'Connols to be sold at 1/3, he to get them for 1/. I also left [one] with Wm Hall, 6 Dr Chalmers @ 5/ he being to get 20 per cent. He paid me his copy 5/. Rev Mr Butler took a copy of map 20/. The fair passed away without a fight, but there was not much business done. These fairs do but little good. At Dr's books.

Thursday, 9th: In the Scotch Village trying to sell maps, did not succeed. Received from Mr [James] Wallis 10/ for a map which Robert Denison of Toronto is to get from S & B. At Mrs [Frances] Stewarts in the evening.

Friday, 10th: Left this morning for the Village of Keene, sold 2 maps one 17/6 & other 20/. Left 3 20/ with Mr.[Thomas] Short for sale & 3 10/ ones, got home about 8 or 9. Very cold.

Saturday, 11th: Today I have been taking orders through the stores [in Peterborough]. Traded one map off for harness & another for silk handkerchief. Sold a Peterboro map to Morrison for 17/6.

Monday, 13th: The most of this week I have been taking orders and trading maps for harness, axes, etc & at Mr [Thomas] Bensons [Mayor of Peterborough, 1850]. Wrote to Father & Scobie & Balfour.

Tuesday, 14th: Received a letter from Father informing me of his having taken the mills on the Humber. I was very glad to hear it, although it is a considerable risk as the milling business may be hurt by the grain law to be passed in the States. I have also written to Mr Alexr Vidal, Port Sarnia, stating that I wished to join his party going to Lake Superior. At a party at Mr Halls, broke up about 2 A.M.

Thursday, 16th: Wrote to Father this morning before going to bed enclosing a check for £10 and also 2 City of Toronto dollar bills. Also wrote to J. Hall Esq in Montreal about surveyors licenses. Selling maps.

Friday, 17th: Today I received an answer from Scobie & Balfour, I also wrote them a reply enclosed £4 which I received from Mr Wallis on their accts. I went up to MacFarlanes mills this morning to make a sketch. Too cold.

Saturday, 18th: Preparing to leave for Port Hope on Monday. Went up to see Mr Rogers in the forenoon. He took a map 17/6. Sent him a 20/ one. Getting things ready to pack up. Do not forget Antoinette.

Monday, 20th: Revolution in France. News came to Peterboro this morning. This morning I intended to have gone with the stage to Port Hope but there was none. Went up to Mr Gilmours with Dr [John] McNabb, he took a map & will pay to MacPhail. It rains a great deal. Afternoon & evening small party at Mrs. H.

Tuesday, 21st: Left Peterboro this morning by stage, sent a philapine to Antoinette. The roads for the first part of the journey are not so bad. Graham paid 4/6 being balance of map after deducting stage fare and expenses going up.

Wednesday, 22nd: Port Hope is very dull, worse than Peterboro. About much trying to get off the maps, did not succeed well, about 6 orders. Got a chance waggon going to Cobourg in afternoon, in the haste of leaving had not time to see Mr Walsh & left a map on the Table. Roads very bad.

Thursday, 23rd: Last night I went up to see Mr Glover. He is somewhat inclined to go with us to the mills. Had a letter this morning from Father. Went up to see Glover again, he promises to go up with me next Tuesday morning. Answered Fathers letter.

Friday, 24th: Today have been trying to get orders for the District map but not very successful. Took a sketch of the Ontario Mills for Mr McKechnie to be engraved about 1/3 the size.

Saturday, 25th: Again trying to dispose [of] the maps. Traded 2 for harness. I have now got a complete set of double harness except one collar. Money is indeed very scarce here. It was never known to be so much so. I intended to have gone to Port Hope today, roads too bad.

Monday, 26th: Wrote a letter to the Cobourg Board of Police urging them to give a reply to the Petition I presented some time ago. They seemed inclined to do something. Mr Glover intends going up with me tomorrow. Up late packing.

Tuesday, 28th: Up at 4 oclock waiting in the Boat all night. I have been at Mr Pratts since Wednesday evening last 5½ days. Lake a sheet of glass, arrived at Toronto. All well but disappointed not hearing from Scotland.

Wednesday, 29th: Went out to the mills with Mr Glover & Whitelaw, he is quite pleased with the mills but think there will be little doing this summer. I had to pay expenses, cost about 11/. Mr Balfour sent up for me while I was away.

Thursday, 30th: Commenced at Scobie & Balfour in the middle of the day, reduce "Ontario Mills." Received a letter from Mr Vidal, Port Sarnia. He has already engaged his chain bearers so that I don't go to Lake Superior.

Friday, 31st: At work Scobie & Balfours. David is uneasy having left Jacques & Hay and not much prospect of getting the mills for want of cash (not having heard from Scotland as expected), he, having taken £30 out of the bank (his earnings in Toronto) and given to Mr Keating, is afraid of losing that too. At S & B today reducing plan of Port Britain. Mr Smith, Mr Howards assistant, is about leaving so I have a chance of getting on there.

April 1848

Monday, 3rd: Yesterday afternoon went along with Mr Smith and Lavery to the Observatory, saw some beautiful instruments, got acquainted with Mr Minnes. Mr Keating has been in — perhaps all will be right yet.

Tuesday, 4th: At S & B forenoon, went with Father and David to McLeans office to see about the mills. We are to have the saw mill just now & the grist mill half or one year after this.

Wednesday, 5th: Making arrangements to go out tomorrow. Packing up the furniture etc. We are to get Jacques & Hays big waggon so that we will be able to take the principal part of the things.

Thursday, 6th: Up early today getting things packed. Got all ready & started, David, Andrew, Henry, Ann & I for the mills, arrived in due time, got the things taken into the house. David returned with the waggon & we slept all night.

Friday, 7th: Up early, beautiful morning, arranged the trunks etc & commenced digging in the Garden. Got a melon bed made in the afternoon. It is very warm today, employed ourselves as we best could.

The Magnetic Observatory (later demolished) on the University of Toronto grounds. From Landmarks Volume 1 *(1894) by J.R. Robertson.*

Saturday, 8th: I left in the stage for Toronto this morning. David went up to the Twelve-mile creek (Mr Whites) in the afternoon to see into the sawing business. Mr Father went out in the evening. Got 20/ (part of the rent).

Monday, 10th: Yesterday afternoon went up Mr. Linn surveyor with Mr. Smith. Mr. Keatings waggon came & the remainder of us & furniture went out in the afternoon. Got 10/ from S & B, paid the balance of rent £4/8/9.

Tuesday, 11th: It is a beautiful day. Hard at work digging, fencing, etc. etc. went to bed about 9 oclock. Began the new road to the saw mill. Keating sent up today for the oxen.

Wednesday, 12th: Up early, began to build abutments for the new bridge into the bush for drawing saw logs over. The oxen came but in very poor condition, we will try them tomorrow.

Thursday, 13th: Taking down part of the old bridge across the Humber & building one to get from the saw mill to the plank road — almost finished it today, many hands make light work.

Friday, 14th: I see I have mistaken a day, what I have written for Thursday should be for today. Its no matter. We were not idle this week. We also planted a few apple trees in the garden.

Saturday, 15th: With the oxen drawing up string pieces from the Humber bridge to the one in the bush. Got abutments up, and after great exertions we got one string piece across. David came tonight, he got £15 from Jacques & Hay.

Monday, 17th: Yesterday David & I went up as far as Pine Grove. Today all engaged getting the other 3 string pieces put across for the bridge. We got some planks drawn too.

Tuesday, 18th: My Father & I went down with Mr Keating to get the lease signed. No letters from Scotland yet, money very scarce. I stopped at Mr Buchans all night as Mr Balfour wants me to stay.

Wednesday, 19th: Commenced taking the view of Horwoods Hotel for S & B. I got from them £5 which with Davids £15 I gave to Mr McLean making in all £50 they have received for rent.

Thursday, 20th: Yesterday I went to Board with Mrs Morrison. At S & B engraving Horwoods Hotel. A tedious piece of business compared with driving saw logs.

Friday, 21st: No letters with the English mail, very much disappointed. My Father expects a money letter from Mr Arnot, Edinburgh. We will have hard scraping to get along if it does not come.

Saturday, 22nd: Still at S & B. Last night I got some flower seeds from Miss Pollock to my sister. Finished part of the thing at S & B will get the remainder done on Monday. Wrote a note in reply to Mrs Benson.

Monday, 24th: Finished at S & B. Got an order on Haworth for 25/ also on Ogilvie & Co for 25/. Wrote to Mr Booth, Board of Police, Cobourg. Got a great quantity of Flower & Garden seeds from Mr Bain (must share the proceeds).

Tuesday, 25th: Started this morning with Mr Hollands buggy, he was kind enough to let me have for a day or two. Mr Pollock went along with me as far as his farm, his plow & drag is worth very little.

Wednesday, 26th: Commenced work at the fences etc and very busy all day. They are getting on very well. David is making a new head block for the saw, it is nicely finished. It is to cut the boards all the way through.

Thursday, 27th: The head block is partly finished today, it promised to work very well, got the west field all fenced in. My Father drove Mother, Ann & Jane as far as Pine Grove in the Buggy. A fine day.

Friday, 28th: Very cold this morning, digging, fencing & garden. Drove up to the Mills above us for Bran, very rough roads, nearly upset the Buggy.

Saturday, 29th: Busy gardening, sowed a good many onions, carrots, melons etc. Drove up the road a little bit with Father to see about hay. In the afternoon left for Toronto. No letters from Scotland yet, expect a mail tomorrow.

May 1848

Monday, 1st: No letters yet. Saw Mr [J. Stoughton] Dennis, Surveyor, and agreed to serve with him 6 months as a step to me getting a license provided I give him during the time 3 months work. Stopping at Mrs. Morrisons.

Tuesday, 2nd: Got a hoe & belt from Mr Haworth. To get another order from S & B. Received from them 15/ each. Purchased straw hats from Henderson & Laidlaw 5/. Started in the stage for home in the afternoon. Called at Mr Dennis, Weston, but not at home.

Wednesday, 3rd: Busy at the mills fencing etc & gardening. There is a credit sale tomorrow about 4 miles from here; my Father and I propose going over to see if we can get a cow or some other stock.

Thursday, 4th: Left about ten oclock this morning for Mr Charltons 15th Lot 4 Concession of York where the sale takes place. Stock went very high but we bought a yoke of good oxen for £22 as we are greatly in want of them.

Friday, 5th: David started this morning for the city to get Jacques & Hay to endorse the note for the oxen for £22 which they did at once on condition of letting the £14 they owe him lye in their hands for the 16 months.

Saturday, 6th: Hard at work on the farm again. The bracket boards on the dam broke today & lowered the water so much that the mill wouldn't go. Had to leave off in the afternoon.

Monday, 8th: The bracket boards being off the dam, this morning early we commenced to put them up. After they were almost right they gave way & threw David in the dam & got a good wetting.

Tuesday, 9th: Yesterday we had a rumpus with Keating about the dam. We have found out he is a bad man void of principles. Afraid of him using us as he has done other people, we have determined to keep the Law.

Wednesday 10th–Friday12th: Mill going as much as possible. Accordingly all this week Andrew & I have kept at her till about 3 in the morning & David & Henry the remainder. We are however a good deal troubled with her breaking down, so that the sawing is stopped. The pit mall broke so that we had to make a new one and the timbers underneath are very loose and shattered. My Father has gone to Mr Orocks on Yonge Street to borrow a little money. He returned today with a cow & calf having got them at Richmond Hill from a neighbour of Mr Pollocks who now lives there.

Saturday, 13th: At work as usual but the saw was stopped in the afternoon by the iron dog breaking. David & Henry went to the smiths 3 miles off to get it repaired. We had a long search after the oxen in the evening.

Monday, 15th: Commenced fencing in the morning. Mr Dennis of Weston sent a letter with Mr Keefer [Samuel Keefer, chief engineer, Department of Public Works; after 1853, Deputy Commissioner] requesting me to go along with him to Brampton, and go over the route of the Hurontario plank road, with a view to me occasionally superintending it.

Tuesday, 16th: Slept at Brampton, went over the road with Mr Keefer and the contractors to Cooksville. Came in to Toronto expecting to see Mr Dennis. Stopped at Mrs Morrisons all night.

Wednesday, 17th: Saw Mr Dennis this morning and went out to Weston with him and from there to home. My engagement to commence on the 3d May last and to give 3 months work during the six.

Thursday, 18th: Left the mills this morning to go to the city with Mr Dennis. He took me along to Mr [John] Howard to see the skeleton plan of the city. Agreed that I should commence on Monday next to reduce it. Got 10/ from S & B. Went home in the stage.

Friday, 19th: Went down in the stage to Weston. Mr Dennis agreed with the stage driver that I should go up and down and to charge the fares to him. Copying plans in Mr Dennis's office & went home in the evening.

Saturday, 20th: Down to Weston this morning drawing in the office. Evening and morning when at home I am engaged in the Garden digging & cultivating etc.

Monday, 22nd: Went down in the stage to Toronto on Mr Dennis's business. Went with him to Mr Howards to reduce large skeleton plan of the city. It being too late before the stage got in I have to wait till tomorrow at 12.

Tuesday, 23rd: Got an order from S & B on Ogilvie & Co for $5 & on Haworth for £1. Haworth still owes me 15/ in goods. Sent some groceries to the mills. Commenced reducing Howards large plan at Upper Canada College.

Wednesday, 24th: At city plan in U[pper].C[anada].College. Very dull place, the windows are high & cant see out. Queens birthday. The stores are all closed in the afternoon. I went along with Mr Laidlaw up the tall church spire. My name is written on the very top.

Thursday, 25th: At Upper Canada College as yesterday. I have called every day this week to see McLean but he is never in his office.

Friday, 26th: At U.C. College same as yesterday. Nothing new going on. There is no letters for us by the English mail yet but 3 papers. No letter from Cobourg.

Saturday, 27th: Finished reducing the plan. Mr Dennis came in today & I am to go out with him & commence plotting the buildings, but unfortunately I lost the stage, it having started before the time.

Monday, 29th: Today Blackies traveller paid me £2/16 being the amount for maps he sold after taking of discount. Got another order from S & B on Ogilvie & Co for $5. Took out a barrel of oatmeal.

Tuesday, 30th: Went down to Weston. Mr Dennis had gone yesterday to Brampton. He expected me to go with him. Commenced plotting in the office. Went home at night.

Wednesday, 31st: Down to Weston again plotting same as yesterday. Very difficult business, the scale is so small being 12 chains to an inch and the survey is not made in the best manner.

June 1848

Thursday, 1st, Friday, 2nd: Drawing in the office as usual. Called on Mr Bain, a magistrate, have to see him about a summons my Father got from some Irishmen who were cutting saw logs. Mr Bain went up in the afternoon with me and got the affair settled (a little bit of experience to us). Drawing as usual at Mr Dennis['s] office at Weston and going home every evening.

Saturday, 3rd: Went down to Weston again & drawing as usual. Took home 100 cabbage plants (1/) and got them planted as it looks like rain. The Garden looks very well.

Monday, 5th: We had a fine shower last evening makes everything look well. Went down to Weston again. At city plan. Got about 100 plants from Mr Card planted in the Garden.

Tuesday, 6th: Went down to Weston again & started in Mr Dennis's Buggy for Brampton. Saw some of the contractors. Travelled over the road to Cooksville & from there to Toronto. Arrived about 10 oclock P.M. Saw Mr Buchan. Stopped at Elgie's.

Wednesday, 7th: Hunted up Mr Brown and measured some parts of the city where I found discrepancies when plotting. Saw Mr Holland. James [Hutchison] has gone down to Peterboro and Mrs Hutchison is to be up on Friday. Left the city for home & brought up my encyclopedias of engineering to Mr Dennis.

Thursday, 8th: Down to Weston and plotting the city plan as before. It is beautiful weather and the Garden is growing but the air is rather cold, in fact there was a little frost last night.

Friday, 9th: At Weston again, the air is very cold. I am very much afraid of the melons & corn, but as yet they have not suffered. The mill is kept going night and day.

Saturday, 10th: At Weston again. The water in the river is falling fast and the dam leaks a great deal. Very cold in the morning but warmer toward evening. Nothing of ours has suffered.

Monday, 12th: At Weston again. I have been very busy every night and morning digging in the garden and getting sowed some white beans I brought from town last week. The cabbage plants are growing fine.

Tuesday, 13th: At Weston again. My Father went down in the stage to Toronto today and got advice about the lease of Keatings place & also the oxen.

Wednesday, 14th: At Weston again. I am to go to Brampton tomorrow and stop there to superintend the plank road and at my leisure time to plot the city plan. The garden is really growing fine but the mill is almost stopped. No water.

Thursday, 15th: There is very little water in the dam, the mill will scarcely go. In the morning working in the garden until Mr Dennis sent up a boy with his Buggy about 10 oclock. Started for Brampton and went over the road on horseback. Buggy returned.

Friday, 16th: It is extremely warm. Staking of the road to the contractors & finding out the old stakes. Went down over Rossiters contract, he has stopped working today for want of planks.

Saturday, 17th: Attending to one of the contractors Graham in the village of Brampton. He knows very little about road work. Went down 5 or 6 miles to Gibsons contract along with 3 of the directors. Getting 'mood' & painting & levelling road.

Monday, 19th: Commenced lay plank on the section. Went down in afternoon to 13 Section to chain & level the long hill, did not finish it as some stakes were pulled out. The weather is excessively warm.

Tuesday, 20th: Went down to Section 12 & 13, finished levelling the hill

& staked off another hill near the big [illegible]. Fine showers today, a great hurricane in the afternoon blew down several trees.

Wednesday, 21st: Directing the men on Section 14 and plotting sections of hill on Section 13. The air is cool and pleasant today. Mr Dennis has not yet come as I expected. I cant go to Gibsons contract for want of a horse.

Thursday, 22nd: Mr Dennis came this forenoon and went up the Center road to lay of a Town Hall. Went to a Methodist Tea Party in the open air in the afternoon. Charge 1/3, a very tame concern. Mr Dennis did not go over the road with me.

Friday, 23rd: Went down with the stage this morning to Gibsons contract. It rains today, had breakfast at the Center house & returned on foot to Brampton. We had a terrible hurricane in the afternoon tearing up trees etc etc.

Saturday, 24th: Went down to Rossiters this morning. Plotting city plan. Got a ride across to St. Andrews village in the afternoon with Mr Wright. Our people are all well and the Garden looks fine. One of the wheels of the tanker broke all to pieces today.

Monday, 26th: Went down to Weston this morning with the stage, finished plan of Klines property. Mr Dennis's man drove me in to town in the afternoon. I stopped at Mrs Morrisons. Mrs Hutchison has gone to Guelph to see her sister.

Tuesday, 27th: Got an order on Haworth from S & Balfour — also 4/. Sent out some articles to the mill with the stage. Saw Mr Milne from Cobourg. The town is very dull. Left in the stage for Cooksville & Brampton, paid to Cooksville 1/10.

Wednesday, 28th: At city plan & looking after men on Section 14. Plotting the city plan is a difficult operation it being so badly measured with a good many omissions and the scale being so very small.

July 1848

Monday, 3rd: According to agreement with Mr Dennis I went down in the stage this morning to Cooksville to meet him, but by some misunderstanding he came across another way. I had to wait till evening and go up in the stage again.

Tuesday, 4th: Mr Dennis left a letter for me with some orders & saying that he would send over for me this week, the directors not being pleased with him not attending personally 2 days a week.

Wednesday, 5th: Attending to the Contractors staking of the embankment at the large culvert, and the level embankment opposite Elliots. Very hot.

Thursday, 6th: Engaged plotting the city plan this forenoon. Mr Dennis came while we were at dinner with Mr Orock. I packed up everything and went down as far as Gibsons and then home all week.

Friday, 7th: Cutting hay the most of the day and working about the mill. I thought I would not go down to Dennis this week.

Saturday, 8th: Cutting hay. Brown & Unwin, Mr Dennis, two apprentices up in the afternoon. They say they have got the survey of the city done except the Garrison & some other little things. I promised to be down to Weston on Monday.

Monday, 10th: Went down to Weston. Dennis has gone to Kingston & Brown to the city. Plotting the plan in the forenoon & walked into the city in the afternoon to make right some discrepancies in the measurements etc.

Tuesday, 11th: Slept at Mrs Hutchisons last night. Commenced survey with Brown before breakfast down towards the Don river and in other parts of the city during the day. Saw Dennis on his way from Kingston.

Wednesday, 12th: Surveying a line from Dundas street down the city limit to the Lake shore in the afternoon. Waiting on some of the Ordinance officers to get admitted into the Garrison to survey, but there is an order against it.

Thursday, 13th: Surveying the new Garrison from the outside as we are not admitted in, and the Lake shore as far as the old Garrison. Saw my Father who came in with Mr Pollock.

Friday, 14th: At the old Garrison, took my Father over to Mrs Hutchisons at noon. In the afternoon we got the survey finished but it was 8 oclock P.M. before we were done. My Father went up with Mr Orock.

Saturday, 15th: This week I had my meals all but 4 at Mrs Morrisons and slept at Mrs Hutchisons. Got an order on Ogilvie & Co. from S & B for 5 dollars and got a barrel of oatmeal. Saw the provincial exhibition today. Came out to the mills with Father.

Monday, 17th: At home plotting the city plan and the other part of the day hoeing corn & working about the mill.

Tuesday, 18th: At the city plan part of the day, but gave it up with disgust. Howards plan is so very incorrect it agrees neither with Browns measurement nor mine.

Saturday, 22nd: All this week I have been hoeing the Indian corn with little John, some of us have had a touch of dysentery. Mr Orock came over for Father, who returned today and brought Mr Orock here with him.

George B. Holland, brother of Mrs. John Hutchison (Martha Holland), who befriended Fleming in Toronto.

Monday, 24th: Yesterday Mr & Mrs Holland & Mrs Hutchison came up to see us. It got so stormy towards night that they were obliged to stop all night and left this morning after an early breakfast. We sent to the city a load of lumber.

Saturday, 29th: Hoeing corn & cutting saw logs all this week. The dog of the saw mill broke today & I went down to Weston & got it repaired. Andrew left for Mr Orocks on my return with his horse & to Mr Strath.

August 1848

Saturday, 5th: Cutting saw logs all this week. Mr Dennis sent up Brown to see how I was getting on with the plan. I went down to Weston. He is much disappointed that I have been doing nothing on it. I agreed to commence in earnest on Monday down at the city.

Monday, 7th: We got a loan of a waggon & Henry and I took a load of lumber down to the city. I have commenced to board at Mrs Hutchisons. Butt will not let us have the waggon without pay part cash.

Saturday, 12th: At the city plan all this week. Henry brought a load today & George & Burton Hutchison & I went up with him. Butt has agreed to let us have the waggon by [giving] him a Note for three months.

Monday, 14th: Started early this morning and got down before the stage with a load of lumber. My Father came down too. We got the waggon up with us. I took the plan up with me so that I could work at home.

Tuesday, 15th: Inking part of City of Toronto plan.

Wednesday, 16th: At city plan.

Thursday, 17th: Came down in the stage this morning. At city plan all week.

Saturday, 19th: At city plan all week although I was part of the time at home & part here. Went up in the stages. James Hutchison was down from Hamilton and came along with me.

Monday, 21st: Down in the stage this morning. Keatings creditors meet today but did no business. They are to meet this day week.

Saturday, 26th: At city plan all week. Went home.

September 1848

Saturday, 2nd: At city plan this week.

Saturday, 9th: At city plan this week.

Saturday, 16th: At city plan this week. Sick about 2 days.

Monday, 18th: Looks rather rainy this morning. Went down in stage to Weston and proceeded with Mr Dennis to Oakwood to lay off some village lots. Mr Dennis went to city & I went to work. Mr Dennis has just got married. Slept at the Peacock.

Tuesday, 19th: Laying off village lots today. Henry & Alexr were at the city with lumber. Went home with them with the horse team. Got very dark and rainy so I stopped at Weston for poor Alexr & the ox team. Dreadful dark & rainy.

Wednesday, 20th: Went down in the stage to Weston (paid 7/2) and proceeded to Oakwood with Mr Dennis. He sent a boy to drive me into the city in the afternoon. There is plenty of water in the mill now.

Thursday, 21st: At city plan.

Friday, 22nd: At city plan.

Saturday, 23rd: At city plan and boarded at Mrs Hutchisons all the time. Went home with Henry in the evening. I intend to be at home all next week to assist in getting down the family etc.

Monday, 25th: Drawing the lumber from the mills up to St. Andrews village all day. Alexr was drawing in saw logs. Very little water in the river.

Tuesday, 26th: Today Henry took a load of lumber down to Mr Smith worth £7 a thousand. Packing and fixing things for our removal. Took up and barrelled the beets & carrots etc etc. Bird took down a load of hay.

Wednesday, 27th: Today I went down with Henry with a load of furniture & Birds waggon. Took a load of hay. Annie & Jane went down with us.

Thursday, 28th: Henry & I went down today also with furniture & oats. Birds waggon went up to load in the afternoon. We didnt go home tonight but stayed at the house all night.

Friday, 29th: Started about ½ past 5 this morning for the mills, brought down a load of furniture, also Mother & John. Bird brought a load today. Our sojourn at the Humber will soon be over.

Saturday, 30th: Henry went up this morning. I bought a pair boots 2/3/6 & got ready to start for Cobourg. Recd 3 dollars on acct from Mr Smith. Arrived at Cobourg in the evening. Stopped at Mr. Pratts.

October 1848

Monday, 2nd: At Church yesterday. Meet the Board of Police today. They agreed to take the Cobourg plans off my hands at ¼ the selling price. Was very glad indeed about this. Saw most all the Cobourg folks.

Tuesday, 3rd: Very stormy, Miss Webster arrived from Kingston this morning and stopped at Mr Lockheads. It rained all day. I did not take Scobie & Balfours articles to the show today on acct of rain.

Wednesday, 4th: Mr Scobie came down last night and went down to Grafton. Today I entered the articles and also a crayon figure I did at Mr Nairns. The weather was fair all day. Went all round the show ground with Mr Scobie & Mr Hind.

Thursday, 5th: Mr Scobie went home last night, he left me a ticket for the Dinner. The show ground was crowded today. Saw a great many Peterboro friends. Went to the Dinner in the evening. About 500 present.

Friday, 6th: The prize list was read over today. I got the first for the crayon drawing £2/10. Went down in Hon Z[acheus]. Burnhams carriage to the steeple chase about 2 miles below town. Packed up the articles & sent them to Toronto by steamer.

Saturday, 7th: This week I received £4/10 from the Board of Police, lent Mr Hall £2/10. Scobie & Balfour prizes amount to £5. My own £1/2/10. Got a check on the bank for the amount. The bazaar this week cost me about 12/6.

Monday, 9th: At Church yesterday. Ordered Paton to make me a black coat and vest. Started after dinner for Peterboro along with Mr Lockhead, Mr McIntyre & his daughter, arrived about 8 oclock and stopped at Davidsons Hotel.

Tuesday, 10th: Saw most of the Peterboro folks today. Walked round the town most of the day with Miss Webster etc. Dined at Mr Hall. Tea at MacPhails. Not much improvement on Peterboro this summer.

Wednesday, 11th: Mr Lockhead started for Cobourg this morning and left a horse he brought for me to bring down on Friday. Collecting some money for the maps. In the afternoon along with Hugh MacPhail planted a weeping willow over poor Dr. Hutchisons grave. At Mr Bensons in the evening.

Thursday, 12th: Collecting etc. Bought from MacPhail London's Architecture £4/7/6 and recd cash £1/7/6 amounting to £5/15. I received an account of S & B to date Nov 1845. At Mrs Stewarts in the evening. Recd from McNeil £3/5/0 cash & note £4/19/9 for Mrs Hutchison. Left notes with MacPhail.

Friday, 13th: Started this morning for Port Hope on horseback, Hotel 18/6 horse shoeing. Received cash from Armour 20/ Armour 20/ Smith 17/6 & sold another to Waddel 17/6 cash. Walsh given up their tavern. Rode on to Cobourg. Very tired. Very tired.

Saturday, 14th: Sent up Mr Albros saddle & bridle, paid in full Pringle, Jeffrey, Nielson, Landon, Paton. Gave Gray & McLean order on Board Police for £4/10. Bought from Lockhead cwt sugar 50/ 16 lb coffee 16/ and got order on Freeland & Taylor for Bar of soap. Gave G. Butler 20/ map. Gave him about 5/. I owe Pratt altogether 17 or 18 days board after deducting map 20/.

Monday, 16th: Arrived here yesterday with the steamer *City*. All well with the exception of Father who has been troubled a good deal with dyspepsia.

Tuesday, 17th: Nothing new going on. We are all settled down in our new house, corner of Richmond & Victoria streets. In my absence they having been making the Garden into a lumber yard.

Wednesday, 18th: Papering the Hall and Room. Mr Anderson the Landlord supplied the paint and paper and we put it on.

Thursday, 19th: Commenced city plan again. While I was at Cobourg Mr Dennis according to agreement gave Mrs Hutchison [blank] dollars. My Father received from Scotland £50 currency.

Friday, 20th: At city plan.

Saturday, 21st: At city plan.

November 1848

Monday, 6th: I think this is the Monday we had a little party. Mr Hall of Peterboro was present among others.

Thursday, 23rd: I have been engaged pretty regularly at city plan, occasionally surveying and plotting. I have been principal person in getting up classes at the Mechanics' Institute for the study of Geometry, Drawing and Arithmetic. The two first are commenced and getting on very well.

Wednesday, 29th: At city plan when not noted to the contrary.

Thursday, 30th: At city plan forenoon previous and making plan of Scobie & Balfours premises afternoon. At Geometry class in the evening.

December 1848

Friday, 1st: At Scobie & Balfour plan all day. At the Drawing class in the evening.

Saturday, 2nd: At city plan today.

Monday, 4th: ½ day working for Scobie & Balfour. Not at city plan today.

Tuesday, 5th: Not at city plan.

Wednesday, 6th: Not at city plan.

Thursday, 7th: At city plan.

Friday, 8th: At city plan.

Saturday, 9th: At city plan.

Saturday, 16th: (At city plan) Until today when I commenced to finish a plan of America for Scobie & Balfour. Little Stokins has behaved so bad that they were obliged to put him away.

Monday 18th: At S & B. Geometry class in the evening.

Tuesday, 19th: At S & B. Drawing class evening.

Wednesday, 20th: S & B. Drawing class evening.

Thursday, 21st: S & B. Geometry class evening.

Friday, 22nd: S & B. Lecture at Institute.

Saturday, 23rd: At S & B.

Monday, 25th: Christmas. James Hutchison came down from Hamilton. Dinner at Mrs Hutchisons.

Tuesday, 26th: S & B. Drawing class.

Wednesday, 27th: S & B. Drawing class.

Thursday, 28th: At S & B. At Geometry class evening.

Friday, 29th: S & B. At lecture Mechanics' Institute by Dr Burns on English Literature.

Saturday, 30th: At S & B. Commenced the fourth sheet of the large map. Received from them 15/. 1848 nearly at a close. Time rolls on. What will another year produce.

[Written on blank page]
May it not truly be said that one's life is made up of good resolutions, and bad actions. How often do we resolve to improve our time by study and self denial and how often does lazy indolence and cunning thoughtlessness come across our path. But let us look forward a few years if our

lives be spared so long and take our choice even in a selfish point of view. Whether we wish then to be the ignorant & depraved or enlightened & useful member of society. Let us once more make perseverence our motto and industry our watchword and firmly resolve to act at least according to the best of our judgement and try to make self denial our great guide.

CHAPTER FIVE
The Canadian Institute 1849

Highlight of the year 1849 was Sandford's trip to Montreal in April to write his Canadian surveyor's exams at the Crown Land Office. James Hall, friend and neighbour of the Hutchisons and MPP for Peterborough, was in the city attending sessions of the House of Assembly. He welcomed his young protege and toured him around the points of interest, including the Parliamentary Library, the Lachine Railway, and the Mechanics' Institute. Hall, who was a member of the Committee on Railways, also introduced Sandford to the committee. He had written to him in February inviting him to send to the committee in advance a model locomotive he had made, and the meeting provided an opportunity to explain and demonstrate its special features. Montreal was a hopeful interlude for the young engineer.

It was an eventful time at the seat of government. Governor General Lord Elgin had given assent to the Rebellion Losses Bill amid strong conservative opposition. Rabid protestors pelted the governor with eggs, and even stones, as his carriage passed through the streets. The dramatic culmination of the revolt was the burning of the parliament buildings. Not only was Sandford a witness, he was proud to record in his diary that he had helped to save Queen Victoria's portrait from the flames, and that he "saved the crown" which was on top of the frame and "had the honour of sleeping with the crown in my bedroom" that night.

After an exciting month in Montreal, Sandford returned to Toronto and resumed his work with Stoughton Dennis. Temporarily he was assigned to survey work in Vaughan, but he soon returned to the City Plan. Work for Scobie and Balfour (including a large map of America and a map of Canada) provided some income, but Dennis was irregular in his salary payments and Fleming frequently records that he had to ask for some pay, and almost as frequently was put off to some later date. At the end of June he was at work at John Allanson's (for Scobie and Balfour), starting to engrave the Toronto map on a large block of stone. Allanson, an experienced European wood-engraver who had arrived in Toronto the year before, was a fellow member of the Mechanics' Institute and of the newly formed Canadian Institute. Fleming continued his classes at the Mechanics' Institute and devoted many hours to designing and then engraving a prize-winning "diploma" for them. While the Mechanics' Institute activities had a serious tone, Fleming and some like-minded colleagues had formed the Young Men's Debating Society, whose "soirees" offered more light-hearted "amusements, comic songs and dancing."

Early in June, Fleming and Frederick Passmore, in a more earnest light, organized a meeting of a group of engineers, surveyors, and architects who gathered in architect Kivas Tully's office to discuss forming an organization to meet regularly to present papers of mutual interest. This was the beginning of the (now Royal) Canadian Institute, a professional institution that occupied much of Sandford's leisure time in the months to come. He played a leading role in organizing and promoting Institute events and was active in extending its membership. At one early meeting only he and Passmore showed up, and the two proceeded to conduct business and pass motions as if the room was full. After some prodding by the two enthusiasts, the session they arranged for the following week was well attended, and in time the Institute became a permanent feature of Toronto life.

A variety of professional activities continued to fill the working hours, including forays out into the field such as joining a survey party out in Thornhill with Passmore in December, which provided a balance to the indoor work at the engraving table. Meanwhile, work on the City Plan was ongoing and continued to require his attention for months to come. It was finally published, after numerous interruptions, in the summer of 1851.

January 1849

Monday, 1st: David and I were foolish enough to go first footing this morning, although an old Scotch custom not a very exemplary way to begin the year. My Father Mother & the rest of the family went to Mr Pollocks at Richmond Hill.

Tuesday, 2nd: A beautiful frosty morning. Commenced work at S & B [Scobie & Balfour] in the afternoon, and attended drawing class at the Mechanics Institute in the evening. Poor Gillespie on the spree.

Wednesday, 3rd: At work at S & B as usual. At present drawing on the stone the last sheet of the large map of America I have promised to let them have 2 or 3 mounted on Monday morning next. At drawing class.

Thursday, 4th: At S & B. The Young Mens Debating Society had a Soiree at the Institute in the evening. It passed off very agreeably with a great variety of amusements, including comic songs, and ended dancing.

Friday, 5th: At S & B. Worked very hard and got the map finished, just as it got dark, to have a proof for tomorrow. Attended a lecture on Education at the Institute by Dr [Joseph] Workman.

Saturday, 6th: At S & B. David and Andrew very busy mounting two maps for Monday morning. Received from S & B 3 dollars.

Monday, 8th: Yesterday was the anniversary of my Birthday. I am now 22 years of age. Old enough to have a vast deal more knowledge & information than I fear I will ever possess. At geometry class in the evening.

Tuesday, 9th: Mounting maps at home but getting on very slow, they are so very large. The weather is now excessively cold, I suppose below zero, most of the time.

Wednesday, 10th: At home during the day. Attended the drawing class from 7 to 8. And then the debating society. Mr Carmichael proposed me as a member. I will probably be elected next Wednesday.

Thursday, 11th: At home during the day. Attended geometry class in the evening. Afterwards went out to Mr Bains expecting to meet a Mr Bridges, a young man just out from Edinburgh.

Friday, 12th: At home. I had a sleigh ride both today and yesterday across to the Island. Attended a lecture at the Institute by Dr [Egerton] Ryerson on the Education of Mechanics. A good one.

Saturday, 13th: At home working at maps, but not getting on very well. The severe frost is now over and it rains today. Received 3 dollars from S & B.

Monday, 15th: When reading "Dick, Scenery of the Heavens" there is a short paragraph on the Density of the Earth, to the effect that "the mean density of the Earth is nearly double the density of the rocks that compose the surface. The density of these rocks is reckoned to be two and a half times the weight of water, consequently the density of the Earth is to that of water as 5 is to 1. As the mean density of the whole earth surface including the ocean, cannot be above twice the density of water, it follows that the interior of the earth must have a much greater density than even 5 times the weight of water, to counterbalance the want of weight on its surface. Hence we are led to conclude that the interior of the earth near the centre must consist of very dense substance, denser than even iron, lead or silver."

Now I think it has been proved that water increases in density as we descend, so that even iron would swim at a greater depth, is it not highly probable that the interior of the earth consists of water, and that the continents are floating on the surface, but connected with each other under water.

The action of volcanoes seems at first sight to be against this theory, but the author of *Fairholmes Geology of Scripture* says [in] Chapter 1: "We cannot consider this awful phenomenon of burning mountains as more than superficial pustules on the mere skin of the earth. It is now pretty generally understood, and acknowledged, that water is one of the most active agents in the production of volcanic fires, and that almost all the active volcanoes now known are situated near the sea coast, and rarely, or never, far in the interior of large continents. We have very great reason to conclude, that the utmost depths of volcanic actions are not much, if at all, greater than those we have reason to consign to the ocean itself —from one to 5 miles.

Catopari, in South America, is perhaps of all volcanic mountains, the most distant from the sea, and yet it is only 140 miles from the shores of the Pacific. This volcano from time to time throws up, not only great quantities of mud, but also innumerable fish. In the mud volcanoes of Trinidad, a white sea shell was picked up, in the act of being thrown out with the mud; a sufficient proof of a subterranean communication with the sea. It is possible so to divide the globe into into two hemispheres, that one shall contain nearly all the land; the other being almost entirely sea; demonstration of a want of absolute equality in the density of the solid material of the two hemispheres. Considering the whole mass of land and water as in a state of equilibrium, it is evident that the half which protrudes must of necessity be buoyant, not of course that we mean to assert it to be lighter than water, but, as compared with the whole globe, in a less degree heavier than that fluid (Herschel's Astronomy).

February 1849

Friday, 2nd: This day to be charged to City Plan.

Saturday, 3rd: For the last three weeks I have been mounting maps & attending the Mechanics Institute in the evening as usual. Nothing strange has happened. Fine clear frosty weather.

Monday, 5th: Putting up pictures at Scobie & Balfours for the sale. Including 2 day previous. 3 days in all must be charged to this. Problem in geometry — given the four sides of a quadrilateral figure inscribed in a circle, to construct.

Tuesday, 6th: I have been almost all day trying to solve the above problem, but not successful. Had two games at chess with Mr Bain.

Wednesday, 7th: Part of the day at above problem — ½ day at City Plan. Last Saturday I received a Bill regarding patents from Mr [James] Hall MPP, Montreal. [Peterborough Member of the Legislative Assembly]

Thursday, 8th: Today at City Plan. Got on pretty well today. Geometry class in the evening.

Friday, 9th: Part of the forenoon at City Plan. Receive a letter from Mr Hall asking me to send down my model locomotive, as he is on the committee on railways & wishes to bring it before them & he may perhaps get enough granted to make an experiment with it — very attentive on his part.

Saturday, 10th: Engaged all day get the spring put on &c. Wrote to Mr Hall & to Mr Dennis.

Monday, 12th: At Timsons getting model repaired. Geometry class evening.

Tuesday, 13th: At Timsons as yesterday. Very severe frost. Drawing class evening.

Wednesday, 14th: At Timsons part of the day. The charges now seven dollars for his trouble.

Thursday, 15th: Working at model at home. Geometry class & theatre in the evening.

Friday, 16th: At model. Mr Dennis called today and we went over the time I had been with him. Promised to let me have some money soon.

Saturday, 17th: At model.

Monday, 19th: At model and writing out a paper showing the advantages of the system and refuting the objections to it.

Tuesday, 20th: Writing paper &c.

Wednesday, 21st: Writing paper and collecting information.

Thursday, 22nd: Same as yesterday.

Friday, 23rd: Got a box made for the model and sent it off by express along with the paper, a letter to Mr Russell — the package cost 5/.

Saturday, 24th: Out surveying part of the Lake shore for City Plan, very cold. Plotting afternoon. Today Mr Dennis gave me £5 (20 dollars).

James Hall, MLA, of Peterborough, introduced Sandford Fleming to the Assembly's railway committee in Montreal and later became his father-in-law.

Monday, 26th: Plotting &c at City Plan today. At class in the evening.

Tuesday, 27th: ½ day at City Plan.

Wednesday, 28th: ½ day at City Plan.

March 1849

Thursday, 1st: All day at City Plan.

Friday, 2nd: Assisting Mr Bain to remove to his new house in the forenoon. I have been looking over Guinness survey this week.

Saturday, 3rd: At City Plan in the afternoon — sketching the hills & trees between Parliament st & River Don.

Monday, 5th: At City Plan today. Napier's circular parts — on the sides, (of right-angled spherical triangles) the complt of angles & complt of hypothenuse vis — I think a simple instrument could be made for putting the eye in the same line as two distant objects, also for lay off regular curves of a large radius, such as railway curves, thus — . The two mirrors could be made to have a small motion so that the rays of light could meet at a an obtuse angle thus.

Received a letter from Mr Hall (At City Plan today) the model is running in the committee room, they are delighted and he is confident of something being done. Received from S & B 10/. Also a letter from Mrs Stewart, Peterboro.

Monday, 12th: The following from Mr Sangs system of surveying — 12 Sept 1842:

> The latitude of any situation is equal to the algebraic
> sum of the latitude of the first station and the product of
> the surveying line by the corion of its bearing; and the

longitude of any station is equal to the algebraic sum of the longitude of the first station and the product of the surveying line by the rim of the bearing.

[pages of technical information here]

Saturday, 17th: (Telegraphed Mr Hall today & wrote him about survey Bill. Mr Leslie also wrote Mr Morrison to speak to Mr Price about it.)

Monday, 19th: Saw survey bill today. Wrote to Mr Hall suggesting some alterations.

Friday, 23rd: Sketching in trees on City Plan today. At Mr Bains with Mr Bridges in the evening.
     Last night the effigies of Mackenzie, Blake & Baldwin were burnt in the streets, and the window at Mackenzie house broke and roughcast with mud.

Saturday, 24th: ½ day at City Plan. Received a letter from Mr Hall in reply to telegraph dispatch, to the effect that I would be in good time to go to Montreal after navigation opens. He wants to know how much would be required to try locomotive. They are all pleased but Gzowski.

Monday, 26th: Saw William Lyon Mackenzie, not unlike Gzowski — da da.

Saturday, 31st: About 2½ days this week at City Plan sketching trees & plotting.

April 1849

Tuesday, 3rd: Recd surveyors Bill today from Mr Hall. Being read a second time.

Thursday, 5th: Went down to Jacques & Hay and got Mrs Morrisons acct £2/2/9 transferred to Davids acct. I also paid her the balance of Boarding amounting to 10/. At City Plan yesterday.

Saturday, 7th: Went out to Weston this afternoon with Mr Brown. Mr Dennis has kindly given me his theodolite to take to Montreal. He will try to give me a little money before I go. Stayed with him till Monday morning.

Monday, 9th: Mr Anderson our Landlord would only take £10 just now as I am going to Montreal, he will get the remaining £4 when I return. I have some intention of going to Montreal tomorrow if Mr Dennis comes to town.

Tuesday, 10th: I have learned that navigation is not open all the way through so I have put off going until Thursday. Scobie & Balfour have given me an order on the Boats all the way down to Montreal.

Wednesday, 11th: Doing odds and ends to put off the time. Attended Debating Society in the evening. Mr [F.F.] Passmore read a very good essay on Geological changes in the earth. Also some good recitations.

Thursday, 12th: Mr Dennis has not come into town. Left in the *Magnet* for Kingston, passage paid by an order from Scobie & Balfour being $4. I had about £8 in my pocket when I left Toronto. Saw one or two of the Cobourg folks when we stopped.

Friday, 13th: Arrived at Kingston this morning and left in the *Highlander* for Dickensons Landing, passage 16/3 which along with a due bill $6 I received from the Purser for my passage up is paid by order from S & B total £2/6/3 — The Thousand Islands really beautiful, but the day was cold and rainy. Took stage from Landing to Cornwall.

Saturday, 14th: Woke up about 3 in the morning. A Propeller can come down to the Rapids and can take us on to Coteau de Lac. The wind was rather strong. We struck on a bank in the middle of Lake St Francis, and lay there all night, about 24 passengers in a cabin about 12 feet square, besides a number of steerage passengers — very cold.

Monday, 16th: We got on board the small steamer *Rob Roy* on her first trip yesterday morning — very glad. Arrived at Coteau de Lac & took the stage to the Cascades, then crowded in a large bateau to the other side of the river where the splendid steamer *Queen* lay. We passed through some very long islands of ice at the foot of the rapids, rather dangerous, bateau loaded with luggage & passengers. Arrived at Lachine and took the stage to Montreal. Put up at Macks Hotel. Could not find Mr Hall at home but saw him at the House today.

Tuesday, 17th: Mr Hall introduced me to the Library of the House of Assembly, which is of great value, it contains some of the most splendid works with plates I ever saw. Spent most of the day in the Library. It is certainly a great privilege to have the run of this Library.

Wednesday, 18th: Attending the Assembly & Library. Went up to the Lachine railway in the afternoon, made myself acquainted with the engine driver who comes from Dundas. He came down to Macks in the evening to talk about the locomotive. He introduced me to the Mechanics Institute.

Thursday, 19th: Commenced this morning to undergo my examination at the Crown Land Office, went through Euclid to Crooks, some trigonometry calculating finding of areas by traverse and other methods. At House of Assembly in the evening.

Friday, 20th: At examination today. Forenoon astronomical questions, finding Latitude &c. Finished very easy. Mr Russell is very agreeable person, examining theodolite in the afternoon. Went up to the railway station to see Mr Greig again.

Saturday, 21st: Met Mr Hall at the Crown Land Office, went down to the House with him and from there to find out some practical Engineer about the locomotive. The committee on railways want to summons two or three to appear before them on Monday, when they make up their report.

Monday, 23rd: Went along with Mr Cane yesterday to Mr MacFarlane, Engineer Civil. Went this morning to the Eagle Foundry to see a Mr

Dunbar. I rather think a locomotive built on my principle would be more complex. Called for Mr Hall. He had gone to Peterboro yesterday morning, one of his children dying.

Tuesday, 24th: Having to get two sureties for £500 I have lost Mr Hall in mean time. However Donald Cameron of Thursk, has kindly offered his name, also James Black, surveyor Blenheim township, both without being asked. I believe Surveyors Bill passed Lower House last night. Mr Russell took me to Mr Logan, geologist, [William E. Logan, director of Canadian Geological Survey] yesterday.

Wednesday, 25th: This is a memorable day. The Governor gave his assent to the Rebellion Losses Bill which not excluding rebels from receiving pay for loss sustained in 1837 gives a great deal of dissatisfaction. The Governor was pelted with eggs when coming out, the windows of Parliament house were smashed by the mob and lastly the building set fire to. Very little was saved. I assisted to save the Queens picture and saved the crown which was on the top from the flames, took it home.

Thursday, 26th: I had the honour of sleeping last night with the crown in my bedroom — wrote to Father. The House is one mass of ruins, the City is boiling with excitement. The leaders of the Government pelted with eggs, and not allowed to travel the streets. The soldiers parading the streets all day. Five gentlemen taken up for speaking at a mass meeting last night, escorted to jail by a company of soldiers. All the soldiers I daresay on duty.

Friday, 27th: Assisting Mr Cane to draw a large map. The Town is in a great state of excitement — no business doing, groups of people all along the streets &c.

Saturday, 28th: This day the Governor [Lord Elgin] came into Town to the Executive Council. On his way home he was pelted with stones and his carriage broken. I saw the troops make a charge on the crowd opposite Macks.

Monday, 30th: The most of this week drawing at Mr Canes map. Saturday the Governor signed my License. The town still very much excited.

May 1849

Tuesday, 1st: [diary pages left blank May 1 to 3 and later filled] July 5. I have neglected to fill up some parts but am at present reading with improvement of the mind, a good work and intend extracting some passages from it. To begin with the following lines from the Pythagoreans are worth waking up to:

> Nor let soft slumber close your eyes
> Before you've recollected thrice
> The train of action through the day;
> Where have my feet chose out their way
> What have I learnt wherein I've been
> From all I've heard, from all I've seen?
> What know I more that's worth the knowing?
> What have I done that's worth the doing?
> What have I sought that I should share?
> What duty have I left undone?
> Or into what new follies run?
> These self inquiries are the road
> That leads to virtue and to God.

Monday, 7th: Yesterday went down to Isle Bourdon with Mr Ross. His Father has a beautiful farm there.

Saturday, 12th: Saw Capt Harrison of the *Cambria*, the Capt our family came out with. Invited me to dinner with him tomorrow — but I dine with Mr McLean and he gave me a drive round the mountain.

Monday, 14th: Borrowed from Mr Hall £2 — gave £2 to Mr Mack. I still owe him £2/7/6 for Board. Mr McLean drove me round the mountain yesterday, fine drive. Left Montreal with the railway at 12 and got the splendid steamer *Passport* at Lachine. Woke up this morning and saw the Thousand Islands gliding past my bedroom window, a most beautiful morning. Caught the *Magnet* at Kingston, play chess several times with Dr Liddel of Montreal on the way up.

Wednesday, 16th: Landed at Toronto about 6 oclock this morning. All well. The town had been a good deal excited by the getting up of some addresses to the Governor.

Thursday, 17th: Saw Mr Dennis today, he said he sent me £2/10 last Monday to Montreal. Went out to Weston with the stage. Mr Dennis wants me to go along with Bridges & Brown to go over our dispute.

Friday, 18th: Survey in Vaughan — went up to Vaughan this morning — survey all day. Slept at Berwick.

Saturday, 19th: Completing survey this morning. Difference between this and former only 5 links. Came down to Weston and from there to Toronto in the evening.

Monday, 21st: Fixing the fence before the house today. Dined at the Buchans yesterday with Mr Cole, an engineer on the Erie Canal. At Mechanics Institute.

Tuesday, 22nd: Received letters from Mr Hall this morning, one enclosing the money letter from Mr Dennis to me which came to Montreal after I left, contained $10. Remitted $8 to Mr Hall.

June 1849

Saturday, 16th: I having spoken to Mr [F.F.] Passmore about getting up a Surveyors Society, we called upon several in town, and agreed to meet on Wednesday next. I wrote out to Mr Dennis.

Wednesday, 20th: Tonight 10 surveyors & engineers met in Mr Kivas

Kivas Tully, prominent Toronto architect with whom Fleming frequently worked on design projects.

Tullys [architect] office for the purpose of getting up an association of surveyors, engineers & architects. We agree to meet again on the 20th of July and to give notice to all those interested in the neighborhood.

Thursday, 28th: Commenced to trace on the stone down at Mr Allansons the City Plan for S & B.

Friday, 29th: At City Plan S & B. Since I came from Montreal I have been about 6 days at City Plan for Mr Dennis.

Saturday, 30th: 1 day at City Plan — made the tracing on Saturday the 16, making in all 4 days work.

July 1849

Monday, 2nd: At Diploma for Institute. Anne & David went over to the Falls today. At Plan engraving ½ day.

Tuesday, 3rd: Finishing design for Diploma, sent it in this evening.

Wednesday, 4th: Engraving City Plan.

Thursday, 5th: Engraving City Plan. Paid the balance of last half years rent to Mr Anderson being £4. He owes us about 6/ for paint & oil for the fence which was not deducted. Wrote to Mr Sang and sent Newcastle Distr map. With Mr Bethune.

Friday, 6th: Engraving City Plan today. The committee are to meet tonight and decide on the Diploma design. I am on the fidgets to see the other two.

Saturday, 7th: Engraving City Plan. Passing along the street after noon I was congratulated on having got the Honorary Premium for the best diploma. I put in as an amateur, the other two competitors styled themselves as professionals, Thomas & Wheeler, but amateur was the successful.

Monday, 9th: ½ day at City Plan.

Saturday, 14th: ½ day at City Plan. All the other [preceding] days full making 5 days. The cholera is in town.

Wednesday, 18th: The committee have agreed that I should engrave the diploma, they are to pay me for my time at 10/ per day. I said thought it would cost them about £20.

Friday, 20th: Recd 20/ lately on acct. maps & refrigerator. Recd 10/ from Scobie & Balfour.

Saturday, 21st: All this week at City Plan.

Monday, 23rd: At City Plan today.

Tuesday, 24th: Commenced to trace Diploma for Mechanics Institute, my own design. I intend to charge 10/ per day and think it will take about two months.

Saturday, 28th: All work since Tuesday at Diploma.

Monday, 30th: At Diploma today. Recd 4 dollars from S & B.

Tuesday, 31st: Making alterations on small map of Canada for Scobie & Balfour.

August 1849

Wednesday, 1st: At Map of Canada.

Thursday, 2nd: At Map of Canada forenoon.

Friday, 3rd: At Map of Canada forenoon. Cholera still in town — 24 cases yesterday.

Saturday, 4th: At Diploma.

Monday, 6th: Last night Mrs Buchan came for me to sit up with John, he had been on the spree & was very bad (the Blues). I thought he was going to have the cholera one time. At Map of Canada today S & B.

Tuesday, 7th: At Diploma today. Received from S & B 5 dollars. I gave Mr Brown 4 dollars for John Pauls subscription to the Globe which I received at Peterboro about 18 months ago.

Wednesday, 8th: At Diploma afternoon. Went down to see John Cochrane with Mr Gillespie. He had been very bad last night & took down Dr Buchanan to see him. Afterwards took down a bottle of wine which cost 4/2. My Mother made some chicken broth which I took down.

Thursday, 9th: At Diploma today.

Friday, 10th: Forenoon at Diploma. Afternoon at Almanac for S & B. Sent up Surveyor Society circular.

Saturday, 11th: At Diploma today. Received 5/ from S & B.

Saturday, 18th: At Diploma engraving all this week.

Saturday, 25th: At Diploma engraving most of this week.

Friday, 31st: ½ day at S & B.

September 1849

Saturday, 1st: At Diploma 5 days say this week — got impression from border.

Thursday, 27th: Mr Gillespie came to board with us today.

December 1849

Friday, 7th: Making survey of south [entry too faint to read].

Monday, 10th: At Diploma title. Writing paper on the Earth this evening.

Thursday, 13th: At Diploma title. Read my paper on the Earth at Bridges, was well received and caused a lengthy discussion. Deep thought, slept very little.

Saturday, 15th: Not very well, took dose of salts & bath. Making plan of theatre for Bernardi.

Monday, 17th: Went out to Thornhill with Passmore, Bridges &c to commence a survey.

Tuesday, 18th: Commenced running a line from the town line 1½ miles below Thornhill to beyond Richmond Hill about 6 miles. Saw Mr Pollock family and walked back to Thornhill in the evening.

Wednesday, 19th: Came down in the stage this morning. Finished a newspaper title for Allanson say 5/. Diploma about ready.

Thursday, 20th: Took down the two stones of Diploma and got a proof this forenoon. It is likely to do pretty well. Mr Gillespie coloring the vignettes of one. At Bridges — Bridges read a good essay on right and wrong.

Friday, 21st: Designing throne chair for Drummond and Thompson. At Kivas Tullys lecture in the evening. Sub &Ventilation.

Saturday, 22nd: Part of forenoon at throne chair. Cleaning up rooms.

Monday, 24th: Made a newspaper title for Mr Allanson.

Tuesday, 25th: Christmas. Mr Russells horses ran off today while I was bringing them to the front door. They ran against a house on Yonge street and knocked the waggon all to pieces.

Wednesday, 26th: Received 10/ from S & B. Read my speech at Debating Society this evening, well received — subject Whether India or Africa suffered most from Europe.

Thursday, 27th: ½ day at City Plan engraving.

Friday, 28th: At City Plan engraving.

Saturday, 29th: Painting fire place. Mr Russell came up from Whitby his waggon is repaired cost 11/3 — I paid him 5/.

Monday, 31st: Painting room today. I intend to paper & clean it up and make an office. Received 15 from S & B. I owe the following persons as far as I can recollect:

Henderson & Laidlaw
Carmichael say 18/
Sterling — Boots plain 15/
Riddell & McLean 25/ [tailors]

[Note on side of page: all paid Jany 9, 1850 S.F.]

CHAPTER SIX
Map of Toronto 1850

Engraving the large Toronto City Plan on stone, the challenging project first begun in May 1848, occupied most of Fleming's working days throughout the year 1850. He felt he was finally making progress in February when he noted that he was spending "about 3 days to a square inch" on it (at a scale of 12 chains to an inch), although Hugh Scobie became impatient with the time it was taking. In July, shortly after he and John Balfour dissolved their partnership, a disgruntled Scobie decided to hold back any further payments until it was finished. Corrections were still being made. Early in the year, Sandford was out sounding on Toronto Bay in wintry weather trying to finalize some details, and in the ensuing months there continued to be other similar interruptions. When the first proof was pulled from the stone on August 3 there was still much to be done and further adjustments needed.

One big bone of contention was the wording of the title and credits on the map. Scobie accepted Stoughton Dennis's version giving credit to himself, with Scobie as publisher and no mention of Sandford Fleming. At this Fleming rebelled. "I have no heart to go on with the map unless I get credit for my work. If I don't choose to finish it, send down the storm." He sent Scobie a bill for fifty pounds. Scobie asked for a "correct note" of the time spent — 97½ days according to Sandford's reply. All was settled amicably and when the finished map finally appeared in 1851, it bore Fleming's name three times "from actual survey by J. Stoughton Dennis... Drawn and Compiled by Sandford A. Fleming, Provincial Land Surveyor ..." and elsewhere "Published by Hugh Scobie ... Engraved on stone by Sandford A. Fleming ..." An inset map of "the Harbour and adjoining coast" was produced from "Fleming's Chart."

Sandford became fascinated by the Toronto Harbour and twice delivered papers on his proposals for the waterfront at meetings of the Canadian Institute, the first in June and another in December. He presented his Harbour Chart to City Officials and was awarded a diploma at the Provincial Exhibition for his Toronto Harbour model. Colleagues met through Institute activities, notably Frederic Cumberland, who was involved in many important local projects, led the way to new opportunities. In October, Sandford was one of a delegation from the Mechanics' Institute that went to Montreal to attend the Provincial Exhibition, a week-long event highlighted by sightseeing in the Bonsecours Market area, and a gala dinner hosted by the Montreal Mechanics' Institute, prize-givings, fireworks, even a ploughing match. He arrived in Montreal to join Cumberland, who had gone down earlier, bringing proofs of the *Canadian Journal* prospectus to distribute there in hopes of attracting subscribers for the new publication.

The creation of the *Journal*, originally suggested by Fleming, was the culmination of months of meetings of a dedicated few, including Fleming, J.O. Browne, and Dr. Henry Melville. It was to provide a permanent record of the Institute's proceedings and papers delivered, many of them by Fleming himself. Members of the Institute continued to be closely associated with the Mechanics' Institute committee, often serving, as Fleming and Cumberland did, on both. In December, William E. Logan, Director of the Geological Survey of Canada, was elected the first chair of the Canadian Institute.

Throughout this year Sandford took on numerous freelance jobs in addition to his work for Dennis. He spent several weeks on surveys in Toronto for William Cayley, MLA, and drawing a perspective view of the Welland Courthouse for architect Kivas Tully. Cumberland asked him to produce a finished sketch of his plans for the new St. James Cathedral being built to replace the old church which was destroyed by fire in a major conflagration in downtown Toronto in April 1849. In November he decided to open an office of his own in rented quarters on Yonge Street, where W.B. Leather, a recently-arrived British engineer, joined him for a year while he (Leather) prepared to write the Canadian surveying exams. Shortly thereafter, young George Stewart came from Peterborough as an apprentice.

January 1850

Tuesday, 1st: New Years morning. David & I was foolish enough to go out first footing and get back about 4 oclock A.M. Visiting a number of friends during the day. Spent the evening at the Bains.

Tuesday, 8th: Showed diploma proof to Mechanics Institute committee tonight. They passed an order to pay me £10. The price of the whole I said would be £30. At drawing class first night.

Wednesday, 9th: Recd from Treasurer of Mechanics Institute £10 — and £12/10 formerly, in all £22/10. Paid Carmichael 18/9, Riddell & McLean £1/5, Sterling 15/. At drawing class. At debating society agreed to read an essay next Wednesday.

Saturday, 12th: This week I have done nothing to City Plan, been cleaning, papering & painting room. Paper cost about 7/.

Monday, 14th: 1 day at City Plan.

Tuesday, 15th: ½ day at City Plan. Also at drawing class. Paid back Father £2/10 which I borrowed. Also lent Father £1/5 in all £3/15.

Wednesday, 16th: At drawing class. Read an essay tonight on the Earth at the Debating Society. McDougall without permission noticed it in the *Globe* and invited the public. However although very much annoyed I read the essay about ½ hour long, and was well received. I introduced my water theory of the interior of the Earth, which brought out a good deal of discussion.

Thursday, 17th: Poor Annie has got rather bad in her mind occasionally, very melancholy. Dr Telfer has been allowing her to go to Asylum for some time past. Mother & I went up with her today. Poor girl a very sorrowful affair. Paid Mother £3/5 & cab 3/9 — £5/8/9. Yesterday Donald Cameron 5/. Also received from Agricultural committee Hamilton Prize for Locomotive model 20/.

Sunday, 20th: The Lord layeth the beams of his chambers in the waters, he maketh the clouds his chariot, he walketh upon the wings of the wind: he maketh the winds his messengers and the lightning his agents. He watereth the mountains from his chambers, the earth is satisfied with the fruit of his works. Psls [Psalms]. God himself that formed the earth and made it, and hath established it created it not in vain; he formed it to be inhabited. Isa[iah].

Monday, 21st: Very idle today. Making sounding lead. By means of the voice we have been enabled to become a civilized people, and have obtained all the blessings peculiar to that state. There is something so fascinating in some of the modulations of the voice that they penetrate our souls, and we acknowledge their influence from the bottom of our hearts. A pleasing and soft voice tuned to the language it utters is irresistible; and we often from the tone of the voice judge the temper of the mind.

Wednesday, 23rd: Went out sounding in the Bay with Gillespie & John, myself on skates using 12 pole chain.

Thursday, 24th: Out sounding with Gillespie & Irishman very disagreeable day. I owe Irish 1/3.

Friday, 25th: Sounding Bay in afternoon with Passmore & Irishman, got on very well with Passmore & I on skates. Gave James 1/3.

Saturday, 26th: In the forenoon plotting soundings. Received 5/ from S & B. Went out in the afternoon with James MacDonald to his Father's farm in Markham.

Sunday, 27th: At Markham, very kind people.

Monday, 28th: Still at Markham, went up as far as Whitchurch.

Tuesday, 29th: Left Markham after breakfast. At drawing class in the evening.

Wednesday, 30th: ½ day at City Plan engraving. At drawing class.

Thursday, 31st: At City Plan evg. At Bridges. Paper had to read, did not come out too bad!

February 1850

Friday, 1st: At City Plan engraving. Letters from Kirkcaldy. Poor William Hutchison is dead. Out first footing & fell over the pier on New Years Day. Most distressing news for his poor Mother. I went down to Mr Holland, did not tell anyone else. He had just written to William last night, urging him to come back immediately. He had got a situation for him.

Saturday, 2nd: ½ day at City Plan. [Indecipherable] first mate on board the *Sovereign* & Mr Bethune wanted him as soon as possible to rigg her up. Mrs Dr Burns told Mrs Hutchison, a painful job, her spirits were so much raised with the expectation of an early visit.

Monday, 4th: Engraving City Plan.

Tuesday, 5th: Engraving City Plan.

Wednesday, 6th: Engraving City Plan. Drawing class evening. Mrs Hutchison is very bad poor body.

Thursday, 7th: Engraving City Plan. Mrs H. a little better. At Bridges. I read a short paper & described the steam from Parks Diagram.

Friday, 8th: At City Plan. Canadian Institute meeting evening. Only Passmore & I present. Passed several resolutions with Mr Browne to send circulars to the members to meet every week. Dennis is for giving it up as a decided failure — a Chuzzlewit affair. Truly a Canadian Institute.

Wednesday, 13th: Making soundings in Bay. Good skating. Drawing class evening.

Friday, 15th: ½ day at Engraving City Plan.

Saturday, 16th: At City Plan.

Monday, 18th: At City Plan.

Tuesday, 19th: At City Plan Engraving.

Wednesday, 20th: ½ day at City Plan Engraving.

Thursday, 21st: Engraving City Plan.

Friday, 22nd: Engraving City Plan.

Saturday, 23rd: Engraving City Plan. Recd from S & B 20/. At Canadian Institute, read a speech.

Monday, 25th: Engraving City Plan.

Tuesday, 26th: Making soundings on Bay. Finished the last two lines I can get done through the ice around Blockhouse Bay. Found very bad, some places rotten through.

Wednesday, 27th: Engraving City Plan.

Thursday, 28th: Father paid Henderson & Laidlaw £2/10.
I also paid them £2/10 which I received today from S & B. At Eng City Plan. Bridges in evening.

March 1850

Friday, 1st: Engraving City Plan, getting on pretty well now, at the rate of about 3 days to a square inch — the centre of the town.

Saturday, 2nd: Engraving City Plan. At Canadian Institute in the evening. This society is likely to get on now, we are to have a short paper read every Saturday.

Monday, 4th: Engraving City Plan.

Tuesday, 5th: Engraving City Plan. At drawing class & committee meeting in the evening.

Wednesday, 6th: Eng City Plan.

Thursday, 7th: Eng City Plan. At Bridges in the evening. He is very sanguine about starting a Review next winter.

Friday, 8th: At City Plan.

Saturday, 9th: At Canadian Institute in the evening. Mr Dennis read a paper suggesting to the Surveyor of Canada some amendments to the Survey Bill. It was sent to the *Packet* for publication.

Monday, 11th: Commenced a perspective view in the evening for Passmore. He is designing a church for London C.W.

Tuesday, 12th: Engraving City Plan.

Wednesday, 13th: Engraving City Plan.

Wednesday, 20th: Engraving City Plan.

Thursday, 21st: Engraving City Plan.

Friday, 22nd: Engraving City Plan. Lent two vols of Gilpin to Mr Ambrose & one to Mr Allanson.

Saturday, 23rd: Engraving City Plan. Gave Henderson & Laidlaw on their acct nearly £3. At Canadian Institute, discuss chair of Engineering in University of Toronto.

Monday, 25th: Engraving City Plan.

Tuesday, 26th: Engraving City Plan.

Wednesday, 27th: Engraving City Plan.

Thursday, 28th: Engraving City Plan ½ day.

Friday, 29th: Good Friday. At Bains helping him put up fences etc. Got a pair of books from Polson price 25/.

Saturday, 30th: Engraving City Plan. At Canadian Institute — discussion about surveying — got a proof of Societies Arms from Mr Allanson. Riddell & McLean sent up my suit of clothes Altogether cost £5/18/9.

Sunday, 31st: [Easter] At St Andrews Church forenoon.

April 1850

Monday, 1st: Engraving City Plan.

Tuesday, 2nd: Engraving City Plan. At drawing class at Mechanics Institute committee in the evening. We had letters from Kirkcaldy. Poor Grandmother <u>Dead</u>, and buried at Kennoway about 85 years of age.

Wednesday, 3rd: Engraving City Plan.

Thursday, 4th: Engraving City Plan ½ day. We have had great rains. The Don bridge and many others swept away. At Bridges in the evening.

Friday, 5th: Commence finishing Diploma. Got a stone for the tint at S & B.

Saturday, 6th: At Diploma tracing. At Canadian Institute in the evening. Discussion about professionalism of Engineering. 50 copies of rules & regulations printed. Received the thanks of meeting for my design of the shield.

Thursday, 11th: At Bridges. He read a paper on Matter.

Saturday, 13th: At Canadian Institute. Mr [J.O.] Browne read a paper on optics and optical instruments used in surveying.

Tuesday, 16th: Last night of drawing class at Mechanics Institute.

Wednesday, 17th: Mr Passmore & I at tea at Mr Russells in the evening.

Thursday, 18th: Mr Russell paid me a visit this afternoon he seemed to be much pleased with my work.

Saturday, 20th: This week & the last I have been preparing a stone for the tint of diploma.

Sunday, 21st: Finished tint stone of diploma yesterday. At Canadian Institute. Passmore read a paper on the Climate of Canada yesterday.

Monday, 22nd: At meeting of Mechanics Institute committee this morning, for the purpose of drawing up suggestions for City Council regarding the city prison. Mr [Frederic] Cumberland came up to see Davids Lions [carvings]. Down with Mr Cayley surveying for him near the Scarboro line. Recd payment 15/.

Tuesday, 23rd: Out in the afternoon surveying north west part of the city for Plan.

Wednesday, 24th: Preparing chalk stone of diploma for printing &c got some proofs of the tint stone thrown off & sponged.

Tuesday, 25th: Looking after the printing of a few diplomas in the morning. Out surveying for City Plan in the afternoon. Trying to get a copy of a pamphlet published by Captain Richardson on Toronto Harbour.

Friday, 26th: Out surveying all day for City Plan. Charles Unwin & John [Fleming, Sandford's youngest brother] is along with me. Lent Unwin *Londons Rural Architecture*.

Saturday, 27th: Plotting surveying of City Plan. Canadian Institute meeting adjourned till next Saturday. Mr Cayley not having had time to prepare his paper on piling.

Tuesday, 30th: Surveying City Plan with Unwin & John.

Frederic Cumberland, fellow founder of the (Royal) Canadian Institute, for whom Fleming worked as assistant chief engineer on the Ontario, Simcoe and Lake Huron (later the Northern) Railway.

Courtesy Toronto Public Library, Special Collections.

May 1850

Wednesday, 1st: Plotting City Plan.

Thursday, 2nd: Plotting City Plan.

Monday, 6th: Started today with Annie for Mr Bethunes. I had 90/ and Father gave me £2. Put up at City Hotel in Hamilton all night.

Tuesday, 7th: Started in the Port Dover stage this morning & landed at Mr Bethunes in the afternoon. They were very glad to see us.

Wednesday, 8th: Left for Henry Flemings this morning. He & Henry were taken by surprise.

Thursday, 9th: Henry Brother drove me up to Jarvis this morning. Saw there Mr Gowans people. Came down in the stage and arrived at Toronto in the evening.

Friday, 10th: Travelling expenses — Boat to Hamilton 8/9, Hotel 12/6, Stage out & sundry 10/. Gave Henry 5/. Stage in 5/, Boat 3/9. [total] £2/5.

Sunday, 12th: Measuring a line for Mr Cayley after 4 oclock in the afternoon at the top of the Avenue to charge 5/ yesterday.

Monday, 13th: Surveying in the forenoon for Mr Cayley staking of row 23 chains for Ave &c &c. John [Fleming, Sandford's youngest brother] was with me plotting in the afternoon.

Saturday, 18th: Writing paper today and during the week. Bought some flowers at a sale 7/6. I intended to read paper tonight but there was no meeting. Mr Hall MPP went down with me to the Institute.

Wednesday, 22nd: Subpoenaed to attend court on account of [David] Gibson re Brampton plank road company — referred to arbitration.

Thursday, 23rd: Part of the day at arbitration. In the afternoon surveying for Cayley.

Friday, 24th: The Queens birthday. Out making soundings at the point of the Queen's wharf. A beautiful morning but afternoon wind & rain rather too rough, so that I could tell little perceptible change on the shoal. Fireworks up the College Avenue in the evening.

Saturday, 25th: In the afternoon out with Passmore running a line for Hon Mr William Cayley from Queen St to the cricket ground. No meeting of Canadian Institute.

Sunday, 26th: Took a walk down to the shore in the afternoon.

Monday, 27th: Plotting survey of City Plan.

Tuesday, 28th: Gave my evidence at the arbitrations. My subpoena was taxed for £2. Survey in forenoon for Cayley. Henry came this evening.

Wednesday, 29th: In the afternoon measuring along Queen St for Cayley with Henry. At meeting of Exhibition committee in the evening.

Thursday, 30th: Delivered Cayleys plans. Showed Captain Harrison my chart of the Bay. Making a little garden at the back of the house. Received a letter from Mrs [Frances] Stewart of Peterboro.

Friday, 31st: Writing paper on the Harbour.

June 1850

Saturday, 1st: Read paper on the Formation & Preservation of Toronto Harbour at the Canadian Institute. It occupied upwards of an hour. It was well received. Had a little discussion and received the thanks of the Society.

Monday, 3rd: Petitioned the corporation for an opportunity of carrying before them my views regarding the Harbour. It was referred to the committee on Wharves & Harbours.

Tuesday, 4th: Today plotting City Plan. At Mechanics Institute committee in the evening.

Wednesday, 5th: Rec'd £4/17/6 for teaching drawing class during the winter for Mechanics Institute. Paid Polson £1/5, Henderson & £1/2/6 new pot, Brown & Child £1/2/6 Boots & shoes, Mr Edwards 7/6 Soiree tickets. Met at Mr Cumberlands house about starting a periodical scientific.

Thursday, 6th: Up at the Crown Land Office. Saw Mr Cayley — he wants me to stake off the line & make a survey for his brothers near the cemetery. Mr Hutchison & I at Mr Cumberland in the evening. Recd £1 from Gibson & his note for £1, being for Lefroy (£2).

Friday, 7th: An article appeared in the *Colonist* today regarding the paper I read last Saturday evening. David has finished the Royals Arms, they are bronzed and put up today above the Speakers chair in the House of Assembly. They give universal satisfaction. Had a bath.

Saturday, 8th: ½ day plotting survey of city. Out staking off Cayley line 2 hours in the afternoon.

Monday, 10th: Mr Cumberland sent for me today. He wants me to assist him in drawing the plans for the English church [St James Cathedral]. Wrote to the secretary of the Board of Trade about Harbour. An article appeared in the *Patriot* today — he calls it "rather a wild speculation."

Tuesday, 11th: At Mr Cumberland today.

Wednesday, 12th: At Mr Cumberland today. Saw Mr Brent. The Board of Trade to meet tomorrow.

Thursday, 13th: At Mr Cumberland. Met the Board of Trade in the evening only 4 present. They thought it better to put off reading the paper till this day [next] week, when the members could be special noticed.

Friday, 14th: Out with Passmore this day levelling across the Don at Cayleys for Mr Cayley. At committee meeting in the evening. Proof of Diploma inscription was sent up to me during the day.

Saturday, 15th: Down at King Street. Surprised to learn that Scobie & Balfour have dissolved partnership. At Cumberlands. Got a blowing up from Mr Scobie about the City Plan in the evening.

Sunday, 16th: Passmore has been writing a long article in reply to the *Patriot*.

Monday, 17th: Plotting section for Cayley. Henry went off today.

Tuesday, 18th: Plotting section and making plan for Cayley. Wrote to Mr Scobie this morning about Plan engraving. Gave Father 4 dollars.

The old Parliament Building in downtown Toronto, circa *1850. From* Landmarks, Volume 1 *(1894) by J.R. Robertson.*

Wednesday, 19th: Commence again to Plot survey of City Plan. David went up to Richmond Hill. At committee in the evening.

Thursday, 20th: Plotting survey of City Plan. I had to attend a special meeting of the Board of Trade the purpose of laying my paper on the Harbour before them. Noone but the secretary Mr Brent appeared. He supposed they had gone to hear Fanny Kemble, or Thursday prayer meeting.

Friday, 21st: Delivered Cayleys section today at the Parliament Buildings. Paid Masterson for painting McLeans boat 5/. Swimming at the Island with MacDonald.

Saturday, 22nd: Plotting City Plan. Mr Hall & Mr Bell member for Lanark called in the afternoon.

Monday, 24th: Plotting City Plan and sketching trees &c at the Grange.

Tuesday, 25th: Passmores letter appeared in the *Colonist* today. Plotting City Plan and making corrections at Crookshank, Denniston &c.

Wednesday, 26th: Plotting City Plan.

Thursday, 27th: Tracing City Plan for stone.

Friday, 28th: Tracing part of City Plan for stone.

Saturday, 29th: With Passmore forenoon. ½ day plotting City Plan. Went out in the evening with James MacDonald to Markham. Wrote to Mrs [Frances] Stewart Peterboro for George to come up to go on a survey with Brigland.

Sunday, 30th: At Markham at Church 6 hours. Boyd & Nesbit preached — sacrament — rain — smoking — fireflies — morning glory's &c.

July 1850

Monday, 1st: Left Markham this morning. Saw an old well digger been digging for 20 years, found no rock between Ontario & Lake Simcoe along Yonge st — some wells 100 & 40 ft deep.

Tuesday, 2nd: Saw Mr [William] Logan [director of Geological Survey] this morning. He wishes to meet the Canadian Institute. ½ day at City Plan.

Wednesday, 3rd: City Plan Engraving.

Thursday, 4th: ½ day City Plan Engraving. Went down to show Jos Boucher my Plan of the Harbour according to his request. He was much pleased and wished two copies when published.

Friday, 5th: City Plan Engraving. Went down with a cab for Mr Logan — from 12 to 20 at the meeting — a conversational.

Saturday, 6th: Today Engraving City Plan. Taking up to Parliament Buildings. Mr Logans box.

Monday, 8th: Engraving City Plan this day.

Tuesday, 9th: Down at Legislative Council at noon for Mr [William] Cayley regarding survey of road. ½ day Engraving City Plan.

Wednesday, 10th: Engraving City Plan. At Industrial Exhibition committee in the evening.

Thursday, 11th: Engraving City Plan.

Friday, 12th: Engraving City Plan.

Saturday, 13th: Engraving City Plan. Mr Scobie refuses me any money until the plan is finished.

Monday, 15th: Engraving trees on City Plan.

Tuesday, 16th: Engraving City Plan. Commenced at Mrs Hutchisons tonight. English composition.

Wednesday, 17th: Engraving City Plan.

Thursday, 18th: Engraving City Plan.

Friday, 19th: Engraving City Plan.

Saturday, 20th: Engraving City Plan.

Monday, 22nd: Engraving City Plan.

Tuesday, 23rd: Engraving City Plan. At Mr Hutchisons.

Wednesday, 24th: Engraving City Plan.

Thursday, 25th: Engraving City Plan.

Friday, 26th: Engraving City plan.

Saturday, 27th: ½ day Engraving City Plan. Afternoon surveying and staking lots for Mr William Cayley.

Monday, 29th: At City Plan Engraving.

Tuesday, 30th: At City Plan Engraving.

Wednesday, 31st: Engraving City Plan.

August 1850

Thursday, 1st: Engraving City Plan ½ day. Plotting &c Necropolis ½ day.

Friday, 2nd: Engraving City Plan.

Saturday, 3rd: Took down the stone and got a proof of the City Plan.

Monday, 5th: Went out to Newmarket in the evening. Borrow 10/ from Father.

Tuesday, 6th: At Sharon with Passmore.

Wednesday, 7th: At Sharon. Came down with Mr Robertson in the evening. Gillespie up late painting America arms.

Thursday, 8th: Great preparations making today for the arrival of the citizens of Buffalo. Spoke to Mr Scobie about title of City Plan.

Friday, 9th: Grand review today — feasting the corporation of Buffalo at the Governors. Thomas Young & I met in Scobie's — spoke about title, afterwards met Dennis in the street. Dennis said that "I should have full credit for everything I had done to the map."

Saturday, 10th: Went up to Crown Land office to get names of streets put in the memo in the forenoon.

Monday, 12th: Sketching alterations in City Plan new buildings &c ½ day.

Tuesday, 13th: Drawing at design for new theodolite. Dennis came up today with title & dedication of map, but gave me no credit for drawing the map. I insisted that my name should be in the title. He promised to come back tomorrow.

Wednesday, 14th: Drawing plan of theodolite. Received £1 from Gibson being half of the subpoena. Paid Father 12/6 borrowed.

Thursday, 15th: Running around between Cumberland & Allanson about periodical. Went down to Scobie about title, he overwhelmed me with abuse. I wished him to appoint an hour tomorrow to talk over it reasonably — at 9 o'clock.

Friday, 16th: Had a blowup with Mr Scobie this morning. He would not satisfy me about the title. I have no heart to go on with the map unless I get the credit of my work. If I don't choose to finish it send down the storm. I demand a settlement first, send in acct for £50.

Saturday, 17th: Preparing to go over to the Island on Monday to finish survey. Making moulds of part of the theodolite. Handed in Mr Cayleys acct.

Monday, 19th: Went over to the Island with David & Andrew who brought the boat. I returned in the evening.

Tuesday, 20th: At home plotting trees & marshes. Received a letter from Scobie requesting a correct note of the time I have been at City Plan.

Wednesday, 21st: Over at Island with Mr McLean & Gillespie — beautiful day. Gill spreeing since Sunday.

Thursday, 22nd: Thursday at home plotting. Saw Cayley quite satisfied with my acct, will pay some soon. Mr Passmore presented me with a handsome Meerschaum pipe today!

Friday, 23rd: Wrote to Scobie informing him that I have been 97½ days employed in work on the stone. Over at Island all day with Gillespie — finished survey on land. Beautiful moon light!

Saturday, 24th: Plotting trees and swamps. Proof book at Scobies 5/. Awful thunder and lightning at night! Mean night!

September 1850

Wednesday, 11th: At Mr Youngs in the forenoon. Took down my design for the Provincial Diploma to Cumberlands office. At Youngs.

Thursday, 12th: At Youngs.

Friday, 13th: Received a letter from the secretary of the Commission they have accepted my Diploma and requested me to make some trifling alterations.

October 1850

Thursday, 3rd: Took up the wood block to Mr Allanson about 2 oclock. Recd £2/10 for little prism. Bought a pair of boots 3½ $. At committee. They handsomely awarded me a discretionary prize of £5 — and suggested to the corporation to consider the model.

Friday, 4th: Expected to see an article in the *Colonist* today but none. Made a sketch of carriage today. Paid Scott and Laidlaw 16/3 for trouser cloth. Bought stationery at Scobies 4/.

Saturday, 5th: Making sketches of carriages for Wheeler, finished 8 of them. At the Mechanics Institute committee at the City Hall in the evening. I intend to go to Montreal to the Provincial Exhibition and will be one of a deputation from the Mechanics Institute. Mr Cumberland spoke of our Periodical at the meeting for the first time. It is likely to take.

Monday, 7th: Thinking of commencing with David, Andrew & Mr Gillespies assistance during the winter to make a model of Canada in blocks of wood 2 ft square, to extend over 1,200 miles and to a scale of 2 miles to an inch with the curvature of the Earth. It would be about 50 feet, being 35 feet broad and about 3 feet deep in the centre rounding off to 2 or 3 inches at the sides. It would show the comparative level of the Great Lakes, the cultivated and forest land, the roads & canals & the geologic features of the country.

Wednesday, 9th: Tonight the Governor General presented the Diplomas at the City Hall. He did very well and shaked the hand of all those who were successful. I got a diploma for Lithographs & another for the model.

Thursday, 10th: Drawing Diploma on block. Recd £5 for prize awarded to me. Paid Riddell & McLean £4 — ordered a greatcoat. Paid Burgen 7/6 for making trousers. Making design for carriage in the evening.

Friday, 11th: Making design for carriage today. Recd £5 for Niagara prize.

Saturday, 12th: Sent off designs for carriage with Mr Cumberland to Montreal. Mr C never having had time to write out prospectus I told him I would get it done and printed ready to bring down with me on Tuesday. Drawing on block afternoon.

Sunday, 13th: Saw Mr Hutchison last night and showed him an outline of the prospectus. He made some alterations and corrections. Making yesterday a view of Sheriff [Henry] Ruttans store [Cobourg]. Mechanics Institute.

Monday, 14th: Gave the Prospectus into the hands of Cleland the printer. Purchased paper at Taylors, paid 5/. Drawing on block for afternoon.

Tuesday, 15th: Recd 30/ from Wheeler for drawings of carriages. I charge him £2 being 5/ each. Started with the steamer for Montreal with a proof of the *Canadian Journal* [prospectus] — 500 to be sent down tomorrow with Mr Bains — $11 in pocket.

Wednesday, 16th: Arrived at Kingston this morning and started with the steamer *Lord Elgin* for Montreal. The vessel very much crowded with passengers going down to see the Provincial Exhibition in connection with the Exhibition of 1851.

Thursday, 17th: Arrived at Montreal this morning and put up at the Macks. They were all glad to see me apparently. Met Cumberland on Notre Dame St, showed him the Prospectus with which he was well pleased. In the afternoon the Exhibition was much crowded and the display very good.

Friday, 18th: Got an invitation to attend the Mechanics Institute Dinner. Bain & young Ridout arrived this morning at Macks. Seeing the sights about town.

Saturday, 19th: Seeing the sights. At the Dinner in the evening, it passed off very well. Mr Speirs the president, Cumberland and I went down to see the Fireworks afterwards.

Sunday, 20th: At Bonsecours Market, the French Church, Sion Church and Methodist Church on St James Street.

Monday, 21st: Cumberland promised me my price of £7/10 for Diplomas today. Saw Mr Logan. Received from him his Geological Report for the Canadian Institute. At Ploughing Match. Ten ploughs & very good ploughing.

Tuesday, 22nd: At the announcement of the prizes last night. David got second for wood carving, I second for Lithography and a Diploma for Toronto Harbour model. Cannot find Cumberland. Bain lent me $10 — and we started on steamer *Ottawa* after paying bills.

Wednesday, 23rd: It being near 12 last night before the steamer started we were just entering the Beauharnois Canal in the morning. Rain — Rain — Rain. Enter the Carillon Canal about dark.

Thursday, 24th: Dull weather but very pleasant boat and passengers. Bain paid my passage $6. Arrived at Kingston about 8 at night — beautiful moon light.

Friday, 25th: Arrived at Cobourg this morning. Saw a great many old friends. Called at Port Hope. Saw MacPhail. Arrived at Toronto about 7 P.M.

Saturday, 26th: Went along to Youngs. I agree to take £4 and the plans & specifications of Normal School for £10 which I was entitled to according to original agreement! He is very hard up.

Sunday, 27th: At Free church morning and evening.

Monday, 28th: Paid Father £4 — the £1 which I borrowed from Bain he has charged to me in Scobies books. Hear Joseph lecture on Temperance tonight.

Wednesday, 30th: Settle up with Father this week allowing 30 for last year Board up to Oct 1 last — I owe him about £10. I owe David £8 or £10.

Thursday, 31st: I have been very idle this week & unsettled, seeing about *Canadian Journal*. Drawing plan of a house for Father. Saw Cumberland. The Montreal Mechanics Institute have agreed to take 50 copies of the *Canadian Journal*. At a meeting of the Mechanics Institute a discussion about the *Journal*. They are likely to patronise it. Recd £7/10 for Diploma Provincial and £2 for prize at Montreal. Paid Father £5 and Riddel & McLean £2/13/6 — I owe them still £2.

November 1850

Saturday, 2nd: First meeting of Canadian Institute tonight, not many present for want of any notice. I paid £1/2/6 my subscription for 1850 & 1851 which pays for 7/6 for Mechanics Institute too.

Monday, 4th: Mr [W.B.] Leather, an English engineer, called on me today and wishes to go with me for twelve months, it being necessary before he can get a license as surveyor.

Tuesday, 5th: Down at Cumberlands house tonight about *Journal*.

Sandford Fleming and William B. Leather became partners in these Yonge Street offices in November 1850.

Wednesday, 6th: Seeing about taking an office.

Thursday, 7th: Took office on Yonge street from a Mr Grant Lawyer for 12 months. Rent £17/10 per annum.

Friday, 8th: Took possession of offices on Yonge street this morning. George Stewart [son of Frances and Thomas A. Stewart] has arrived from the bush and wishes to be with me all winter. I have partly agreed he is to likewise have 30$ as a premium. Recd from treasurer Mechanics Institute £7/12/0.

Saturday, 9th: At Office. Mr Leather & Stewart cleaning up & making catalogue of Books &c.

Monday, 11th: At Office. Went down to Cumberlands house and got manuscript of new prospectus, with orders to print the same and send to Hamilton tomorrow. Designing & drawing ornamental "T" [symbol] for new prospectus. Leather & Stewart writing out letters to be sent to architects &c regarding *Canadian Journal.*

Tuesday, 13th: Finished small drawing of "T" for prospectus. Received proof of the same and sent off by Hamilton Boat to Cumberland.

Monday, 18th: Surveying for Mr Cayley near City Hall say /5.

Thursday, 21st: Drawing diploma on wood.

Friday, 22nd: Making wooden chain for measuring distance on surface of water — 7 chains long.

Saturday, 23rd: Making wooden chain. At Canadian Institute auditing accounts.

Monday, 25th: Preparing to go out sounding forenoon. Got an iron tripod made for a station on the shoal, had great difficulty in placing it as the wind blew so hard. Leather and I had a hard pull up against the wind. Dennis came about City Plan today.

Tuesday, 26th: Rain & wind — too rough on the Bay. Finished drawing Provincial Diploma on wood. Prospectus appeared in *Packet* today.

Wednesday, 27th: Went out to the shoal with Leather and Mr Lamby & Gillespie, a beautiful day. The wooden chain answered very well but was rather difficult to sketch not being accustomed to it. Got the sections about half made and the levelling staff.

Thursday, 28th: Very strong morning. Went down to the boats. They were both adrift. Mr Craigs is split up through the middle probably a total wreck. McLeans we got hauled up after a great deal of trouble and a thorough wetting. Laying out part of St Georges Square for Mr Cayley with Leather say 10/ or 7/6. Afternoon passed at Bridges first time.

Friday, 29th: It still blows on the lake a little. Tried to get a boat but could not. Went up to Queen's Wharf — tripod standing. We have to make out plans for supplying the city with water for Mr Furniss. Mr Browne to meet us at 9 oclock tomorrow.

Saturday, 30th: Drawing out plans for Furniss. They have to be ready by Monday morning to lay before the Council. Mr Scobie sent for me he is very anxious to go on with the City Plan.

December 1850

Sunday, 1st: At Leathers.

Monday, 2nd: Making calculations &c for Furniss. Alone experiment with pipe in afternoon.

Tuesday, 3rd: Calculation & plans for Furniss. Reservoir under street &c. went up with him to the ground.

Wednesday, 4th: Calculations & plans of water works. Recd from Geo Stewart £1/8/9.

Thursday, 5th: Paid Mr Edwards. Plans &c Furniss.

Friday, 6th: At Furniss's plan this morning, he waited till we were down about 12 oclock. Received letter from Ruttan. Went up to Queen's Wharf, found tripod gone, lighthouse man saw it on Tuesday last.

Saturday, 7th: Went down to Scobie but could not speak to him about time of payment. Snowing hard. At Canadian Institute. Election of members, associates & officers. Logan made president. Normal School competition. Culls paper on harbour. Requested to bring mine next night. Sleighing.

Monday, 9th: Received from Mr Scobie £5. Settled Gillespies charge for door plate 15/. Paid Father £2/10. Cutting hole through partition for storm pipe afternoon. Writing over paper on Harbour evening. Brick pipe for stove pipe 10d. Paid tinsmith12/9 for stovepipe, Boy at boat 1/3, Jacques for wooden chairs &c 5/, Old Craig treat for men, drawing out boat 3/9.

Saturday, 14th: Mr [Edward L.] Cull read his paper tonight at the Canadian Institute. 24 Gentlemen present — a good discussion.

Monday, 16th: Commence engraving on stone plan of city the weather being so cold it is necessary to heat the stove every morning — say ½ day at work all this week.

Saturday, 21st: Read paper on Toronto Harbour second time at Canadian Institute — large attendance, 3 of Harbour Commissioners present. Lost at the meeting plan of soundings at Queen's Wharf.

Sunday, 22nd: Tully.

Monday, 23rd: Making perspective view of Welland Courthouse for Kivas Tully. Sent off printed circulars to all who had been present at meeting on Saturday about lost plan.

Tuesday, 24th: Today engraving City Plan. Lent Father 15/.

Wednesday, 25th: Christmas. Went out Yonge street with Ogilvie, Mac-Donald & Primrose in sleigh. Plenty of snow and fine sleighing.

Thursday, 26th: Paid taxes for Father £2/10. ½ day engraving City Plan.

Friday, 27th: ½ day Engraving City Plan.

Saturday, 28th: ½ day Engraving City Plan.

Monday, 30th: At City Plan Engraving.

Tuesday, 31st: At City Plan Engraving. Recd from Hugh MacPhail 7 dollars which he owed me for two orders on Wheeler & Gillespie also 4 dollars which he owed David in all $11.

CHAPTER SEVEN
The Toronto Harbour 1851

The Canadian Institute quickly developed into an important institution among Toronto's professional men. The *Canadian Journal* recorded the proceedings almost from its very beginnings and all of Toronto's senior scientists, doctors, university professors, architects, surveyors, and engineers were numbered among its members, many of them taking their turns contributing learned papers at the Saturday evening meetings. Fleming devoted much of his time and energy to Institute activities. The *Journal* was just one of his interests. A Museum Committee was established and he took advantage of his survey trips in the backcountry to contact interested collectors and to gather specimens himself. Meetings were held to draw up formal Rules and Regulations and to discuss obtaining a Charter. Highlight of the spring of 1851 was the Conversazione, a gala social evening organized by Fleming, attended by 70 or 80 Institute members.

Fleming made many friends through the Institute and close contact with the city's leading architects consolidated his place in his professional world. His drawing skills were much in demand and as time went on he got numerous surveying assignments from fellow Institute members like Frederic Cumberland, who asked for his help with his design for the replacement of the burnt-out St. James Cathedral, and on plans for the City's Normal and Model Schools. Kivas Tully employed him frequently on a variety of projects, including his design for the first Trinity College, on Queen Street, and on several out-of-town jobs. Through much of 1851 he was engaged, often with Leather, on plans and construction of the city waterworks, a project marked on opening day in December with a celebration dinner at St. Lawrence Hall.

Corrections on the City Plan were ongoing. In February he was at work engraving the controversial "Titles," but it wasn't until mid-August that he mounted a final copy — three years and three months after he first began the project. He continued fine-tuning his ideas about the development of the Toronto Harbour and attempting to interest the Harbour officials in his plan. A design of another sort was offered to Postmaster General James Morris over breakfast one morning and Sandford Fleming's "Beaver" became Canada's first adhesive postage stamp.

His working life brought a great variety of activities. In September, he and Frederick Passmore spent a week in Peterborough, plotting the roads and pathways for the new Little Lake Cemetery, and then went on a canoe trip to the Back Lakes, camping out as they passed through Pigeon Lake, Bobcaygeon, Sturgeon Lake, Fenelon Falls, Cameron, and Balsam Lakes to Beaverton. On October 1, they headed back south, crossing Lake Simcoe by steamer and returning by stage to Toronto.

Railways were always in the back of his mind, and this year saw some small steps toward what was to become his full-time career. After surveying the Don Danforth plank road for J.O. Browne, deputy provincial surveyor, in May, he began work on a survey of the Toronto & Kingston Railway. There was much railway talk in the air. Discussions with Judge Brown of Ogdensburg, New York, led to an assignment in the Barrie area for the St. Lawrence and Huron Railway, which was later expanded to include a survey of Gloucester Bay Harbour at Nottawasaga Bay. Both he and Leather put out feelers about the Guelph and Toronto Railway. Late in November he talked to Scobie and Charles Berczy about possibilities with the Northern Railway. Eventually it would all bear fruit.

On the home front things became more settled. Andrew and Elizabeth purchased a farm west of the city in Etobicoke and moved the family out there in the early spring. Sandford, who had been living in Toronto with his parents, became a boarder with Martha Hutchison, who had recently moved from Peterborough to be near her relatives. Frequently he was out at the farm helping his father get established, his first chore to purchase some fruit trees and plant a little orchard, but more and more his time was taken up with his professional activities. In November he and Leather dissolved their year-long partnership, with Fleming retaining the office. At the end of the year he was delighted to be appointed to survey the new Military Reserve, an assignment that further broadened his circle.

January 1851

[Diary blank to January 28]

Tuesday, 28th: Meeting tonight in my office about *Journal.* Dr Melville, Browne came.

Wednesday, 29th: At Allansons drawing second block of Diploma.

Thursday, 30th: Drawing second block of Diploma.

Friday, 31st: The City Plan stone having cracked I have been endeavoring to find a plan to make it secure. During this month say engraving altogether from 6 to 8 days.

February 1851

Saturday, 1st: Canadian Institute, Mr Lyons comments.

Thursday, 6th: Engraving the two titles for City Plan during the last week.

Friday, 7th: Commence to make a perspective view of a design of Mr Tully for him of designs for proposed Trinity College. He promised to give me £10 for it. Mr Cumberland also asked me to help him.

Saturday, 8th: Perspective view. Canadian Institute Museum committee proposed.

Tuesday, 11th: *Canadian Journal* meeting at my office, present [Henry Youle] Hind, [Professor H.H.] Croft, [Dr. Henry] Melville, [J.O.] Browne, [John] Allanson.

Thursday, 13th: Up till this day at large perspective view for Mr Tully. Up until 5 oclock this morning and very late hours during the whole time.

Saturday, 15th: Canadian Institute, Mr Ellis paper. Charter Council proposed.

Wednesday, 19th: This week at second perspective view.

Thursday, 20th: Second perspective view not required. Mr Tully is appointed architect.

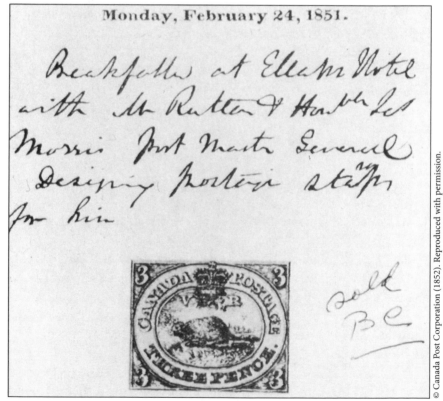

This Beaver stamp designed for Postmaster General James Morris by Sandford Fleming was Canada's first adhesive postage stamp.

Saturday, 22nd: Meeting of Canadian Institute. Mr Ridout on geologics of the Falls.

Monday, 24th: Breakfast at Elsaps Hotel with Mr Ruttan & Honble Jas Morris Postmaster General — Designing postage stamps for him — 3d Beaver stamp.

[Page removed from diary by a Fleming descendant, given to H. Borden Clark, book dealer, with proof of stamp.]

March 1851

Monday, 3rd: Measuring near city hall for Mr Cayley and making sketch 7/6 say. Making calculations & areas of property say 2/6.

Tuesday, 4th: Making drawing for patent yesterday & today, received £2.

Wednesday, 5th: Worked this day at Mr Tully's.

Thursday, 6th: At Mr Tully's roof plan.

Friday, 7th: At Mr Tully's.

Saturday, 8th: At Mr Tully's. 13 meeting Canadian Institute. Alfred Brunel elected. Level of Lake Erie — Mr [Henry Youle] Hind.

Tuesday, 11th: Sent off proof to Mr Ruttan.

Wednesday, 12th: At Mr Hollands plan.

Thursday, 13th: At Mr Cayleys.

Friday, 14th: At Mr Cayleys cottage.

Saturday 15th: Up in the afternoon staking of ground for excavation Trinity College. 14th Canadian Institute. Mr Tully on piling.

Wednesday, 19th: Gave Mr Ruttan his last perspective of store in measurements 15s. Sundry plans sections & tracings £2/5/0. Engraving in stone £2/10. Total £5/10.

Thursday, 20th: Preparing paper & diagrams for Saturday evening.

Friday, 21st: Writing paper.

Saturday, 22nd: This letter appeared in the *Patriot* without my consent. Meyer without my consent went & got it inserted. Read a second paper on the Harbour having prepared altogether about 29 diagrams. Very few present. 15th meeting.

Monday, 24th: Reducing plan of College.

Tuesday, 25th: Borrowed from Father £1.

Wednesday, 26th: At committee meeting in the evening — they make a report in favour of me continuing the experiment on the Harbour.

Friday, 28th: At office reducing College. Recd from Mr Tully £20 — £10 for myself & £10 for Mr Leather.

Saturday, 29th: Paid in full the following accts — Scott & Laidlaw £3/14/10, Riddell & McLean £2, John Balfour £1/1/0 (*Illustrated News*), John Henderson £ 2/8/2 ½, Boots 17/6. [Total] £10/1/7. Recd from Cumberland £3 for four days work last summer. Also recd on *Canadian Journal* acct his share £2/0/6. With my 7s I paid Clelands bill.

Monday, 31st: Paid Father £10 — which deducting £1 which I borrowed last week makes £9 to account. Paid David £1 which I got from Hugh MacPhail some time ago to give him. Out at the farm in Etobicoke which Father is buying from Mrs Lea family yesterday.

April 1851

Wednesday, 2nd: Making designs for Foundation Stone trowel [for Trinity College] for Kivas Tully.

Thursday, 3rd: Do Do. [Ditto]

Tuesday, 8th: Out surveying for Mr DeGrassi at his place up the Don. Gave David £1 which I got from H MacPhail which he owed him.

Wednesday, 9th: David left today for Scotland.

Thursday, 24th: Making preliminary survey with J.O. Browne [deputy provincial surveyor] of Don & Danforth plank road.

Friday, 25th: Plotting survey for J.O. Browne.

Monday, 28th: Out on the Don & Danforth plank road chaining and laying out center line. Mr Browne at home. Got home about ½ past 8.

Tuesday, 29th: Out with Mr Browne staking out center line & levelling.

Wednesday, 30th: At the laying of Foundation stone Trinity College. At meeting in Mr Tullys office about Converzatione. Mr Culls Lemonade.

May 1851

Thursday, 1st: Showing Mr Cumberland plans of Harbour &c he wrote me a reply to see a reply to my letter. Ordering circulars for Institute. At Mr Brownes making up levels afternoon.

The first Trinity College on Queen Street, designed by Kivas Tully. From Landmarks, *Volume 3 (1896) by J.R. Robertson.*

Saturday, 3rd: Got a bad cold. Out at the farm helping Henry & Alex to plant some fruit trees & bushes. These cost me 10s at the nursery.

Monday, 5th: Election of Mechanics Institute. Cumberland president, Hind vice.

Tuesday, 6th: On the Don & Danforth plank rd levelling &c found levels perfectly correct. Made levels also between Section 1 – Playters.

Friday, 9th: Making plan of York Scarborough & Pickering lake shore — for scheming railway on.

Saturday, 10th: Making preparations fitting up room &c &c for Conversazione in the evening. Went off very well between 70 & 80 present. Refreshments coffee, tea & sherbet.

Monday, 12th: Taking the various articles which we loaned for the evening to their owners. In the morning examining hydrants all over the city.

Tuesday, 13th: Both *Colonist* & *Patriot* have a very good notice of the Conversazione this morning. Making preparations for proposed experiment tomorrow morning.

Wednesday, 14th: Up the morning at 3 oclock with Mr Leather, J.O. Browne &c making experiments with hydrant & engine for Water Company Cab 2/6. Making out report of d[itt]o.

Thursday, 15th: Afternoon engraving chart at bottom of City Plan.

Friday, 16th: Engraving chart at foot of City Plan all day. Evening making plan of tanks for Mr Furniss.

Saturday, 17th: Attending court all day. City of Toronto against City Waterworks.

Monday, 19th: Attending court all day. Toronto water works. Jury return a verdict against Furniss £2,000 charge. Leather & I against S. Keefer, Cumberland & Howard.

Tuesday, 20th: Borrowed $10 from Laidlaw $10 from Mr Leather — paid rent £4/7/6. At J.G. Josephs plan of shop front.

Wednesday, 21st: Canton was the first to prove light compressible, and Oersted proved every additional atmosphere (or pressure of 15 lbs on the square inch) water was compressed rather more than 46 millionths of its volume, alcohol, 21, and ether, 61 million – (*Natural Philosophy* Tomlinson page 60).

Monday, 26th: Saw Mr [Thomas] Young — promised to assist noone else but him with the university.

Tuesday, 27th: Borrowed 15s from Father and paid Laidlaw £2/10 borrowed last Monday.

Wednesday, 28th: Surveying in the forenoon for Mr Humphrey. At Trinity College meeting.

Thursday, 29th: Making calculations of work done at Trinity College.

June 1851

Monday, 2nd: Sent out to Daws Tavern by J.O. Browne to commence survey of Toronto & Kingston. Railway. Expenses 6/7. Home at night George & self.

Tuesday, 3rd: Commenced chaining from Evans — T & K Railway.

Wednesday, 4th: T & K R.R.[Toronto & Kingston Rail Road] survey.

Thursday, 5th: T & K Railway survey.

Friday, 6th: Toronto & Kingston Railway survey, very wet all day. At Belle Tavern in Scarboro.

Saturday, 7th: T & K Railway — in Scarboro.

Friday, 13th: Surveying levelling up to this date on the T & K Railway. Finished levelling tonight.

Saturday, 14th: Making up levels.

Monday, 16th: T & K Railway.

Tuesday, 17th: T & K Railway.

Friday, 20th: Surveying Lot for Mr Humphrey on Queen St, this $4 and formerly $3.

Saturday, 21st: Drawing plan for Mr Lemon to process patent recd 20s. Measuring ground for Crooks.

Monday, 23rd: Designing two wholesale buildings for Mr Crooks.

Tuesday, 24th: As yesterday.

Wednesday, 25th: Getting frame mark and stretching paper &c &c for perspective view.

Thursday, 26th: Commenced making a perspective view for Messrs Cumberland & Ridout of Normal & Model Schools.

Friday, 27th: At perspective view of Normal & Model Schools for Mr Cumberland. The stone was reserved at Scobies today.

Saturday, 28th: At perspective view. Levelling along Queen St & down Nelson St for the piping of the water works.

Monday, 30th: At perspective view.

Fleming drew plans for the Toronto Normal School, Gould Street, one of Frederic Cumberland's projects. From Landmarks, Volume 3 *(1896) by J.R. Robertson.*

July 1851

Tuesday, 1st: At perspective view. At York Mills with Mr Leather in the evening.

Wednesday, 2nd: Up at 4 oclock near Yorkville looking out for a site for Reservoir — digging for clay. Finished perspective view. Stone here.

Friday, 4th: Recd from Mr Leather the sum of £9/7/6, the half of his quarter salary.

Monday, 7th: Gave Father £5 & $5 which I borrowed formerly and which he did not charge. Anne £1 for two shirts £2 for trousers vest & summer coat.

Friday, 11th: At Crooks building &c. Getting rings made for Canton hose &c.

Saturday, 12th: Making drawings for Hazlehurst &c.

Monday, 14th: At Parker Edwards about hydrant & valves.

Tuesday, 15th: Scale at Queen's Wharf 2.9 inches. Line to move tripod which was hurt last fall.

Thursday, 17th: At Parliament Buildings in the evening, met Mr Leask.

Friday, 18th: Running about getting gooseneck and names ready — tried the same in the evening. Worked very well, very wet.

Saturday, 19th: Three days this week making corrections on City Plan over different parts of the survey.

Sunday, 20th: At Knox's church morning and evening.

Monday, 21st: Recd from W.H. Boulton 10s for making perspective view of Grange staircase.

Friday, 25th: Laying out Lots at the front of Jarvis street for Mr Cayley.

Saturday, 26th: 2 hours each day 5 days this week engraving City Plan down at Scobies. Went up to lay out Lot on Jarvis st.

Sunday, 27th: At Knox Church twice, Roman Catholic for the first time in the afternoon. Mummery & Humbug.

Monday, 28th: 2 hours making additions to City Plan.

Tuesday, 29th: ½ day engraving City Plan. ½ to Dennis.

Wednesday, 30, Thursday, 31st: 1 day making additions & 1 day engraving since Tuesday.

August 1851

Friday, 1st: Got check from Mr Cumberland for £10 for drawing diploma on wood & alterations.

Saturday, 2nd: 1 day engraving City Plan. Got cash for check at Upper Canada Bank. I paid Father £10.

Sunday, 3rd: At church.

Monday, 4th: ½ day engraving City Plan. Afternoon at Crooks store.

Tuesday, 5th: Survey Lots on Toronto St. Afternoon &c on Jarvis south of Shuter.

Wednesday, 6th: Laying off Lots on Toronto Street with levelling. Seeing about hydrants afternoon. Drawing Leasks forenoon.

Thursday, 7th: Sent in to Mr Leask a coloured sketch of his store. Endeavoring to to obtain specifications of Shaws Building from Hooper. I tried hydrant with the Mayor, 4 chief engineers in the evening.

Friday, 8th: Drawing section of Crooks stones and commence writing specifications in the evening. At Priests found the Lake making great encroachments at the neck of the peninsula, washed off upwards of a chain since last fall.

Sunday, 10th: Recd from J.O. Browne the sum of £5 to acct.

Monday, 11th–Wednesday, 13th: At Crooks plans, specifications and water works & drains.

Friday, 15th: Mounting proof of City Plan.

Saturday, 16th: Obtain proof of City Plan & mounting the same on frame — coloring & burnishing.

Sunday, 17th: Church morning & evening. Wooden plug blown out corner of Yonge & King men working afternoon & evening.

Monday, 18th: With Mr Leather staking out Yonge st & at the birthday lady from our corner of Queen st & Yonge st until 3 oclock on Tuesday morning. Mr Browne & Mr [Charles] Berczy.

Tuesday, 19th: Paid Mr Grant the Rent of office £4/7/6 & Mr Leather rent £4/7/6.

Wednesday, 20th: Recd from Mr Ruttan £5 in full of acct. Recd of Mr Leather £2/10.
    Paid to testimonial £8/18/9. Drawing in wood angels &c starch label. Recd from Geo Humphrey £1/15.

Thursday, 21st: Staking out church & Toronto streets. Afternoon boring for clay on site of Reservoir and levelling. Presented Edwards testimonial at his house.

Friday, 22nd: Finishing Crooks plans. Sent off Dennis acct £23/7/6. Drawing Leasks store on wood.

Saturday, 23rd: Reducing Trinity College to a small scale for a copper engraving.

Monday, 25th: Survey ravine in College Park for Mr Young. Lent Andrew £1.

Tuesday, 26th: Levelling on Church & Adelaide streets and staking out d[itt]o. Plotting Youngs survey.

Friday, 29th: Up at Government House with Mr Ridout about Charter of Canadian Institute. Surveying Lot on Jarvis street for Walter MacFarlane Esq. Article about City Plan appeared in the *Colonist* today.

Sunday, 31st: Leveling at Reservoir and down Yonge street. Parliament prorogued today. Finished Youngs plan. Lent Hugh MacPhail 10s yesterday.

September 1851

Monday, 1st: Sore eyes.

Tuesday, 2nd: College grounds. Large stone. Moonlight.

Thursday, 4th: Cemetery Meeting.

Friday, 5th: Engaged for most of this week assisting Mr Leather with plans & specifications of Clover Hill Reservoir.

Saturday, 6th: Coloring elevations of Thorold Church for Mr Tully ½ day. Recd from Andrew £1. River Don, lost large knife.

Sunday, 7th: At Knox's Church. Took a walk to the River Don this morning before breakfast. Bathing.

Monday, 8th: Borrow £1 from Father. Left in steamer *Magnet* with Passmore, Tully & Short for Cobourg. Saw & greet many old friends. Milner, Brock. Prayer meeting. Lochead &c.

Tuesday, 9th: At present on board steamer *Forester*, Otonabee River with Passmore. Delightful day. Old Traill [Thomas Traill, husband of Catharine Parr Traill], Major Falconer [Judge William Falkner], Indian girl, Rice Lake &c &c. Put up at Chambers Hotel, Peterborough.

Wednesday, 10 Went down to Cemetery ground. Reconnoitering — chaining. Very Hot.

Thursday, 11th: Making survey of grounds. Young Shortt came from Port Hope in the afternoon. Post broken & stretched.

Friday, 12th: Plotting &c &c surveying. The young men head for Warsaw. Very hot.

Saturday, 13th: Plotting &c &c, designing the laying out of the cemetery. The member for Port Sarnia. In the afternoon surveying. Very cold & wet.

Sunday, 14th: Much pleased to receive a paper from Toronto. Went up to Stewarts & visit in the afternoon. Saw Mrs Stewart — Louise. Went up to Mud Lake and agreed with Dunbar to take us to Balsam Lake for $5.

Monday, 15th: The member for Sarnia & his constituents. The secretary of the Board of Examiners.

Tuesday, 16th: Laying out the grounds. The Directors have accepted my design. The member for the St Lawrence board.

Wednesday, 17th: Short has to leave for Toronto, having heard of his Grandmother's death.

Thursday, 18th: Laying out the walks.

Friday, 19th: Laying out grounds — worked hard.

Saturday, 20th: Hard at work cutting out walks through the young bush. Finished about sundown — very heavy thunderstorm.

Sunday, 21st: At Mr Rogers church forenoon. At Stewarts afternoon.

Monday, 22nd: Decided upon not leaving for the Lakes until tomorrow. Went to call on Mr Rogers & endeavored to get some geological specimens for the Canadian Institute. He has a fine encrusted slate. Spent the evening at Mr Bensons very agreeably.

Tuesday, 23rd: Very stormy & rainy all day — very dark accordingly, the weather looks set in bad and all the prophets say it will last for a week. Spent the evening at Miss Halls.

Wednesday, 24th: Fine morning, left Peterboro for Back Lakes, sent out luggage by Mr Chambers to Toronto. Mrs Benson very kind. Send over for a boiled ham. Paddle along nicely and camped out — Passmore, our guide, Dunbar, and I — quite new to us.

Thursday, 25th: Left our camp at the foot of Pigeon Lake about 6 A.M. slept comfortably, Dunbar shot a duck. Arrived at Bobcaygeon about 11. Mr [Mossom] Boyd asked us to his house and gave us two fine large eels. Paddle along Sturgeon Lake & camped for the night near Sturgeon Point. Wind blew pretty fresh. Dunbar cooked the eels — stewed duck & eels & fresh bread for breakfast. The wind ahead. Arrived at Fenelon Falls, got two pair large stag horns. Camerons Lake very rough. Boat nearly foundered on stones, enter Burnt River with difficulty & Camerons Rapids. Land on 1,200 acre island on Balsams Lake but very poor camping ground. Went over to Bexley Point and camped in an old hut — very stormy.

Saturday, 27th: Wind has changed to the north. Rowed over to the portage & introduced ourselves to Mr Stevenson, Admiral VanSittarts father in law. He volunteered to send us over on horseback to Lake Simcoe.

Sunday, 28th: Prayers in the morning. Old Mr Stevenson excessively kind. He is English but his parents were both Scotch & he talks much of Scotland. We enjoy very much his comfortable home.

Monday, 29th: Out shooting and looking for the horses. The boat does not leave Beaverton until Wednesday so we need not leave until tomorrow.

Tuesday, 30th: Left Balsam Lake thanking in our hearts Mr Stevenson and his good family. Little Henry accompanies us with a horse to carry the luggage. Henry shot for us 4 brace of partridge.

October 1851

Wednesday, 1st: Left Beaverton this morning in steamer *Beaver*, sailed across Lake Simcoe to Holland Landing. No paper at Post Office. Stage to Toronto & arrived about 10 P.M. At home glad to see me — thought I had been lost.

Thursday, 2nd: At Reservoir at Yorkville in the morning, seeing about other things during the day. Delivered Capt Richardson pamphlet.

Friday, 3rd: Drawing Whyllis store for wood block. At Mechanics Institute.

Saturday, 4th: Went down to Mr Jas Liddells and got orders to make plans for a curing house immediately. Drawing d[itt]o. Surveying Lot at the top of College grounds for Mr Grant. To charge £1.

Monday, 6th: Drawing Liddells plans and writing out specifications. Spending the evening at Mr Leathers.

Tuesday, 7th: Delivered Mr Liddells plan. Drawing Mr Whyllis store for wood cut. Borrowed £2/10 from Father. Paid Keillor £2/15 for Canadian Institute Conversazione.

Wednesday, 8th: Drawing on wood block Whyllis store.

Thursday, 9th: Drawing on wood Leasks store small scale. Went down to Mr Culls about Canadian Institute Charter.

Friday, 10th: Recd Gas Company acct £1/5. Making tide registering machine. Paid Father £1 which I borrowed before going to Peterboro.

Saturday, 11th: Getting tide registering machine made, also inscription printed in Provincial Commission Diploma.

Sunday, 12th: Making machine.

Monday, 13th: Making tide gauge.

Tuesday, 14th: Took down tide gauge.

Wednesday, 15th: Helping Tully ½ day coloring Thorold Church plans. Called at Mr Leask's.

Thursday, 16th: Saw Mr & Mrs L at Exhibition ½ past 3 oclock. Walked up to Trinity College in the afternoon. Met William at Spadina Avenue.

Friday, 17th: Getting Mr Gillespie to paint an allegorical picture for Jenny Lind's concert.

Sunday, 19th: The polar distance of the star on the 1st of January 1830 was 1" 35' 51" and its annual diminution is 19.3" — to find the azimuth. As Radius is to the secant of the latitude of the place, so is the sum of the polar distance to the azimuth.

Monday, 20th: Saw Jenny Lind.

Tuesday, 21st: At the Exhibition in the afternoon. Took down the pictures to the concert room. Jenny Lind singing.

Wednesday, 22nd: Getting up stone, paid for fitting up stone &c 5/7 ½. Passmore lent me £10 today. Wonderful exciting Jenny Lind. Recd £1 from Walter MacFarlane for surveying Lot on Jarvis st.

Thursday, 23rd: David came from Scotland today. Heard Jenny Lind ... Got a cord of wood for office & Mr Leather from Father $3.

Friday, 24th: Writing specifications & finishing Humphreys plans.

Saturday, 25th: Wrote to the Harbour Master offering to dispose of my plans of the Harbour to the Commission. Also to Mr Stevenson at Balsam Lake. Recd from Hugh MacPhail 10s which he borrowed formerly.

Sunday, 26th: At Free church morning & evening. With Mr Grant afternoon. Mr Laidlaw to tea.

Monday, 27th: Recd the address of (M.M.) this morning for newspaper correspondence. Capt Richardson called, he wished to know how much I would expect for the plan of the Harbour. £50 I said would be about right, but he was authorized to offer me £5. I think if I was not good natured I might have taken it as an insult. I told him it was rather little.

Tuesday, 28th: Making sketch of Mr Grants Lots yesterday laid out as a garden. Mr Tully wishes me to go with to make an exploration survey between the Holland Marsh and the River Humber, proposing to start on Thursday. Mr Leather wrote to the Governor & I to Mr Taylor of Peterboro about the engineering of the Guelph & Toronto Railway. Sent in to the president two applications, one from Fleming & Leather & one from Mr Leather. Wrote a second letter to the Harbour Commission asking if the Board would countenance my publishing of the Chart in any way.

Fleming advertised his services in the York County Directory *(Volume 1, Toronto) in 1851.*

Thursday, 30th: Made sketch of wheel barn at Railway Office, took out to Insurance Co. Had some words with O'Brien. Preparing to start this afternoon, took out seat for three oclock stage, waited at Mr Allansons till 5, stage full, couldnt get on (M.M. on board). Dreadfully put out all night.

Friday, 31st: Gave Father £2/10 yesterday. Recd 11/10½ from Gas Company for expenditures on Jenny Lind picture. Saw Scobie & Mr Berczy about a job on the Northern Railway. Preparing to go off tomorrow. Danzic Beer to M.M.

November 1851

Saturday, 1st: Called on Mr Bowes, showed him the testimonial letters about chart. Started in stage with Tully, Witham & Short. Stage upset near Weston with about 18 passengers, none badly hurt, plank rd very bad. Tea at Pine Grove. Rain and bad roads. Arrived at Loydton about one oclock on morning. Had tea & went to bed at 2.

Sunday, 2nd: Rain all Sunday. Rather unwell. I think indigestion, perhaps smoked too much yesterday. Sunday evening sitting in Mrs Steads tavern writing now. Rather comfortable country inn.

Monday, 3rd: Rather cloudy. Hired a waggon and went over bag & baggage to about the center of the ridge. Raised the tent. Mr Tully & I went out exploring. The two boys left in charge of the camp. Walked perhaps about ten miles before returning to the camp.

Tuesday, 4th: Camp very comfortable, perhaps a little cold, in the morning about six inches of snow had fallen, fire nearly out and everything covered with snow. Got breakfast and away out to work. Tully, Short & I went through some of the roughest ground I have seen, sent Short home to the camp, while we commenced levelling. Got dark & took refuge in a farm where we were very comfortable.

Wednesday, 5th: Had early breakfast & levelled homewards towards the camp. Ground covered with snow & mud. Had lunch at camp and continued on until we finished just about dark having gone over about 7 miles with long sights. Walked home to the camp & spent the night very well.

Thursday, 6th: Up about 6 oclock & had a good breakfast, the waggon having been ordered arrived about 8 oclock. Shaved & dressed by the camp fire & packed off for Bradford. Dinner at Browntown where the boys were left for tomorrows stage. Mr Tully & I arrived at Amsterdam about dark & had tea on board the boat.

Friday, 7th: Spent the night on board the boat & caught cold. Then started for Barrie, but it happened this boat went to Orillia. Mr Tully went out at Jacksons Point, and I went on. The passengers very agreeable. Arrived at Orillia about 2 oclock. Walked all over the town. Called at Mr Patersons for tobac. Had a chit at a horrible concert.

Saturday, 8th: Boat started this morning about 10 — no fresh passengers according to expectations, much disappointed. Nothing wonderful happened on the way smoking smoking. Boat & stage arrived in town about 11 oclock P.M.

Sunday, 9th: Up very late. At church saw two snake bonnets. Received a letter from Revd Mr [R.J.C.] Taylor, inclosing introduction to the Mayor.

Monday, 10th: Wrote this morning to M.M. Recd cash from Mr Leather to pay Mr Grant which I did for office & Mr L house. I received from Mr G £1 for surveying his Lot at College Park.

Tuesday, 11th: Getting instructions about schools for which plans are required.

Wednesday, 12th: Recd a reply from M.M. Called on Mr Bowes with letter of introduction. Board of Directors to meet tomorrow.

Thursday, 13th: Mr Leask introduced me to Mr Fisken. Helping Tully with Thorold plans afternoon. Paid Joseph for scale 22/6.

Friday, 14th: Commenced to make plans of common schools, paper 3/9, Barnards Architecture 10s.

Sunday, 16th: Saw Mr Hall at church, he wishes to introduce me to Judge Brown of Ogdensburg who is principal man about the St Lawrence & Lake Huron Railway.

Monday, 17th: Saw Judge Brown, he came to the office two or three times.

Tuesday, 18th: Gave Judge Brown a copy of Newcastle & Colborne District map. Mr Hall left for Peterboro & I wrote to Mr [Wilson] Conger, chrm of Railway committee.

Wednesday, 19th: Judge Brown left and gave me instructions to go to Barrie on business of his and requested me to look after the interests of the St L & Huron Rly.

Saturday, 22nd: At plans of city schools and drawing a sketch of the line of railway to be engineered.

Courtesy Trent Valley Archives.

Sunday, 23rd: At plans of schools & writing (last week) to Judge Brown, the boat having stopped on Lake Simcoe. A Walk.

Monday, 24th: At school plans. Mr Leather wishes to have a separation which I at once consent to.

Wednesday, 26th: Walked up Yonge st with Mrs Leask &c.

Sheriff Wilson Conger was also a railway entrepreneur. He became mayor of Peterborough in 1856.

Thursday, 27th: Out sounding at the Queen's Wharf — Stewart, W Skirbing & self, rather cold, exactly 12 months today since I sounded here before.

Friday, 28th: At lecture Mechanics Institute — Rev Dr Burns. A walk afterwards.

Saturday, 29th: At plans & specifications of school all this week. The dissolution of partnership of Fleming & Leather in the *Colonist*. I retain the office.

Sunday, 30th: At Knox Church morning & evening. Took a walk after church (M.M.).

December 1851

Monday, 1st: At school plans. At St Andrews supper in the evening, got home before 5 oclock next morning.

Tuesday, 2nd: Working at plans, but don't feel exactly all right. Gave Gillespie £1 & order at Burgen & Leishman for £5. Finished description & specifications.

Wednesday, 3rd: Working at plans. Mr Passmore assisted afternoon. Delivered them at 6 oclock P.M. Called at Mr Leask.

Thursday, 4th: Writing letter for *Patriot* in reply to "a Voyageur."

Friday, 5th: Writing. Mr Bucklands lecture.

Saturday, 6th: Writing. Surveying William Burks Lot on Jarvis st ordered by Mr Cameron. Meeting Canadian Institute. Walked up to Spadina avenue in the morning.

Sunday, 7th: At Knox Church twice. (A light at the door.)

Monday, 8th: Writing. Called on Dr McCaul with Mr Youngs order, he referred me to the Bursar.

Tuesday, 9th: Called on the Bursar and received £5 for Fleming & Leather from Thos Young. Election going on.

Wednesday, 10th: Writing Rules & Regulations for Canadian Institute. Elections going on.

Thursday, 11th: Sent in letter with wood cut to Editor of *Patriot*. Writing Rules & Regulations. Cull & Passmore met in my office at night.

Friday, 12th: Last night Mr Leather informed me that a man had called at noon when I was out with a letter from the Crown Land Office wishing me to do some work. Went up but they knew nothing of it. Went down to Royal Engineers office. Lieut Cream & the others knew of nothing, but the porter had taken a letter to me from Lieut de Moleyers to the post. Came home and was much pleased to find that I had been appointed to make a survey of Toronto Military Reserve. Called on de Moleyers & saw the papers. At school trustees meeting at St Lawrence Hall. Did not go to lecture but had a moonlight walk, met [William G.] Storm & Passmore on Yonge st.

Saturday, 13th: Saturday morning met Mr Lancaster & went down to the Engineers office & the Garrison Reserve, very cold. Writing Rules & Regulations &c. At Canadian Institute. On Friday morning my "letter" appeared in the *Patriot*. A good deal of talk about it. (A short walk, snowing hard.)

Monday, 15th: Wrote to Lieut de Moleyers and Sheriff [Wilson] Conger [later Mayor of Peterborough] enclosing wood cut. Started for Barrie in the stage. Good sleighing. Went with Mr Savigny from Bradford to Barrie, very cold. Arrived about 2 oclock in the morning.

Tuesday, 16th: Finding out the names of the owners of land at the Crown office & Registry office. Paid Mr Marks for Mr Patersons trunk bringing from Bradford by stage 2/6.

Wednesday, 17th: Left Barrie this morning about sunrise, very cold head wind, had breakfast after traveling 13 miles. Cold cold southeast wind all the way but good sleighing, 60 miles in 12 hours including a great many stoppages.

Thursday, 18th: Pretty late in getting up this morning after the long cold ride. Received 10s from Mr de Grassi, balance of old acct. Working out list of lands in Tiny & Tay [townships] &c. Expenses going to Barrie — Stage up & meals 15/, down 15/, Registry 15/, Hotel & other exp 11/3, [total] £2/16/3.

Friday, 19th: Called a Mr Gwynn, secretary of the Guelph Railway. Wrote to Judge Brown, with list of Lands &c &c letter, also to Sheriff [Henry] Ruttan [Sheriff of Newcastle District, 1827–57]. Called on Lieut de Moleyers, and received instructions regarding the Military survey. Called also on Mr Hawkins but had not returned from England (evening at Mr L).

Saturday, 20th: "A Voyageur" replied to my letter in Thursdays *Patriot* in very flattering terms. Writing Rules & Regulations Canadian Institute. At Institute meeting discussion about "regulations."

Sunday, 21st: At Knox Church twice. Walked round by the College avenue, all snow.

Monday, 22nd: Hunting up evidence regarding the Reserve survey at City Hall. Howard, Chewit, Dennison, Passmore & [I] wrote to Dennis. Recd instruction from Peterboro [Conger] to make a survey for a Harbour at Gloucester Bay for St L & Lake Huron Rlwy. Saw great puff in Peterboro *Despatch* about my letter to the *Patriot*. Recd £5 from Passmore which with £10 on 22 Nov makes £15 for share of Welland County Court House premium. Answered Mr Congers letter.

Tuesday, 23rd: At Royal Eng office hunting up plans, at Registry office &c endeavoring to get information about boundaries of Reserve. Heard from Mr Dennis. Telegraph & Quebec — cost 3/9. Paid Mr Bridges 6/3, seat rent until March next. Tracing map of Gloucester Bay & making all enquiries after Bayfields chart, writing to Mr Russell & Dennis. Mrs Allanson died this morning.

Wednesday, 24th: Telegraphed Mr Divine for tracing a chart of Gloucester Bay paid 3/9. Making out accts & writing to various parties. Received £5/10 from Mr Cayley allowed 12/6 discount. Received £1 from Jos Sheard being for surveying Insurance Co. Lot. Christmas gift — John coat £1/8/9, Necessities £1/5, E.M. 10s, [indecipherable] £1/6, [total] £4/8/9.

Thursday, 25th: Very cold. At Office making sketch for Mr Allanson. At Mrs Allansons funeral, and at Mr A all afternoon. Tea at Mrs Hutchisons and spent the evening.

Friday, 26th: Very cold. Capt Lefroy. Say from 7 to 8 A.M. the coldest here this winter as yet — 14 below zero. Saw W Ogilvie who came last night from New York. Trying to find out the windmill line for setting out Jacques & Hay wharf. At Observatory transferring meridian to the ordnance reserve. Called in the evening at Mr Leask for Will Ogilvie. Mr L. & M.M. A bad cold.

Saturday, 27th: Started this morning to make survey every 33 feet at the Queen's Wharf, the ice being sound yesterday had everything prepared, but the ice was gone. Surveyed 3 water Lots for Jacques & Hay. Saw Mr Gwynn with regard to the west boundary of reserve, to see Dr George on Monday. At presentation dinner in the St Lawrence Hall, opening of the water works &c &c.

Sunday, 28th: At church twice. A great many people have influenza — or bad colds.

Monday, 29th: Got a new chain from Simpson, paid him 25/. Called on Dr George twice but did not obtain his affidavit. Got Major Denisons evidence, also Robert B Denisons, running about among them all day. Paid for Buggy hire 7/6. Handed over the Institute charter and proposed Regulations to Carter & Thomas to be printed.

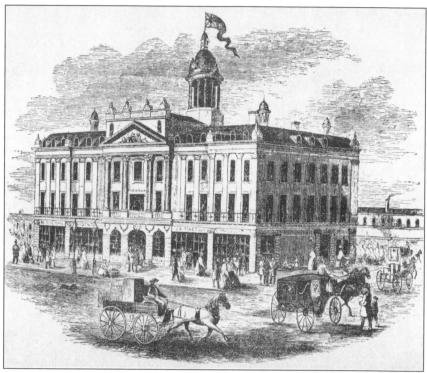

St. Lawrence Hall, designed by William Thomas, was the setting for many special events in Toronto in the 1850s. From Landmarks, Volume 3 *(1896) by J.R. Robertson.*

Tuesday, 30th: Ordering various articles necessary to take with us. Received tracing from Devine. Wrote to Mr Hawks. After calling on Howard, left with Lieut de Moleyer all the paper & maps I received from him except instructions. Very wet, cant go to the Lighthouse. Paid for tape 7/6 — cake 5/10 — biscuit 8/9 — line 3/8 — shortbread 2/6. Saw M.M. at Leasks.

Wednesday, 31st: Got ham from Mr Liddel which cost 12/6 & cash £1/17/6 in all £2/10. Left my plans of the Harbour in Shaw, Turnbull &c safe, in case of fire. Saw M.M. Yonge st. Went up to Mr Farr and got his affidavit bus 4d. Paid for box of herring 4/6. Leask acct for various articles necessary for the survey £3/16/6.

CHAPTER EIGHT
The Ontario Northern Railway 1852

A wintry campsite near Nottawasaga Bay provided the setting for Fleming's twenty-fifth birthday celebration on January 7, 1852. Optimistically he sent out invitations to friends to join the survey crew at a "tea party" at the camp on Sturgeon Point and the host provided "cake and hot scotch" to mark the occasion. The group had been chaining the route from Orillia via Coldwater to Nottawasaga Bay for several days, covering eight or nine miles a day in bitter windy conditions and the entertainment provided a little respite.

Through his acquaintance with Judge Brown of Ogdensburg, and Wilson S. Conger of Peterborough, Sandford had been engaged to do exploratory work for the St. Lawrence and Lake Huron Railway around Nottawasaga Bay and to map the proposed Gloucester Bay Harbour. At the same time, he had been approached by several interested parties to be on the lookout for available land that might prove a good investment in an area that seemed destined to be opened up by expanding railway interests.

During the early months of the year he juggled two projects. Work went on with his field crew making their way north on snowshoes toward Georgian Bay, while in Toronto he was planning and plotting his survey of the new Military Reserve and Garrison, west of Queen's Wharf (where the Old Garrison was located) along the Lake Ontario shoreline. The latter involved a large tract of land that stretched between the lake and Queen Street West with a section set aside for the Lunatic Asylum at 999 Queen. Heavy snow and ice in the bay slowed their progress in the early part of March but conditions improved as spring drew nearer, and on May 11 he reported that chaining at the Reserve Wharf was complete. By the end of the month he had begun to draw the map, though work went on in the field throughout the process.

Another undertaking mid-year was the preliminary mapping for the Central Railway committee, including Sheriff Conger, of an overland route from Toronto to Peterborough via Markham, Brooklin, Scugog, Manvers, and Cavan. In July, a group of interested railway officials and local politicians had an excursion along the route ending with a "magnificent dinner" at Chambers Hotel in Peterborough. Two days later the travellers had a "champagne dinner" at Cobourg before returning to Toronto, leaving Fleming and John W. Tate, who had also been involved with the St. Lawrence and Lake Huron Railway, with instructions to begin surveying the line.

That summer marked a major turning point in Fleming's career. In July, the Ontario, Simcoe and Lake Huron Railway (later the Northern) named Frederic Cumberland chief engineer. Rumours abounded and friends began congratulating Fleming on his new role as assistant engineer, but it wasn't until August 11 that he received a letter from Charles Berczy, president of the line, confirming his appointment. The very next day he went out with his survey party to begin examining the partially completed route from Toronto to Barrie, and to assess the needs there. Extending the line northward was to be Fleming's main responsibility. September was a busy month and diary entries are very sparse, but by October they were working their way north from Barrie, up the Penetanguishene road toward Sturgeon Creek and Nottawasaga Bay. There was time in late August for another group excursion by steamer to Buffalo with Cumberland and members of the Ontario, Simcoe & Huron Board to attend the opening and celebratory dinner for the Niagara Falls Bridge — "Gigantic structure. Great dinner. Very hot!" From then on, work went on in earnest defining the route of the "Ontario Northern."

It was a busy year for the Canadian Institute, too. From the beginning, Fleming had been performing organizational and secretarial roles, and in March, at the first formal elections held under their new Charter, he was elected secretary of the organization, a job he had already been doing since the founding. Geologist William E. Logan (later Sir William) was elected president, and Captain John H. Lefroy, Director of the Royal Magnetic Observatory on the university grounds, vice-president. Another milestone for the Institute, after months of meetings and preparations, was the appearance of the first issue of the *Canadian Journal* in July, with Henry Yule Hind as editor. Fleming's article on the Notta-wasaga valley appeared in an early issue and his contributions appeared frequently throughout the rest of his lifetime.

January 1852

Thursday, 1st: New Years Day! Wrote to Mr Divine about Town plot Nottawasaga River for Mr MacNabb [Saugeen] (enclosing 10s). To Judge Brown list of Macdonalds lands in Tay. To Sheriff Ruttan & to Lieut de Moleyers. Visiting during the day. Dined with Passmore & had tea at Miss Macdonalds. Took out seat to go tomorrow to Barrie & Orillia.

Friday, 2nd: Left this morning in the stage with £12/17/6, then paid stage for George and I to Bradford including meals 17s 6d; ditto to Barrie 10s; ditto for MacNabb 5s. Engaged MacNabb at 5s per day. W. Ogilvie accompanies us, arrived at Barrie. Nothing particular happened.

Saturday, 3rd: Left Barrie for Orillia, Hotel 7s 6d; Conveyance to Orillia for £2/15/0; paid ditto for Charlie 5s; Iron bars for sounding 15s; Camp-ing kettle 3s; Frying pans &c &c at Patersons 10s. George & I at Mr Pat-erson at tea & spending the evening. The Town Reeve, Mr Drinkwater, Dr Cordach, & other persons interested in the Railroad came to see us.

Sunday, 4th: At Church forenoon. Dined at Mr Patersons. Sent circulars to Toronto inviting some friends to attend a tea party at the camp on Sturgeon Point on Wednesday evening next. Left for Coldwater, paid 7s 6d; Sleigh 12s 6d. Ogilvie goes down tomorrow.

Monday, 5th: Left for Sturgeon Point with Caswells team & traps, pd him 15s 7½d train expenses & whisky; pd G.Bob 7½d. Employed three Indians &c &c G & J Boland & Winters also Charles Day & J Macdonald @ 3s 9d per day. Chain today about 6½ miles and cut many soundings. Fine day. Camped out at Sturgeon Point.

Tuesday, 6th: Pretty comfortable in camp. Snow nearly all day, nevertheless we chain nearly 9 miles. Very cold toward night. Amuse the hands by reading from Antoine in the camp.

Wednesday, 7th: A bitter cold morning, wind from N.West. Several of us get nose, ears and fingers a little frozen. Chained today about 8 miles. My Birthday [age 25] anniversary in the camp, had a blow out after tea with Cake and Hot Scotch. Laid down star line about ½ past nine. Clear cold moonlight!

Thursday, 8th: (Mr Robinson of Orillia said the thermometer yesterday was 24 below zero. I think it was perhaps not so low) — Very cold today. Chain about 8¾ miles & finish Hog Bay [Victoria Harbour]. Very smoky in the camp & snows a little.

Friday, 9th: Surveying at Sturgeon Bay. Snow in the afternoon, chain upwards of 8 miles. Paid MacNabb 25s. Moved our camp over to the empty tavern at the Landing and camped on the floor.

Saturday, 10th: Had a good potato breakfast, beautiful clear day. Keen frosty morning, beautiful mirage on the ice. Measured upwards of 11 miles today and finished chaining at 7 o'clock P.M. Good supper and left with Mr Caswell for Coldwater. Paid John Macdonald 25s; Tom Winters 15s 7½d; John Boland 22s 6d; Charlie Day 17s 6d; George Boland 11s 3d and cooking utensils. Recd from George Stewart 10s 7½d.

Sunday, 11th: Had a good night rest and breakfast. Mr Caswell drove us to Orillia Evg 1s 3d. Met Mr [John W.] Tate who has just come to Orillia in advance of surveying party. No Letter! In my arm chair at Mr Patersons.

Monday, 12th: Left Orillia this morning with dispatch from Mr Paterson. Recd from Mr Tate £2/10 — to be arranged with the council. Paid Garret 7s 6d; Mark 2s 6d & 1s 3d; Mrs Bustle 3s 9d & 1s 3d. Saw old Mr Galbraith in Oro [township]. He is to let me know when he is to open an Indian mound in the spring.

Tuesday, 13th: Left before breakfast. Paid May 3s 11d. Steel, Finch &c for dinner & breakfast paid 3s 9d — also paid Caswell for conveyance from Coldwater £2. On arrival found letter from Judge Brown, also from Mr Conger informing me that the secretary had instructed me to examine Thunder Bay and find on the vacant lands.

Wednesday, 14th: Sheet of paper at Scobie for Harbour Survey 5s at Scobies. Plotting survey — paper at Rowsell 3s [Henry & William Rowsell Stationers]. Recd from Donald Cameron 5s which he borrowed long ago. From Mother 10s which I lent to pay biscuit, also from Arnold for T & L S Ry celebration10s. Paid George 10s 7½d which I borrowed at Orillia. Called on Mr L in the evening.

Thursday, 15th: Bought boots 17s 6d. Called on de Moleyers. Plotting Harbour survey. Wrote to Mr [Wilson S.] Conger and Judge Brown.

Friday, 16th: Received letter from secretary of Railway Committee instructing me to extend my examination to Thunder Bay, the letter had been at Orillia the day after I left. Plotting survey of Harbour. Recd from Lieut de Moleyers specifications of detail surveys of Toronto & London in the afternoon. At lecture, not many there.

Saturday, 17th: Plotting survey of Hog & Sturgeon Bays. Short of tracing paper at Scobie's 1s 3d. Measuring distances for M.C. Cameron on Yonge st south of Bettey and King with wooden rod say 7s 6d. Drawing until midnight. Recd proof of Charter & Regulations of Canadian Institute.

Monday, 19th: Intended going over to the Island to set back meridian but wind blowing & exceedingly cold, called on Lieut de Moleyers who thinks that I had better finish my drawing at Gloucester Bay immediately while the weather is rough & attend to this afterward. George [Stewart] finishing Ruttans [Cobourg] drawings. Borrow Mr Leather theodolite.

Tuesday, 20th: One of the coldest & most stormy days of the year. Traced chart of Hog & Sturgeon Bay, enclosed the same to Mr [Thomas] Benson [Peterborough], secretary of the Ry committee. Wrote to John W Tate, Orillia.

Wednesday, 21st: Milder today, but blowing & snowing. Recd proofs of regulations Canadian Institute from printer, took same up to [Frederick] Passmore. Called on Crooks, he is to give a check on Saturday.

Friday, 23rd: No letter from Peterboro this morning. Went up to see Major Denison concerning boundary marks on Queen st, he was just going out in his sleigh so I could not get his evidence. At Queen's Wharf. The ice extends from the Lighthouse Pt to the point this side of Humber Bay.

Saturday, 24th: No letter this morning. Canadian Institute. Scobie *Almanac*. Observations at Balsam Lake. Denison called. History of Toronto with plates.

Monday, 26th: Recd letter from Peterboro. Made a draft on Conger for £12 and made preparations for starting. Expenses — Pork 9s 9d; Biscuit 8s 9d; Gloves 8s 9d; George £2/10; Stage 12s 6d; Cake 3s; [indecipherable] 7½d; Groceries Mr [James] Leask 11s 7½d. [Total] £5/5.

Tuesday, 27th: Prepared to go with the morning stage but lost, had to stay until afternoon. Left on stage with £7/1/10. Tea 2s 6d. Expenses at Bradford 3s.

Wednesday, 28th: Left Bradford in teams for Orillia. Snow deep & snowing. Send John Galbraith Charter. Breakfast at Boults 3s; Hire of team to Orillia £2. Saw Mr Barlow. Dinner at Marks 2s 6d. Arrived at Orillia. Met Mr Tate & party at the Tavern. Jolly set! At Mr Patersons & stayed the night.

Thursday, 29th: Started from Orillia with John Boland & John Bickerton & George.

Line 2s; expenses [total] 3s; Team to Coldwater 15s. Engaged Joe Cradock, John Macdonald team to Coldwater, Mr Casswell & team and George Boland went on to Sturgeon Bay and slept at John Macdonalds. W Boland & George Dunford to come over tomorrow. Paid John Bickerton 10s.

Friday, 30th: Water on scale 1.7 ft at Sturgeon Pt. Spent the night with all the party at Mr Macdonalds. Started with Caswells team for Mundys Bay. Commenced George [Stewart] on the survey and with J Boland & the team went on to the only house on the Bay, Richd Murphy. Left the luggage there and came along an awful road to Penetanguishene. Snowing all day & very deep. Drew upon Conger at Penetang for £15/10, expenses.

Saturday, 31st: Expenses at Selby Tavern 8s, meal 1s 3d. Started for Thunder Bay. J Boland, Caswell & team. Snow from 4 to 5 ft deep, got to the French settlement and had dinner at a Frenchmans named Lamoreux — and change the team for a new horse train. Road very badly [hooked?] arrived at Labate at Thunder Bay about ½ past three. Walk on snowshoes with John to the point west side of Bay & half way across to round island about 13 miles, arrived at Labates about ½ past 12. Supper of preserves & French cakes. Decent old French people. Indian kettle.

February 1852

Monday, 2nd: Travelled with John Boland on snowshoes yesterday from Thunder Bay to Penetanguishene, very very tired. Caswell team went on to Murphys. Boland, Winters and I walked over to Mundys Bay. Gave Mrs Labate 10s; Bread 1s 3d; Snowshoes 12s 6d, 12s 6d, 11s 3d; Jeffrey Bile 10s; Articles at Hamilton 10s. Snow about 4 ft deep in the woods. Meet George near the mouth of the Wye. Spent the night. Eleven of us at Murphys miserable hut. Endeavor to make all jolly after plotting survey.

Tuesday, 3rd: Left Murphys. Gave Winters 3s 6d; Mrs Murphy for board £1/5. This morning Caswell went on to Coldwater with the team. George to make some more soundings in Mundys Bay & tie it with Hog. John Boland & I went on to examine the land at the head of Hog Bay. Made a good many more in Hogs Bay & completed after dark. Walk over to Mr Macdonalds, arrive about 9 oclock very very hungry & tired.

Wednesday, 4th: Changed my mind this morning and went back to Hog Bay [Victoria Harbour] to endeavor to find two support rocks and make more soundings. Snow on the ice wet and very heavy to walk on — rain part of the day. Finish after dark and walked over to John Macdonalds. Had comfortable supper. Ankle sprained from walking on snowshoes. After a smoke went to bed. George Dunford & Caswell went home this morning.

Thursday, 5th: Started off on snowshoes by the road for Coldwater. Pd Mr Macdonald for boarding last two nights £1/11/3; Paid John Bickerton 6 days @ 5s — £1/10; John Macdonald 6 days @ 5s — £1/10; John Boland 6 days @ 5s — £1/10; William Boland 5 days @ 3/9 — 18s 9d; George Boland 6 days @ 2/6 — £1/5; George Dunford 4 days — 12s 6d; Joseph Cradock 6 days — £1/5. Hired Caswell team to Orillia. Found lots of newspapers & letter from Mr Benson & Mr Barlow. Saw Mr Tate, told him my decision as to Hog Bay being the best harbour.

Friday, 6th: Left Orillia this morning with Mrs Paterson & Maggie. Expenses at Janets and by the way 8s 9d; Harvey team Mr P 7s 6d; George & self 12s 6d; Marks Hotel 3s 9d; [Total] £1/5. Deduct snowshoes sold to Mr Tate 12s 6d. [Total] 12s 6d. (I have yet to send Mr Caswell 15 dollars.) (paid April 6.)

Saturday, 7th: Left Barrie this morning and had breakfast at Bulls with Mr P, 2s 6d; Stage to Bradford 2 @ 5s — 10s; Dinner 1s 10½d — 2s 6d; Stage to Toronto — 8s 1½ — 12s 6d. Paid back on 13th — 26s 10½d. [total] £1/7/6. Dr Burns came down with us from Bradford. Maggie very chatty. At Canadian Institute meeting.

Monday, 9th: Plotting. Called on Mr de Moleyers, not in. Wrote to Secty Mr Benson enclosing tracing of Town Plot & about vacant lands, too late for post. Saw Mrs Paterson.

Tuesday, 10th: Plotting survey forenoon. Wrote to Judge Brown about lands. Over at the Lighthouse setting back meridinal angle to Garrison common George & 1½ day. At Cumberlands evening. Sleigh.

Wednesday, 11th: Plotting survey all day. The wind blows too hard to go out on the survey. Borrowed 5s from Passmore & purchase one doz drawing pins at Josephs. Plotting until past 12 o'clock.

Thursday, 12th: Plotting & making soundings. Recd letter from Mr [Henry] Ruttan [Cobourg]. Prepared to go out today but could not the wind blows so hard. Saw Lieut de Moleyers. Saw Mr Cayley. Wrote to Mr Ruttan.

Friday, 13th: Snow & windy. Lighthouse not seen. Cant go out. Making measurements for Mr Cayley near city hall say 7s 6d — or 5s. Got lithograph stone from Scobie for Ruttan drawings. Bought cotton from Mr Leask for mounting paper 1/8. Received from Mr Leask expenses of Mrs Paterson paid by me coming from Orillia £1/6/10½. Mounting paper for Gloucester Bay plans.

Saturday, 14th: Out on the reserve survey. George, Donald, Grant & I. Grant took sick. Gave him 2s 6d. Run a random line through to the first concession, and found bearing &c. Expense for lunch 2s 2d. At Canadian Institute, passed regulations. F.C. [Cumberland] very quarrelsome. At Kivas Tully afterwards.

Monday, 16th: On the reserve survey. George, Thomas, Remnant & self chaining along Queen street & preparing for astronomical observations, Biscuit & beer 1s. Laying down meridian at night Passmore & I. Paid for lamp 8s 9d; Cab & 3s 9d, Cab & assistant say 13s 3d.

Tuesday, 17th: Snow & stormy, not out. Writing to Mr Russell, Gibson & Smith about west boundary of reserve bearing.

Wednesday, 18th: Writing report of Harbour survey this week. George drawing on stone Sheriff Ruttans drawings. In the evening saw Mrs Paterson and James.

Friday, 20th: Our on reserve survey today picketing & chaining along Queen st. George & Thomas Remnant expenses 1s 3d. Preparing to go out to lay down meridian in the evening with de Moleyers, but he was not in. At Lecture. Sliding with Passmore on King street.

Monday, 23rd: Out on survey today, Thomas & Peter. Received letter from Charles L. Schlatter. Chief engin. St Lawrence & Lake Huron Ry, also Judge Brown pamphlet. In the evening making drawings to send to Mr Sang. Received from Andrew £9/15 also from Mr Crooks part of account by check for £7/10. At short walk.

Tuesday, 24th: Snow & stormy, not out. Getting proof of Ruttans drawing. At Miss Websters funeral in the afternoon. She is gone poor girl, so is Billings, & Miss Willard. Called at Commercial Bank to get cash on Thursday. Mr [Edward L.] Cull rules & regulations evening.

Wednesday, 25th: Wrote Charles L. Schlatter, chief engineer. Out on reserve survey — George, Thomas, Peter & soldier. Expenses 6d. Finishing letter to Mr Sang. Saw Mrs Paterson in the evening & Maggie. Also Mr Cumberland. Issued circular for his paper on Saturday.

Thursday, 26th: Very stormy today, not out. Get Mr Crooks check for £7/10 cashed at Commercial Bank, and enclose letter of credit to Mr Sang, ordering theodolite — £10 sterling or £12/10/7. Plotting survey of reserve, Mr de Moleyers called & promised to send paper connected with London survey. Finishing Ruttans drawing on stone.

Friday, 27th: Finished Ruttans drawing on stone and got taken down to Scobie, ordered Bain to print 50 & send down to Cobourg. Very keen frost. Plotting part of ordnance survey. Wrote to Mr Benson, secty to Mr Ruttan, Dr Bethune & Charles Copland. Paid Peter Tenny for two days amount 6s 3d.

Saturday, 28th: Received papers connected with the London survey from de Moleyers. Made application for an instalment and enclosed copy of diary. Paid Thomas Remnant 15s 7½d, David Wilkie 3s 1½d. Canadian Institute. Cumberland's paper. Very stormy. Deep snow cottage grounds. Large scale.

March 1852

Monday, 1st: Deep snow. Received a reply from Mr Russell. Writing report of Harbour survey. Regulations of Canadian Institute badly printed, to be sent back. Paid for broom 1s. Order bacon stain Jacques & Hay 6s 3d. Order circular at Scobies.

Wednesday, 3rd: Enclosed to Lieut de Moleyers copy of drawing up to 28 Feby, account of time & expenses is £18/2/52. Dennis & Brownes certificates of usual things by surveyor letter of date Feby 29 on March 3. Sent off 30 circulars Canadian Institute — Brownes paper. At Mr Leask about specifications.

Thursday, 4th: Recd letter from Mr Charles L Schlatter asking me to come down with Mr T.L. Ogden, Writing to Capt [J.H.] Lefroy enclosing paper connected with Canadian Institute. Sent back proof to Carter & Thomas. Am reading over with George his copies of London survey papers.

Friday, 5th: Putting in lines of equal depth on plans of Mundy & Hog Bays.

Saturday, 6th: At large plan of Harbour. Copying from Bayfield & Township maps. At Canada Compy copying. George reducing plans of Hog &c Bays to scale 40. At Canadian Institute. Acting as secretary. Brownes paper.

Monday, 8th: On Reserve survey all day, already snow very deep, level with the top of fence in some places. Recd a letter from Capt Lefroy consenting to the nomination. Canadian Institute.

Tuesday, 9th: At de Moleyer for tracing of Penetanguishene &c, say ½ day to Georges Harbour large plan. Bought sector 7s 6d; Books 9s.

Wednesday, 10th: On Reserve survey. George, Daniel, Thomas & Artillery man expenses 1s 9d. Received tracing of Penetanguishene for de Moleyers. Visitor in the evening M.M.

Thursday, 11th: Sent down plan (original) of Peterboro to Captain Renwick. On Reserve survey, George, Thomas & Daniel. Expenses 1s 6d.

Friday, 12th: Recd a letter from Mr Tate from Peterboro, also from Passmore. Making up notes and calculating position of Stations on Reserve survey — one day. Recd from Moberly copy of survey at present built at Toronto.

Saturday, 13th: Making calculations for position of stations Military Reserve survey (say 1 day) 9/s 4½d. Paid Daniel Wilkie 9s 4½d; Thomas Remnant £9/4½; paid Father 5s. At large map of Georgian Bay Harbour — (say 1 day). George having been reducing yesterday & today, myself at it part of afternoon & evening. At Canadian Institute. Very stormy. Capt Lefroy people.

Sunday, 16th: At Church evening.

Monday, 15th: Enlarging part of ordnance map of Penetanguishene for chart of Mundys Bay, putting in lines of equal depth in ditto & gave the whole over to Mr Leather to copy — say ½ day. Plotting & protracting to scale 1 chain to an inch part of survey for the purpose of depicting curve. Say 1 day (extra hours).

Tuesday, 16th: Paid George which I borrowed formerly 3s 9d. Out on Reserve survey. George, Thomas & Dan expenses 2s. Beautiful day — got on well.

Wednesday, 17th: Survey of Reserve. Putting in details at Old Garrison, got on very well. Expenses George, Thomas & Dan 1s 9d. Very tired. At Mr L in the evening.

Thursday, 18th: Snow & stormy. Plotting part of survey to scale of 1 chain to an inch. Paid Daniel to acct 1s 3d. Made a few corrections on stone of Ruttans diagrams and order 150 more to be printed.

Friday, 19th: Snow on the ground, hard frost. On Reserve survey part of the day & plotting afterwards. Daniel & Thomas, say one day. Father returned 5s. Barrack master stopped me on the ground & gave me a check for £18, being an instalment on survey. Paid rent £4/7/6; £3 for office furniture to Grant, Henderson. £1/9/10 — Riddell & McLean £2/10 [tailors]. McLean for telescope £1/5. Paid Daniel Wilkie for 3½ days including 1/3 given formerly. Received letter from Mr Benson.

Saturday, 20th: Calculating distances and protracting chain lines to large scale 4 chains to an inch. At Canadian Institute — nomination of Officers and Council. Browne read paper. Paid Thomas Remnant 3 days 9s 4d.

Sunday, 21st: Sunday evening ½ 9.

Monday, 22nd: Endeavoring to find a curve which will pass through the various points as fixes my measurements given on the [Garrison surb-vey] plan, and after repeated trials found two which seemed to answer every purpose, putting them in ink.

Tuesday, 23rd: Went to consult Mr Hawkins and show him the plan of the curves. He gave me further data as to the establishing of the curve such as old field notes at Engineers office & plotting Mr Hawkins measurements.

Wednesday, 24th: Making trials with various curves, with the view of finding arcs of circles which correspond with part of the curves so that it can be properly described hereafter, found that a curve composed of three arcs of various lengths & radii nearly through all the points. Snow since Saturday and even a little sleighing.

Thursday, 25th: Plotting Garrison survey ½ day. Cumberland & I met McLean and his two editors Rev McGeorge & Dr H. Melville about publishing.

Friday, 26th: Plotting Garrison survey. Paid Passmore 5s 7d borrowed a few weeks back — and £2/10 borrowed out of Canadian [Institute] funds long ago.

Saturday, 27th: Plotting survey, am making measurements on plan for the purpose of planting boundary stakes. Paid Dan to acct 5s. Canadian

Institute election of Officers & Council according to new Charter, elected me secretary. ½ hour walk.

Monday, 29th: Out today, called on Mr Hawkins, showed him the curve as now proposed. Had a conversation about other points. Making measurements for some detail along Niagara st — measuring and pointing out places to dig for the purpose of planting stakes. Expenses 7½d, Dan 3s 11½d. Passmore at Canada Company.

Tuesday, 30th: Snow & very stormy. At large plan of Harbour Georgian Bay. Andrew 5s for varnish. Passmore takes 20. C.C. Meeting in my office about Conversazione. Very cold. Dan & I at circular until after 12.

Wednesday, 31st: Sending out circular now with P.O about D. Lett.

April 1852

Thursday, 1st: Sending off circular Canadian Institute Conversazione. Capt Lefroy & other members of the Council of Canadian Institute met in my office in the afternoon. This is the first meeting of the Council elected by the Royal Charter.

Friday, 2nd: David Wilkins settled for Monday last.

Saturday, 3rd: Preparing for Conversazione most all this week. It came off tonight and was very successful, was well attended — 35 persons put down their names. One of the happiest nights in my life. All were delighted & excited. Lost a good part of the nights sleep.

Monday, 5th: To make survey for Northern Railway Co & description of property examined.

Tuesday, 6th: Recd $15 from Cumberland 3s 15d & sent the same to Caswell, Coldwater 3s 15d.

Wednesday, 7th: Commenced making calculations for Mr [William] Cayley. At Mr Leask.

Thursday, 8th: At calculations for Mr Cayley & plan of property at Grays say 12s 6d. At title of [Gloucester] Harbour plan St Lawrence & Lake Huron Railway.

Friday, 9th: [Good Friday] On Reserve survey. Very muddy. Duncan, Thomas & Dan expenses 3s 12d.

Saturday, 10th: On Reserve survey. Expenses Donovan, Thomas 1s 3d; Dan per day 2s 6d. These two last days get on very well, beautiful weather but muddy. Canadian Institute new members proposed. Walk miles.

Monday, 12th: Out on Reserve survey putting in detail, artillery stables &c and fixing some points for Northern Ry survey. Expenses 1s 6d. At Mechanics Institute soiree in the evening, went off very well. Cumberland a very good address. Paid Daniel to acct 2s 6d.

Tuesday, 13th: Out on Reserve survey, chaining and running lines along King street. Very foggy, putting in detail between Queen's Wharf and Old Fort. Expenses 9d. Survey lot for officers. Expenses 2s. Evening paid 10s.

A section of King Street, which was the commercial hub of Toronto in the 1850s. From Landmarks, Volume 1 *(1894) by J.R. Robertson.*

Wednesday, 14th: Rain, calculating ordinates of station for Reserve survey. Paid Dan up to date balance of wages (in all 12s 6d paid working at night say 1¼ day) 7s 6d. Donovan at [John] Radenhurst plan.

Thursday, 15th: On Reserve survey. Donovan, Thomas & Dan. Expenses 1s 6d. At Council Canadian Institute evening. Received letter from Mr Sang in reply to mine enclosing order for £10 sterling. He has commissioned Christie make my instrument.

Friday, 16th: On Reserve survey. Donovan, Thomas & Dan. Expenses 1s 6d. David left for Hamilton today.

Saturday, 17th: Adjusting bearings & obtain calculating ordinates &c. Donovan at Radenhurst plans.

Monday, 19th: Calculating distances for protracting.

Tuesday, 20th: Calculating distances for protracting & planting boundary stakes, also plotting. Finish design for McLean. Cover for *Anglo American* say £1/5.

Wednesday, 21st: On Reserve survey. Planting pickets for Lieut Crean & survey in rear of asylum & hospital. Donovan, Thomas & Dan. Expenses 7½d. Gave Mr Leather order on Leask for £4. Recd from Father £1/5 & Andrew £1/5. Paid back to Father £1/5. Sending off circulars Canadian Institute.

Thursday, 22nd: In the office plotting for description of property on Reserve for Ontario Simcoe & Huron Railway Co — and also for Reserve survey. Bought Mr Leather small [indecipherable] for £15 — and settled up with him to this date. I owe him a balance of £11/11/6 and the accounts unpaid to F & L are all due to me. Paid Dan in full to this date.

Friday, 23rd: On Reserve survey. Thomas measuring & planting boundary stakes at Toll gate and some Asylum property. Expenses 1s 3d.

Saturday, 24th: At court all day as witness for Passmore. At Canadian Institute in the evening. Finished Radenhurst plan to be sent him on Monday. 1s 5d.

Monday, 26th: Plotting Reserve survey all day. Paid Thomas Remnant in full to date £1/5, being 8 days @ 3½. Rain! Walk M.M. William Mac-Donald opened store.

Tuesday, 27th: Blows & looks rainy! Plotting and mapping Reserve survey inking part of ditto. Duncan copying meteorological observations at Lake Balsam.

Wednesday, 28th: Blowing fresh! Too much so to go on Reserve survey. Out with Mr Leland & Donovan to have some stakes pointed out on Railway line, plotting the same and calculating distances and bearings for description. Up very late!

Thursday, 29th: On Reserve survey. Donovan & McBride. Planting stakes around Faris property and at the end of the curve, also detail survey at top of valley. At night making out description of property required by Northern Railway Company until nearly 2 oclock A.M. Paid artillery man 2/6.

Friday, 30th: On Reserve survey, Donovan & McBride. Expenses 7d. Detail of valley between Queen & below King street. Making out 2nd description for Railway Company at night. Paid rent of Canadian Institute to Mechanics Institute £3/15.

May 1852

Saturday, 1st: Sent in 2nd description of Railway land, say worth £10 or £12/10. Plotting Reserve survey all day. Canadian Institute. Capt Lefroy read a paper on a number of Indian tribes &c Grimes also read paper.

Monday, 3rd: On Reserve survey (Donovan & McBride) surveying lake shore west of the garrison & commence detail of new Garrison. Expenses 1s. Mechanics Institute election.

Tuesday, 4th: Reserve survey (Donovan & McBride) putting in detail of new Garrison and portion of ravine. Expenses 1s 3d. Sending off circulars of general meeting of Canadian Institute.

Wednesday, 5th: Calculating distances &c for protracting Reserve survey. Supper at Mr Leask. Met Mr Ferguson from Glasgow.

Thursday, 6th: Plotting new Garrison & ravine, working late. Say 1½ days.

Friday, 7th: On Reserve survey (Donovan & McBride) with Capt Renwick, Lieut de Moleyers & Lieut Wilkinson pointing out boundary stakes & the boundaries defined by me. Discover traces of old lockspitting (by the shade of the path) on curve which could not before be detected, found the same to agree with my stakes, markings ditto & chaining at SW angle of common. Expenses 1s 3d.

Saturday, 8th: On Reserve survey (Donovan & McBride) in front of Parliament Buildings, getting paper mounted. Paid Michael McBride 6 days @ 3/12 —18s 7d. At Canadian Institute general meeting. Decided on going on with *Canadian Journal.*

Monday, 10th: On Reserve survey (Donovan & McBride). Dividing rear of Faris Lot for Capt Renwick's lockspitting and completing chaining at Reserve Wharf. Expenses 1s 3d. Beautiful cool evening, walked down to the Queen's Wharf in the gloaming, came past the Parliament Buildings.

Tuesday, 11th: Pd T Donovan for 16 days @ 5/ per day — £4, being for April 9, 10, 12, 13, 15, 16, 21, 23, 28, 29, 30, May 3, 4, 7, 8, 10, in all 16 days. Plotting survey of ravine and coast at the new Garrison.

Wednesday, 12th: On Reserve survey, measuring angles of that portion near the Parliament Buildings with Mr Short. Paid McBride for Monday 3/s 1½d. Expenses 6d. Calculating ordinates in the evening.

Thursday, 13th: Plotting survey between Reserve Wharf and R.E. [Royal Engineers] office, inking ditto and other parts of the survey. College avenue. Old May day.

Friday, 14th: Finding names of owners of property abutting on the ordnance at the Registry office. Expenses 10s. Recd from Mr Cameron my fee as witness at the court Saturday 10s. Mapping &c &c.

Saturday, 15th: Mapping and chaining curves military Reserve plan ½ day. Making out 3d description of land required for Toronto, S[imcoe] & Lake Huron Railway. Meeting Council Canadian Institute. Present letter. Lefroy, Cull, Cumberland & I.

Monday, 17th: Making out description Huron Railway Company. Working late.

Tuesday, 18th: On Reserve survey Donovan & John Hunter. Paid Donovan 5s, expenses 1s 3d. Recd letter from Mr Russell about situation in Quebec & Richmond Railway … wrote to Mr Russell. Paid man for getting office cleaned 2s 6d.

Wednesday, 19th: Protracting & plotting yesterday's work.

Thursday, 20th: Plotting & inking &c as yesterday. Recd £10 from W Smith for G Stewart; paid James Hutchison £5 and £2/10 to myself which I lent George formerly. (Evening Mrs L). Made out 4th description for Northern Railway Company.

Friday, 21st: Commenced making fair copy of plan (picking off &c).

Saturday, 22nd: Fair copy (mapping) pencil. At Canadian Institute Council. Tender for printing, Scobie accepted. Wrote Mr Paterson, Orillia, also G Stewart. M.M. Jarvis street.

Monday, 24th: Writing to Lieut Wilkinson at Engineers Office agreeable to his request. Sketching in hills on each side of valley, also detail at Old Fort &c. Expenses 7½d.

Tuesday, 25th: Mapping Reserve survey. Paid Mr Anderson for Father $15 which with 15s lent Father about a week ago make $18 (£4/10). Walked round by top of Crookshank lane and down the valley to Queen st.

Wednesday, 26th: Mapping Reserve survey (perhaps ½ day). Mr Conger, Peterboro, called and saw Railway Harbour plans. Paid printer (M McIntosh) for rent of room Conversazione of Canadian Institute £1.

Thursday, 27th: Recd orders to picket curved boundary, every chain making calculation for the purpose of doing so by angles from the extremities of the three curves. Queen's Wharf.

Friday, 28th: Writing Harbour report. Paid for candlestick Canadian Institute £1/12; Ink stands 7s 6d; Candles 1s 10d.

Saturday, 29th: Sectioning [Walter] MacFarlanes Lot (say 10s).

Monday, 31st: Out with Mr Cumberland all day calling on professors at the colleges & others about proposed *Journal*. Cab 16s 6d. Showing Mr Cumberland boundary of Asylum grounds.

June 1852

Tuesday, 1st: At Engineers office about boundary of Reserve round Lunatic Asylum grounds &c. Left all papers connected with survey there. Make plans of Asylum boundaries for Mr Cumberland say £1. Paid Scott & Laidlaw for cover for Canadian Institute letters £2.

Wednesday, 2nd: Recd letter from Judge Brown & replied that I would be down on Friday. On Reserve survey defining boundary of office block, commissariat &c. [Alfred] Brunel. Canadian Institute evening.

Thursday, 3rd: Rain. Sent in acct Ontario, Simcoe & Lake Huron Ry. Received payment from contractors for ditto £16/17/6. Preparing to go to Ogdensburg tomorrow. Paid Andrew what I borrowed lately £1.5. Called to see Mr Paterson evening.

Friday, 4th: Out on Reserve survey, defining boundaries Victoria Square west end of Front Street, and laying off corner stakes every chain. Moberly & Donovan. Left on steamer *Baystate* for Ogdensburg. Cab 1s 10½d; Boat fare £1/5 [total] £1/7.

Saturday, 5th: At Ogdensburg. Saw Judge Brown and went down the Railway 60 miles to Malone. Meet Col Schlatter.

Monday, 7th: Waited today to see if Mr Tate comes. Saw Mr Shanly at Prescott. Went to hear Cathric harp 10s.

Tuesday, 8th: Mr Tate not come. Paid bill at Hotel. Left in steamer *Champlain*. Fare £1/5.

Wednesday, 9th: Pretty rough on the lake. Arrived about noon. Henry bad with ague. Saw Mr Cumberland about Railway.

Thursday, 10th: At Mr Cumberlands & Canada Company. Saw Mr Hall & Cunningham at Capt Lefroys about mine Lake Superior. Paid *Family Herald* for Canadian Institute £1/5. After tea.

Friday, 11th: Saw Capt Wallace of Cobourg. Put notice regarding Central Railway in *Globe*. Wrote to Mr Hall also to Mr Russell about mine Lake Superior. Paid rent to Mr Grant up to May last £4/7/6. Sent £2/10 to George Stewart.

Saturday, 12th: Recd from draft on committee for £30 — £29/15. Paid Mr Leask (still due £3/16/10) £5. Paid Andrew (on bill £4/15/0) £5; Scott & Laidlaw (£1/17/11) £2/10; Paid *Family Herald* on the 10th £1/5; Paid treasurer Canadian Institute £8/5/7½. J.O. Browne paid to acct £5 — still due £5/12/6. Canadian Institute hired editor [Henry Yule Hind].

Monday, 14th: Wrote to Mr Sang enclosing draft for £10, 2nd instalment on instruments £12/10. Left in steamer *Magnet* for Peterboro.

Landed at Port Hope. Hired buggy & went as far as Grahams Tavern. 12 oclock P.M.

Tuesday, 15th: Breakfast at Grahams Tavern & arrived at Peterboro about 10 oclock. Saw the Peterboro folks & Mr Tate of Ogdensburg. Left Peterboro at ½ 4 oclock to catch boat at Port Hope. Arrived just in time to get on board *Magnet* at 12 PM. Left horse & buggy on the wharf. Expense tolls 7s 6d; Boat fare 10s. Sent down 15s to Mr McIntyre to pay for buggy. I brought the man's whip with me in the hurry.

Wednesday, 16th: Left with John Wallace in team for Barrie. Stop at Mays at night.

Thursday, 17th: Left Mays & arrived afternoon at Barrie. Land all taken up. Went to dig Indian mounds. Very hot & muscatos.

Friday, 18th: Left Barrie, Team on board steamer, met Dr Harris from Balmoral, arrived at Bradford. We came down Yonge street: Organ Grinder! Capt Wallace takes 600 acres of Canada Company.

Saturday, 19th: Letters from Mr Russell, Peterboro & Mr Worthington. Saw Mr Berczy. Map for Scobie Almanac.

Monday, 21st: Out on Reserve staking off curves next Queen street. Moberly expenses 1s 6d. Donovan & 10 soldiers working.

Tuesday, 22nd: Out on Reserve lockspitting & curves Stewart & self. Donovan & soldiers working. Evening making out description No.5 for O.A.L.H. Railway Co — say £1/5.

Wednesday, 23rd: Out on Reserve going over centre curves, Stewart & self lockspitting. Called on Howard about [indecipherable] Foundry. Recd letter from McNeil. Mr Sootheran called for me to go to Hamilton about proposed water works. Recd letter from Smithsonian Institute, Washington.

Thursday, 24th: Left for Hamilton, fare 7s 6d. Went up the mountain and examined the springs.

Friday, 25th: Hire a buggy this morning to examine the country in the rear of the mountain. Drove down with David to Stoney Creek to see Mr Ridout. Buggy 7s 6d. He was at Hamilton, saw him there. Went to the mountain afterward for specimen of water. Specimen vials 1s 10d; Bill at hotel 12s 6d. Left in steamer for Toronto 7s 6d ; Cab 1s 3d; [Total] £1/18/9. Saw Shanly, made promise if the Goderich road goes on.

Monday, 28th: Writing letter to Mr Sootheran relating to Hamilton water works. Seeing Dr Croft about analyzing water.

Tuesday, 29th: Writing letter to Sootheran. Met W. Ogilvie from New York.

Wednesday, 30th: Drawing plan of the village of Acton. Recd for this £1. Saw Mr Paterson.

July 1852

Thursday, 1st: Drawing up papers & plans connected with Tiffanys patent. Heard that Cumberland was about to be appointed engineer of North Railway. Wrote to him at Quebec, also to Judge Hall of Peterboro. Saw Mr & Mrs Paterson.

Friday, 2nd: At Tiffanys patent papers, to charge him £2. Recd cash £1/5. Surveying Leisters south on Mutual street for Jarvis 10s. At Barnum Museum.

Saturday, 3rd: Making additions to plan of Acton Recd 5s. To go to Hamilton with Mr Sootheran tomorrow morning at 8 oclock. At Engineers office making arrangements to place stone monuments on Monday.

Monday, 5th: Went to Hamilton last night. Met Mr Sootheran. Saw Bridges. Expenses Boat 7s 6d; Hotel &c 6s 3d ; Boat 7s 6d [Total] £1/1/3. Came down this morning. Went up to Engineers office pointing out boundaries of d[itt]o. Instructing about planting stones. Say ½ day.

Tuesday, 6th: Superintending the planting of stones round Engineers Block on Front street 1 day. Men employed by ordnance.

Wednesday, 7th: Commence making copy of general harbour plan. Mr Conger called, round with him about various matters.

Thursday, 8th: Recd letter from Col Schlatter this morning asking for Report of Harbour. Writing ditto.

Friday, 9th: Writing Harbour Report.

Saturday, 10th: Harbour Report finished and sent off (19 pages). Left for Acton with Mr Adams. Tolls 1s 3d. At Streetsville 3s 1½d.

Monday, 12th: Writing early history of Canadian Institute at Streetsville yesterday. Tea at Hornby 1s. Walk into Stuart town last night, took stage 6 miles this morning to Acton. Valuing property for Mr Adams & left for Georgetown.

Tuesday, 13th: Left Georgetown for home. Bed 7½, stage 3s 9d [Total] 4s 4½d. Saw Sheriff Conger & Tate up about Central Railway & printing of Report. Mr Ross, Engineer for English capitals & T[homas].Keefer expected up tomorrow to go over this.

Wednesday, 14th: Making various arrangements about Central Railway scheme. Saw Cumberland on his arrival from Quebec. Reported on balance of Mr Adams land at Acton. Fee £2/10, expenses 12s 3d.

Thursday, 15th: Making arrangements to start overland to Peterboro, copying plans &c of route.

Friday, 16th: Paid Brandy &c for Mr Conger 12s 6d. Started with Mr [John] Ross, Keefer, Conger, Tate, Cottingham for Lake Scugog — through Scarboro, Markham, Pickering &c. Arrived at Brooklin. Smoking cigars &c &c.

Saturday, 17th: Left in steam boat for Lindsay. Met James Hall, [John] Langton MPP & Judge [George Barker] Hall, a deputation with carriages, went over to Peterboro 30 miles in 3½ hours. Magnificent dinner at Chambers for the distinguished experts.

Monday, 19th: Left for Cobourg, Ross, Keefer, Tate, Conger, & Judge Hall. Champagne dinner at Cobourg — feted well. Tate & I received instructions through [Samuel] Keefer to commence survey of long line through Peterboro, my section to be from Peterboro westward, to touch Lake Scugog and join the survey lines of Trunk Railway at most favorable point towards Toronto. Arrived at Toronto this morning. Boat 10s. Making preparations to start. Purchased level from Mr Percival for 70 dollars to be paid £5, balance in six months.

Wednesday, 21st: Paid Timson old acct in full £1/5; 100 ft chain to cost £2/10. Recd from Capt Wallace for three month (to pay at Commercial Bank) £10. Left Toronto in buggy for Peterboro £11/12/6. Tolls & meals to Perry's Corners 2s 6d.

Thursday, 22nd: From Perry's Corners to the Bay in search of section of plank road. Expenses 3s 9d. To Brooklin & Reach & Cartwright examining the country. Put up at McQuades Tavern. Supper porridge (pudding) & milk. Expenses horse & self 3s 9d. Exploring through Manvers morn 1s 3d; Through Cavan expenses & tolls 1s. Arrived at Peterboro about 8 oclock, put up at Chambers.

Saturday, 24th: Saw Tate who is about to be married. Stewart &c. Copying plans, sections &c at Courthouse. Over at Judge Halls. Recd from him £20 on acct of St.L.& L.H. Ry. Drove out towards Smith [township] & to Stewarts.

Monday, 26th: Sent to Father check for exp 1/3 — £20. Bill at Chambers yet to pay £1. Sent buggy round by boat & started on horseback to explore for Railway line towards Toronto. Expenses at Mount Pleasant 1s 3d. At NW corner of Cavan by moonlight — arrived at Metcalfs.

Tuesday, 27th: Expenses at Metcalf 4s 6d. Accompanied by Dr Irons & W. Matchett, through part of Ops, Manvers, NW corner of Cavan & returned to Metcalfs.

Wednesday, 28th: Expenses at Metcalfs 6s 3d; Horse & shoes 3s 9d. Accompanied by Dr Irons as far as Manvers, exploring to NW corner. Fed at Mr Giles who accompanied across floating bridge to path into Cartwright, difficult keeping path. Landed at Malcolms (from Fife).

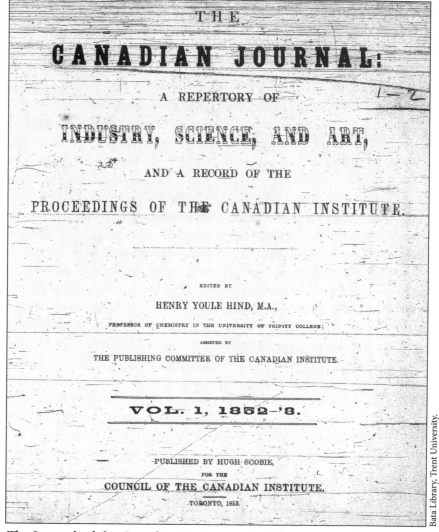

The Journal *of the Canadian Institute, edited by Henry Yule Hind, first appeared in 1853.*

Thursday, 29th: Left Mr Malcolms, feed at Tullys 6d. Dinner at Coveys 2s 6d. Through Reach, Whitby & Pickering to Claremont. Thunder & lightning.

Friday, 30th: Expenses at Clairmont 3s 9d. Exploring towards Toronto. Expenses at Markham village & tolls 2s; at Powers &c 3s 3d. Arrived at Toronto, attended Council meeting of Canadian Institute. Proof first sheet of *Journal.*

Saturday, 31st: Paid Rowsell [stationers] account 5s 7d. At Engineers Royal office, composing plans with Mr Walker — ½ [day]. Paid for horse hire, Grantham £5. Saw Mr Sootheran. David burnt out at Hamilton, lost all his carving tools. Paid Cruthers for coat £1/15. Newspaper from Orillia.

August 1852

Monday, 2nd: At Royal Engineers office composing plans &c. Received letter from Mr Sang, instrument ready. Instructed him to send it by steam care John M Mackay, 121 Water street, New York. Wrote also to Mr Leather & Orillia.

Tuesday, 3rd: On Reserve survey with Mr Walker & Donovan planting stakes round asylum property as requested by Mr Wilkinson. Expenses 2s 6d.

Wednesday, 4th: On Reserve survey, verifying measurements of boundaries. Donovan & self. Saw Mr Sootheran.

Thursday, 5th: Calculating distances of boundary lines & bearings for description. No news from Quebec. Wrote second letter to Mr Sootheran, water supply of Hamilton.

Friday, 6th: At Royal Engineers office. Mappings &c. Meeting of publishing committee. Recd Report of Harbour from Mr Cull. He has been looking over and correcting.

Saturday, 7th: At Engineers office comparing & assimilating plans, making measurements for such about Old Fort & Queen's Wharf, measuring Railway Bridge &c &c calculating position — westward line. No letter from Peterboro people! At Henrys farm today, Father & David.

Monday, 9th: Met Mr Cumberland, long conversation to appoint me Assistant Engineer Toronto, Simcoe & Lake Huron Railway, to be confirmed tomorrow. Quite unexpected!!! ——————————— At Engineers office (Ordnance) placing stakes with Mr Walker & Lefroy commissariat portion of Reserve, also mapping & assimilating. Council meeting evening.

Tuesday, 10th: Writing letter to Lieut Wilkinson concerning the difference between plans & expenses of my paper measuring distances on plan & calculating bearings of remainder of boundary line — say ½ day. Met Mr Berczy, president of Ontario, Simcoe & Lake Huron Railway who congratulated me on my appointment as Assistant Engineership on his line. Have not seen Mr Cumberland yet. (Poor Jane [sister] went this morning.)

Wednesday, 11th: Recd letter from Mr [Charles] Berczy, president O.S. & L.H. Railway informing me of my appointment as Assistant Engineer under Mr Cumberland! Examining plans and making preparations to start with party to examine & look over line tomorrow. Paid for small trunk 12s 6d.

Thursday, 12th: Commenced making general survey of Railway from Toronto towards Barrie. Expenses 5s 3d. Put up with party at Peacocks.

Friday, 13th: Expenses at Peacocks 15s. Left Mr King, Cambie & Marshall behind.

Saturday, 14th: Expenses at Curtis 7s 6d; Dinner &c. Burwick 5s; Sent £5 to Mr Leather; Buggy 5s.

Monday, 16th: Expenses of King party at Thornhill & waggon £1/7/3. Party at Binghams £1/2/6.

Tuesday, 17th: Expenses at Playters 10s. Dinner at Newmarket 4s.

Wednesday, 19th: At Holland Landing 11s 3d; At Bradford 4s.

Thursday, 19th: At Mr Sprys 8s 9d. Dinner at Wallaces 3s.

Friday, 20th: Paid at Shaws 6s 3d; At Thomsons 3s 9d.

Saturday, 21st: At Barrie 10s 6d; Barrie to Toronto 10s. [Total for week] £8/9.

Monday, 23rd: Made arrangements to settle with men. Stewart commenced plotting section.

Tuesday, 24th, Wednesday, 25th: Paid men & expenses in full. Recd money for such and other expenses from Cumberland. Left with Cumberland, Board &c &c to see Bridge open beyond Buffalo at Niagara Falls. At Buffalo cars to portage. Gigantic structure. Great dinner. Very hot!

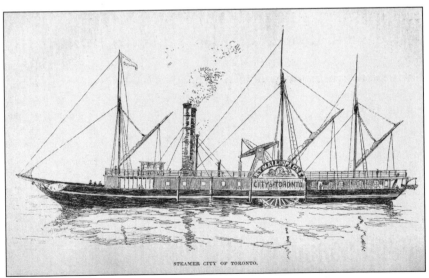

The steamer City of Toronto *carried passengers across Lake Ontario between Toronto and Queenston. From* Landmarks Volume 2 *(1896) by J.R. Robertson.*

Thursday, 26th: Left Buffalo by boat. Lost carpet bag, found it at Manchester. Buggy to Queenston. Slept on board steamer *City of Toronto.*

Friday, 27th: Return to Toronto. Trip would cost £3 or £4. At section and making out report.

Saturday, 28th: At Estimates of quantities. Made draft on Railway committee at Peterboro £32/12/9, less 8s 2d, £32/4/7 being in full of acct. Paid Webb B Canadian Institute £5. Buger & Leesom (Gillespie) £5, rent of office £4/7/6. Watch chain & repair £1/6/3. [Total] £16/13/9.

Monday, 30th: This week at approximate Estimates of quantities on line &c &c.

September 1852

[Diaries blank for numerous days in September]

Monday, 6th: At drawings of alterations & changes of line &c &c.

Wednesday, 8th: Cumberland & Braund gone to Quebec.

Saturday, 11th: Description No. 6 Contractor of O.S. & L.H. Ry. Say 1s 5d. Mr Ruttan [Cobourg] paid acct in full £4/10.

Monday, 13th: Monday evening left town with carriage, Stewart & Marshall £7/5. Tolls & expenses of party at Brougham 13/3.

Tuesday, 14th: At Elgin Mills station carriage broke down. Expenses 8s 6d. Board & lodging 12s 3d.

Wednesday, 15th: At Mitchell's Corners [Machell's Corners, now Aurora]. Tolls & dinner 4s 6d. Arrived at Newmarket. Tolls & expenses, hotel 12s 6d.

Thursday, 16th: At Newmarket 3s 6d. Arrived at Holland Landing. Maj Horn & party 16s.

Friday, 17th: Feed for horses, meals, tolls &c 8s; Paid Marshall 4 days @ 3s 9d — 15s; Carriage £3.

Saturday, 18th: Total recorded daily expenses — £7/14/4. Instrument arrived from Kirkcaldy.
Paid Twysir for dressing case £1/2/6.

October 1852

Tuesday, 5th: Left Toronto for Barrie with £3/12; Stage 10s; Meals 2s 6s. Saw Mr Gibbon & agreed with him to start tomorrow exploring.

Wednesday, 6th: With W Gibbon by Olivers. Mite & Monroe. Mr Gardner & party arrived.

Thursday, 7th: With Gibbon & Gardner up Penetanguishene road & Olivers Mill. Had Marks horse. Gardner to commence survey down Willow Creek [indecipherable] he went home. Heavy rain now by town line. Flos & Vesper. Put up at Mr Brown.

Friday, 8th: Paid Mr Brown 7s 6d. Up Penetanguishene road, Wood bridge road, Sturgeon Creek & Hog Creek summits. Put up at Hamilton.

Saturday, 9th: Rode up to Archys before breakfast. Paid Hamilton 8s 9d; Mr Brown 2s 6d. Rained for three days.

Sunday, 10th: Ostler at Marks 1s 3d.

Monday, 11th: Left for Nottawasaga. Feed at Roots 1s 3d. At Mr Cummer 1s 3d. Very bad roads. Put up at Crows.

Tuesday, 12th: Examining the mouth of the river & adjoining country. At Crows exp 15s.

Wednesday, 13th: Left for Barrie. Fed at Roots 1s 3d. Mr Campbell not come. Gardner finished section to Willow Creek — practicable!

Thursday, 14th: With Mr Gibbon examining valley of Willow Creek. Campbell not come. Instructed Gardner to continue running line to Sturgeon Bay.

Friday, 15th: Left for Toronto. Stage & meals 12s 6d; Total paid £3/3/9. In pocket 8s 9d.

Saturday, 16th: Ride on locomotive 12 miles up the lines. James Block, surveyor, paid £1. Canadian Institute.

Sunday, 17th: Wrote to Wilkinson about London survey yesterday.

Monday, 18th: Recd from Mr Courtright £25; Gave George £6; Paid stage 5s; Bus to Richmond Hill (meals 2s 6d) 4s 6d. Having lost stage Brigham drove me up to *Amsterdam*. Slept on board steamer.

Wednesday, 20th: Left Coldwater for Sturgeon Bay & Penetang. John Macdonald boat — fine day & breeze. Old Lake Beach train road Peters Bay about 100 feet. 5s Coldwater; 1s 10½d Sturgeon Bay; Paid Caswell $10 boat.

Thursday, 21st: Left Penetanguishene for Barrie. Paid Tavern at Penetang 7s 6d. Dinner at Hamiltons 3s 9d; Mrs Brown 1s 3d.

Friday, 22nd: Left Barrie for Nottawasaga. Roots 1s; O Conner 3s ½d.

Saturday, 23rd: Left Crows for mouth of Rivers & Hurontario Mills. Crows say 7s 6d

Sunday, 24th: Left Hurontario Mills for Barrie. Paid at Honeygoods 1s 3d. Hurontario Tavern 11s 3d. Cumberland refunded expenses paid by me on town road last week commencing at Orillia. I have yet to pay Crow 7s 6d. Cash balances correct. In pocket £20/10.

Monday, 25th: Cumberland left for Toronto. Gibbon & party commenced before him. Gardner and ditto from Sundance to Hen & Chickens. Origin for sounding cut. Preparing to make survey of Harbour Nottawasaga Bay. [illegible here] Marks pd in full up to this morning for 22nd and horse team. [some illegible accounts here] Went out to Willow Creek portage. Engaged Smith and boat to convey self & supplies for Gibbons party.

Wednesday, 27th: Marks team to portage and down river with Smith. Put up at Crows.

Thursday, 28th: Rain & N.W. storm. Cant go on. Crows team hauling team over portage.

Friday, 29th: Paid Mr Crow 1s 10½d part for Cumberlands horses & 5s ox team to haul boat over. Also meals & bed for Smith. Started for Hurontario. Rain & wind. Put up at Markles.

Saturday, 30th: Sound Harbour & Island, putting up flags stations &c. Commenced picketing base line. Smith & Hickley.

Sunday, 31st: Dinner at Buirts.

November 1852

Monday, 1st: Windy morning. Cutting base line along beach. Smith, Markle & Hickley. Gardner & party arrived. Sounding afternoon.

Tuesday, 2nd: Sounding with team round to North West, measuring angles & men at Base line. Smith, Archy & Clark.

Sandford Fleming in the field on survey in mid-life.

Wednesday, 3rd: Blows hard from N.West, impossible to go out. Men cutting out base line. Smith, Archy & Clark.

Thursday, 4th: Stormy. Left men to cut out base line & started for river to see Sibbald. Stopped at Crows with Sibbald. Letter at post office.

Friday, 5th: Saw Gibbons party. All well. Left for Hurontario.

Saturday, 6th: Out forenoon. Smith, Markle & Hickley. Very stormy, hail & rain. Could do nothing. In pocket today £14/2/0. Should be £14/5/6. At Hurontario Mills.

Sunday, 7th: Mr Gibbon, Stewart, [Clarence W.] Moberly, Tim & Jim arrived from River mouth. Recd from Mr Gibbon $15.

Monday, 8th: Calm! Sounding.

Tuesday, 9th: Sounding! Blows fresh.

Wednesday, 10th: (Borrowed from Stewart £2/10) (paid on the 15th) Paid board & lodging for Smith & self £2/5; 2½ days of Markle @ 5s — 12s 6d; 2½ days Hillock @ 5s — 12s 6d ;12 yds cotton @ 7d — 7s 6d.

December 1852

[days missing in November and December]

Wednesday, 15th: Moved up to Mrs Buchans.

Monday, 20th: Borrowed from Mr Leask £5.

Tuesday, 21st: Left for Barrie.

Wednesday, 22nd: Paid Mr Alexander for Mr Cumberland £2/10.

Thursday, 23rd: Returned from Barrie. Expenses £1/12/6.

Tuesday, 28th: Lent Father £1. Paid *Globe* for Railway to Peterboro advertisement £2/4. Cumberland to pay half. Note at Commercial [Bank] dates from today, due in 3 months.

Thursday, 30th: Bill discounted at Commercial Bank for £50 — disc 15s 8d. Paid Mr Leask, borrowed later £5. Mr Ambrose for coupon £10.

Friday, 31st: Pd Andrew in full up to date £6; Paid McBean & Withrow £8/17/4.

CHAPTER NINE
The Grand Esplanade 1853

Eight years after eighteen-year-old Sandford Fleming decided to leave his Scottish homeland, the young surveyor at last felt secure. With a position as assistant engineer for the Ontario, Simcoe and Huron Railway (later the Northern), the first railway in what is now the province of Ontario, the future looked bright. In his first months on the job, since his appointment in August 1852, he had already finalized the route north from Barrie, and his survey crew worked through the fall doing soundings around Nottawasaga Harbour, where Hen and Chickens, renamed Collingwood, had been chosen as the O.S. & H. terminus.

The southern section, from Toronto to Barrie, was already well advanced, and although there were still numerous details requiring his attention, the first passenger train ran from the city to Aurora on May 16, 1853, and by June 13, it extended to Bradford. His supervisory duties took him down to Toronto frequently and the introduction of train service replacing the stagecoach, steamer, horse, and canoe he had used in the past greatly shortened the trip. Often he managed to be on hand for Canadian Institute meetings on Saturday nights. In February, he himself delivered an illustrated paper describing Nottawasaga Bay and environs, later published in the *Canadian Journal*, and in May he produced a lithographed map of the Nottawasaga Valley.

At the same time he was still obsessed with visionary schemes for the Toronto Harbour.

The day after he presented his Nottawasaga paper at the Institute, he awoke after a sleepless night: "Mind a good deal excited — couldn't sleep well — got up to get a smoke between 2 and 3 oclock. Conceived an idea of a Grand Esplanade Toronto Harbour. Front street planted with trees — arrangements for 5 Railway termini — space for 10 tracks — site for Canadian Museum at intersection of Esplanade & Yonge St —!!"

Within a few days he had drawn a sketch of the Esplanade plan and on March 1 he submitted the design to Cumberland, the O.S. & H. chief engineer, as his plan for the Toronto railway terminus. Although Cumberland had little to say at the time, Fleming noted in his diary on August 1 that "he has adopted & recommended my plan in Report to Directors. City Papers taking notice of Report calling it Cumberland's plan. My name not known in the matter."

While terminus buildings and other structures were part of his job, Fleming spent much of his time in the field with his survey crew. June and July they spent sounding among the islands off the northern Bruce Peninsula and Saugeen. After a rather roundabout journey by steamers from Toronto via Lake Ontario, the Welland Canal, Lake Erie, the Detroit River, Lake St. Clair, the St. Clair River, and Lake Huron to Manitoulin Island, they visited several Native villages on the island. Fleming did a number of sketches here, but was unable to get any of the Natives to lend or sell them a canoe to do some exploring. With provisions very low, storm clouds threatening, and only one old rowboat at their disposal, they decided to head back to Tobermory, strong winds or no. It was several days before they arrived at Saugeen where they learned that rescue parties had been sent out for them and the residents had chartered a schooner to join the search. A few weeks later the Directors sent a letter of thanks and a cheque for twenty-five pounds to the Saugeen people in appreciation. The response was that they had decided to create a library and name it the Fleming Library, a move that the directors declined, though Fleming was greatly flattered.

Back in Toronto, Fleming's personal life was becoming a little complicated. For some time there had been brief references in his diary of walks with "B," but an exchange of letters in May revealed that Sandford was cooling and "B" was not happy about it. After spending most of the spring and summer in the field, Fleming was back in Toronto in October, and they resumed their discussions. Fleming had not changed and "Bessie" was upset; on November 1 he notes "short walk with B — probably the last one." On November 2 — "Poor Bessie!!!" The identity of "B" is somewhat mysterious, but that he had to make explanations to Mr. and Mrs. Leask indicate some connection there. Not until the last diary entry of the year was her name revealed: "Poor Miss Mitchell."

Meantime, Miss Jean Hall had been paying visits to Martha Hutchison in Toronto and she and Fleming met often when she was in the city. Jeanie Hall was a fourteen-year-old when Fleming first arrived in Peterborough and they had become friends as part of the group that got together for parties and picnics during the time he spent there. After Sandford moved to Toronto, their friendship grew on his frequent returns to Peterborough when he never failed to visit the Halls. Jeanie's father, James Hall, was one of Fleming's mentors and had done much to help him get established in his career. "Walks with Miss Hall" became a frequent entry in the diary when Fleming came down from his duties in the north. On Christmas Day, Fleming and Jeanie Hall attended services at St. James Cathedral. In his New Year's Eve reflections, Fleming notes: "An intimacy growing up with Miss Hall of Peterboro. How it may terminate I don't know."

The year 1853 was a landmark year for Sandford Fleming, both in his personal and professional life. It saw the beginning of the courtship that would lead to his marriage to Miss Ann Jean Hall on January 3, 1855, and it launched him on the path to ever more important railway building projects. In July 1855, he succeeded Cumberland as chief engineer of the Ontario, Simcoe & Huron Railway, the first of his major railway appointments. With his mapping of the Intercolonial to Halifax in the sixties and his westward survey to the Pacific for the Canadian Pacific Railway in the seventies, he became the architect of Canada's rail routes coast to coast.

January 1853

Saturday, 1st: New Years day! Brings to our memory in the middle of business & certain life that another milestone of the journey of life is just passing by and that we are another year nearer the terminus of this uncertain and to all of us untravelled road. Something melancholy in the thought and we cannot help seeing that we pilgrim on happiest in making others happy, that we do not live for ourselves only, but that each of us have our allotted duty to perform to the community in which we live, and to our fellow pilgrims. Ought I not to be thankful for the many blessings bestowed and the success showered upon me during the past year — and ought not I resolve now to act in all cases my part well because it is for eternity and nothing can recall what is past, no not even a second ago. Every action is as it were recorded on the minutes of time for ever and ever! I do not regret the time I have spent (although I deeply regret many other things) and the zeal shown in bringing into existence and into active operation the "Canadian Institute" because I believe it is calculated to do great good to my adopted country, and to begin the New Year well have now resolved to provide for it an endowment of £1,000 when all that is mortal of me returns to its mother dust, the interest of which to be annually expended in furthering the objects of the society. To effect this object I have already taken steps to assure my life for that sum and may the over master of all things enable this humble creature while he likes to lack no opportunity in carrying this scheme out as cheerfully and as easily as it is now commenced.

With last year my success in Canada & good fortune seem to be commenced, whether may it continue remains for future to tell. The "floods" of the tide of my "affairs" seem to have occurred on the 2nd of January when I started to make survey of Harbour on Gloucester Bay — besides being consistently honorably and profitably employed ever since — have secured (through Mr Passmore) 400 acres of land and a span of S.W. at that place and 200 at Hurontario Mills / proposed terminus of Toronto R.R. to both of which places R[ailwa]ys are likely to go and these lands of course will be highly valuable. My present appointment on the O.S. & H. Ry as asst engineer which commenced on August 10th last is £250 a year and £100 for personal expenses, in all £350.

Tuesday, 4th: At R.R. Office as usual. Having been busily engaged all day & evening lately the chief has allowed me a day or two to finish up ordnance plans which I commenced today.

Wednesday, 5th: Directors went up the line as far as Matchells Corners [now Aurora] in 2nd class carriage — in sleighs from there to McGaffeys (contractor) where we partook of his open hearted hospitality. Arrived in Toronto about ½ past six. John Buchan on the [indecipherable] Wrote to Mr Stevenson at Lake Balsam.

Thursday, 6th: At plan of ordnance reserve. Board of directors meet tonight to receive Chief Engineers Report on Harbour &c &c. At Council meeting Canadian Institute.

Friday, 7th: This is my birthday! And I believe I am now 26 years of age — and must therefore have been born in the year 1827. At the office. Sent Mr Walker £1/10. Recd letter from Melville. His mills returning £5. Called at assurance office but papers not ready yet. At Capt [J.H.] Lefroys evening, tea. Mention proposed endowment of £1,000 but not the name of the proposed donor. Saw Dr Primrose at Ls.

Saturday, 8th: Last night writing description of land &c for Rlwy. At office this morning. At ordnance plan afternoon. Canadian Institute meeting in the evening well attended. Chief Justice [Robinson] & 34 others. Rules & regulations and annual address of president. Very good indeed. Excellent man Capt Lefroy. Invitation from Passmore to dine at Douglas tomorrow.

Sunday, 9th: Not at church today. Sorting letters forenoon. Dined with Mr Douglas. Up to Yorkville and home at ½ past nine. Met Brown, Humphrey, Lawrence & sisters at Douglas's, and Urquhart at Buchans. John in bed a little high.

Monday, 10th: Getting description of lands from Dr Beattie. At ordnance plan and during evening. Mr Smith at Cumberlands afternoon. Directors met tonight.

Tuesday, 11th: At ordnance plan morning. Left both at engineers office. Instructed to go with Directors tomorrow to visit harbours on Lake Huron. Making preparations, plans, &c &c. At Leasks. Preparing for tomorrow.

Wednesday, 12th: Left Toronto at 9 oclock by railway along with Directors. Cheney, A. Morrison, [E.C.] Hancock, Macdonald, Gilmour, for the north. Sleigh from Matchells Corners [Aurora] to Barrie. Dined at Bartles. Arrived at Barrie, deputation of inhabitants met Directors. Put up at Frasers. Wine, drinking &c. Slept on floor with Hancock about 2 hours.

Thursday, 13th: Left for Hen & Chickens [Collingwood]. Sheriff [B.W.] Smith, Lount, MacNabb, OBrien, Cameron, Romaine, Boy's, Sanford &c — great procession across plains terrain or old beach on Lororontio. Perhaps same as Penetanguishene, curious position of two streams, one perhaps 20 ft above the other separated by narrow ridges of tenacious clay. Websters clean mills. Nottawasaga village. Bag piper, dinner (haggis), dancing, laughing, sleeping on floor at McGlashens. 1½ hours sleep.

Friday, 14th: Left a daybreak for Hurontario mills. Breakfast. Walked over to little harbour named by Sheriff Collingwood Harbour. Boat race to island, dinner at Buists. Bagpipes. Sleighs to Stephens. Champagne. Hancock, Lount, sleep on floor.

Saturday, 15th: Breakfast at Stephens. Judge poorly. Good sleighing. Arrived at Crows in Sunnidale. Lunch. Proceed to river mouth, bitter cold N.W. wind, breakers rolling in. Plans unrolled. Very cold. Sheriff named Harbour Nottawasga. Returned to Crows, first rate dinner, champagne, smoking. Pretty children. Hancock full of fun after going to bed. Magicians &c &c.

Sunday, 16th: Left Crows. Good sleighing, corduroy road filled with snow. Arrived at Barrie in good time. Dinner. Tea. Champagne. Oyster supper. Dr Hancock very quiet. Only three words. Go to bed. Comfortable nights sleep.

Monday, 17th: Left Barrie. Deputation Judge &c &c. Amsterdam. Champagne dinner at Matchells Corners. At Finchs. Champagne supper. Very Happy. Arrived at Toronto late. Sleighing very bad.

Tuesday 18th: Get up late. At office. Ordered "Maple Leaf" paid. 5/. Saw Cumberland. At description of lands &c &c. Dined at Hancocks in evening, wine. Drawing up report of survey to the north. Home about 12 oclock.

Wednesday, 19th: Got up about 9 oclock. Capt McCall at office. Saw By on King st. DeWitt & Judge Orton in office. £9/2/6 for first semiannual premium on policy of £1,000 in Canada Life Assurance office. At Royal

Engineers office. Walker at plan. John Macdonald from Sturgeon Bay — they had extensive preparations for arrival of Directors, disappointed.

Thursday, 20th: At office as usual. Meeting of Board at night. Directors decided on terminating at Hen & Chickens, now Collingwood Harbour — fortunate to have received 200 acres near it. Called at Mr Allansons. Very low poor man & circumstances low also. Gave him £2/10 for parks account.

Friday, 21st: At Mr Cumberlands house, assist with plans of University grounds for proposed site for Government House. Paid Stewart tailor £1/5.

Saturday, 22nd: Called at office in the morning. At Mr Cumberlands day & evening at Canadian Institute. Interesting paper by [Henry Youle] Hind on geology of Toronto. Brandy & cigars. Passmore & Cole.

Sunday, 23rd: Up late this morning. At home forenoon. At Cumberlands afternoon & evening. Wrote to Mr Sang & Gibbon, also officially to McGaffey.

Monday, 24th: Newspaper from Peterboro this morning. Railway meetings going on. Mary Benson married [newspaper clipping of notice of her marriage to Thomas R. Merritt, of St Catharines stuck on page]. Wrote to Melville (Collingwood). At Royal Engineers office. Staking out terminus at foot of Yonge & Bay streets. At Cumberlands afternoon & evening. Old Tom Ridout came in.

Tuesday, 25th: At Cumberlands in the morning. Planting stake at Ewarts lots on Yonge street terminus, broke axe, also crowbar. Cost 2/6 [plus] 2/5 — [total] 5s. At Cumberlands afternoon & evening. Preparing to go tomorrow with engineer to Matchells Corners.

Wednesday, 26th: Up at 7 oclock to be at Queen's Wharf at 8. Very cold. Engineer didnt go. At R.E. office all day making out description of reserve with Mr Walker. At Cumberlands in the evening. Letter from Mr MacNabb, Saugeen.

Thursday, 27th: Excessively cold, water in urn frozen. At Office and at Cumberlands. Willie Bell. At Mr L evening, supper.

Friday, 28th: At office in the morning, Cumberlands afternoon. Commenced writing paper on Nottawasaga. Cameron called, talked a good deal, remained until near 11 — angry! Sat up nearly to 2 oclock.

Saturday, 29th: Making drawings for paper on Nottawasaga forenoon, Cumberlands afternoon. At Canadian Institute. Fortunately chairman has a paper on currency of Canada, Britain & U States which he read. Mr Valentine C.E. at meeting.

Sunday, 30th: At home forenoon & afternoon reading &c. Walked round to Cumberlands afternoon but didnt go in. At church evening — walked round with B, saw light in Cumberlands, walked as far as avenue.

Monday, 31st: At Cumberlands early. Plan of Government dock all day and evening. Posted description of Reserves to Lieut Wilkinson this morning.

February 1853

Tuesday, 1st: At Cumberlands forenoon. Went up to Royal Engineers office. Cumberland again afternoon, finishing plans of Government House — putting on motto in Indian. Interpretation — the Great Chiefs home [these plans were rejected and Cumberland tried again in 1859]. Dinner with him in evening. Mrs C, Miss C, Smith & [William George] Storm [Cumberland's partner]. Home about eleven.

Wednesday, 2nd: Tire of locomotive broke. Went up in stage to Newmarket. Expenses 7/6. Went down in sleigh to see Searls. Paid at R[ichmond] Hill — $5 to Bingham for driving me up to Amsterdam last fall £1/5. Call at Mr Roe's evening. Miss R plays piano well. Two Miss Lawtons. Saw also Col Colton.

Thursday, 3rd: First brick house built in Toronto in 1811 on S.E. corner of King & Frederick near Canada Company office by Quentin St George, Mr Roe says. Matchells Corners & Newmarket ascertaining boundaries between properties on new line. Drove down to Matchells Corners afterwards to see timetable. At Mr Roe's evening — chat with him about American War in 1812.

Friday, 4th: Left in stage for home. Paid hotel 11/3, stage & breakfast 6/3. At office afternoon. Also at Royal Engineers office. At home evening. Cameron called, did nothing.

Saturday, 5th: Making out description for land at Queen's Wharf for terminus. Took down transit to office. Recd letter from Mr Stevenson of Bexley. Canadian Institute evening, paper by Capt Lefroy on the winds.

Sunday, 6th: At Dr Burns [Knox] church in forenoon. Dinner at Mrs Hutchisons. Called at Hollands, also at Drummonds on Gerrard street. Arranging letters of Canadian Institute in the evening.

Monday, 7th: Took down all letters and papers connected with C[anadian] Institute to [Alfred] Brunel. Plotting survey of Newmarket lands & at Queen's Wharf station. At Royal Engineers office, calculating areas &c in the evening up very late (2 oclock) writing out the dates by which the boundaries were defined. Paid for watch key 3/9.

Tuesday, 8th: Getting papers prepared by Gamble for the purpose of making final arrangements about Newmarket & Holland Landing stations. Saw Cumberland — getting better. Too late for stage. Saw Shanlys report on Toronto Harbour. Writing reply until past 1 oclock. Passmore at tea.

Wednesday, 9th: Left Toronto by stage this morning to arrange about Newmarket & Holland Landing stations. Arrived at Newmarket. Saw Col Cotter. He will either make up or guarantee to the Coy the difference of cost between two plans or not, the amount to be upwards of £2,000 — he yet not arranged — so I instructed A.A. McGaffey to proceed grading ground for station at Lounts. At Oaka Tubers concert in the evening. Chat with Mr Cawthra and he afterwards.

Thursday, 10th: Left in sleigh for Holland Landing. Saw McMaster & Chapman. All day with the latter and succeeded in making an arrangement — he is to see Rogers tomorrow who has a mortgage on the land. In the evening making plan of depot grounds and rewriting deed of conveyance. To bed about 12 oclock.

Friday, 11th: All day negotiating with McMaster, Rogers & Chapman. Succeeded in making arrangements. McMaster took up mortgage & I gave him a check on Mr C. Strong & Co for £105.10. Got deed of conveyance signed by Chapman & wife, also release from Rogers. Went over to Newmarket. Paid May 11/6.

Saturday, 12th: Paid Forsyth 8/9. Left in stage for Toronto 7/0. Arrived about noon. Poor Allanson dead! Yesterday morning! Received quarters pay £87/10. Letter of credit for Mr Sang £31/5 (£25 sterling). Called on Mr Allansons family! At Canadian Institute. Mr Hershfilder read paper on Oriental Literature.

Sunday, 13th: At church forenoon. Mr Allansons funeral afternoon. Death, from Dr Chambers — Manhood will come, and old age will come, and the dying but will come, and the very last look you shall ever cast on your acquaintances will come, and the agony of parting breath will come, and the time when you are stretched a lifeless corpse before the eyes of weeping relations will come, and the coffin that is to enclose you will come, and that house when the company assembles to carry you to the churchyard will come, and that minute when you are put into the ground will come, and the throwing in of loose earth into the narrow house where you are laid, and the spreading of green sod over it. All all come to every living creature.

Monday, 14th: At office & at Cumberlands. He is writing review of Shanly's report. Peter Cameron in the evening — "Logic"! Wrote to Stewart to come up & telegraph 2/6. Paid Mrs Buchan for months lodging £3. Paid David for tripod making £1/2.

Tuesday, 15th: [entered in diary as Monday the 14th] At office seeing about Holland Landing station. McMaster in town. Cumberland writing review of Shanly's report on Toronto Harbour. At Island with B in sleigh. Beach near [indecipherable] filled up. Paid Scott & Laidlaw £5 leaving balance of £1/9/8. Paid Jas W Macdonald in full £5. Paid Mother to date £5. All this happened on Tuesday [15] instead of Monday.

Wednesday, 16th: Wrote to Mr Sang enclosing draft for £25 sterling. Wrote to Percival enclosing check £12/10. Survey of line from Custom House to Gas Works. Very wet & sloppy. At paper evening.

Thursday, 17th: Plotting yesterdays survey. Writing paper on Nottawasaga in the evening, up late! Recd from Mr Cumberland (paid by me to Mr Alexander of Barrie) £2/10. To advertisement Peterboro railway 1/2.

Friday, 18th: Design for Timmons forenoon. Description of Trents lot & writing paper. This evening also at Council meeting. Saw Locomotive at Goods foundry afterwards. Telegraph to Stewart 2/6. Recd from Mr Smith for Canadian Institute 15/. Lent to Father £3. Lent to Dennis £1/3/9.

Saturday, 19th: J. Stoughton Dennis paid on acct £10/1/3. Finishing sketch of arrangement of buildings for proposed terminus at foot of Yonge street. Templeton Brown from Peterboro called. Lent him Leathers level for G. Stewart. Saw Mr James Hall who says stock of Grand Junction Railway all taken up in England. Read paper on Nottawasaga Valley at the Canadian Institute. Attendance about 30 including Chief Justice Robinson, Justice Draper, Arnold, Baldwin, [Henry] Scadding and others — paper well received and requested to be published in *Canadian Journal* by the president.

Sunday, 20th: (Mind a good deal excited — couldn't sleep well — got up to get a smoke between 2 and 3 oclock Conceived an idea of Grand Esplanade Toronto Harbour. Front street planted with trees — arrangements for 5 Railway termini — space for 10 tracks — site for Canadian Museum at intersection of Esplanade & Yonge St —!!) At church forenoon & evening. David there evening. Beautiful clear moonlight. Went to Mrs Hutchison. Romping with the children.

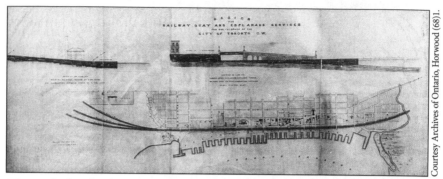

Courtesy Archives of Ontario, Horwood (68)1.

Fleming's plan for the "Grand Esplanade" railway terminal, park, and museum.

Monday, 21st: At office. Timmins design. At Queen's Wharf laying out windmill & sitting at wharf at Yonge street terminus. Plan of Trents Lot for Dr Beattie. At Cumberlands. — he tells me that my paper on Saturday night last was the most successful of the session. Peter Cameron called, to have Logic on Wednesday. Called on B — long lecture about conversation &c. Home about ½ past ten. Reading Smith of England.

Tuesday, 22nd: Commenced copying Chart of Collingwood Harbour to send to Quebec. Recd letter from John Stevenson dated Feby 12. He has sent down thermometer to get proved. Pd Parker Brothers for tripod shoes 11/3. At Mr Cumberlands evening, met Chairman [Henry Youle] Hind & [Professor Henry] Croft about proposed testimonial to Capt Lefroy on his leaving Canada. Telegraph Stewart at Port Hope 1/3.

Wednesday, 23rd: At chart of Collingwood Harbour. At sale of poor Allansons pictures. Cameron & Passmore came over, Logic! Paid David for old services £5. Consider that I still owe him £5.

Thursday, 24th: Finished chart of Collingwood Harbour & Nottawasaga for Quebec. Paid Wakefield for purchase of sketches at sale of Allansons pictures yesterday £1/13. Paid Harrison for boots £1/2/6. Agreed with Sterling that John should have engraving tools &c for cash lent formerly (£2/10). Saw B, walked up Yonge street & avenue. Percival returned note £12/10 today.

Friday, 25th: Making tracing of terminus blocks for corporation. Thermometer from Balsam Lake comes. Brunel left for Barrie. At Dr Goadbys lecture on Natural History. Making sketch of Esplanade until 1 oclock.

Saturday, 26th: Finishing tracing for corporation. George Stewart arrived from Peterboro. Review of Shanlys report out in Journal. Seeing crib work at terminus. At Cumberlands. Canadian Institute evening. Paper by Allen on birds &c. Well attended as at last meeting. Several donations.

Sunday, 27th: Arranging letters &c. Read the "Cotters Saturday Night" by Burns. At church evening. Very wet sleet, walked to Spadina avenue.

Monday, 28th: Ordering maps for report and attending publishing the same. Telegraphed Leather to send down London Reserve papers. 2/3. Revising report. Passmore called in evening. David got hurt on Saturday night.

March 1853

Tuesday, 1st: Revising report. Handed the same to printer. Submitted design of Esplanade &c &c to Cumberland and Storm. Writing up business diary from August 1852 in the evening.

Wednesday, 2nd: At office as usual. Logic in the evening.

Thursday, 3rd: Settled with Mr Crawford to this date for Canadian Institute accts as per book. A short walk.

Friday, 4th: At office as usual. Getting out Report "to office superintendent". At lecture M[echanics] I[nstitute]. At Mr Douglas afterwards.

Saturday, 5th: Paper by Dr McCaul on "… some ancient classical authors."

Sunday, 6th: At Mr Barclays church forenoon. At home in the evening.

Monday, 7th: Busy getting out Report. Cameron in the evening. Passmore did not come.

Tuesday, 8th: Brunel left this morning. Sent off 5 copies of Report & Chart of Harbour to Quebec. Writing out acct of Ordnance survey in the evening.

Wednesday, 9th: Valuing water lots foot of Yonge street. George levelling. Cameron! Logic in evening.

Thursday, 10th: Stewart levelling. Valuing water lots. Board meeting evening. Mr L— evening.

Friday, 11th: At bridge for Thomsons creek. Lecture evening with Passmore — Yorkville!

Saturday, 12th: At bridge and locating buildings at station plans. Acting as secretary Canadian Institute. Verbal discourse by Dr Bovell.

Sunday, 13th: At Knox's church morning. At home evening.

Monday, 14th: Evening called on Dr Stratford. Good architectural work.

Tuesday, 15th: Logic tonight.

Wednesday, 16th: Paid Mrs Buchan for months board £3. Leland returned from Hen & Chickens [Collingwood]. Good profile. At Dr Goadbys lecture on caterpillars. MacDonalds afterwards. Great nonsense.

Thursday, 17th: Preparing plans of stations grounds. In the evening preparing & mounting paper for "A Thought" about city improvements. Cumberland came to Board meeting tonight. He is out first time for 2 months.

Friday, 18th: Reducing drawings for Nottawasaga paper in *Canadian Journal*.

Saturday, 19th: Paper by Buckland on Ornamental planting at Canadian Institute.

Sunday, 20th: At "A Thought" forenoon. Called at Mr Cumberland afternoon. Church evening. Walked up near Yorkville. Poor B. I felt a good deal grieved. Writing or rather copying review of Chief Engineers Report for *Canadian Journal* (written by himself).

Monday, 21st: At office. John commenced to engrave cuts for paper "Nottawasaga Valley." David left for Barrie this morning to take up land. Gave him instructions & £21. Called on Cumberland after 6 oclock, wants a survey to Owen Sound & Saugeen. Gave me £1. I start tomorrow morning. Preparing to go.

Tuesday, 22nd: Left this morning in stage in pocket £10/5. Stage & meals 7/6. Hire horse at Bradford and proceeded by moonlight to Bond Head & Cooksville. At corner of Essa, Tecumseh & Innisfil. To change tomorrow for sleigh.

Wednesday, 23rd: Left in sleigh through Tecumseh, Essa. Lororontio pine plains to Websters and on to MacNabbs corners in Nottawasaga. Stormy afternoon. Expenses 7/6.

Thursday, 24th: Left MacNabbs after a miserable breakfast (potatoes & poor tea) for Ospry. Snow drifting & very deep. Horses went off the track floundering in the snow 4 or 5 ft deep, allright again! Whippletrees break &c. Dinner at Sings mill on branch of Mud river! Rocky falls. Arrival at S.E. corner of the Melangthorn. Saw Gibson (surveyors father) and Sir James Hay, a fine old poor gentleman with family settled in this back part. Spent the evening with him. Exp 17/6.

Friday, 25th: Left Ospry this morning down second concession of Melangthorn. Send across to to Beechells tavern to dinner. Some of the largest maple & beech yesterday & today have seen in Canada. Land along road (new line) from Beechells through Melangthorn very poor & swampy, said to get better & hardwood to the right or east. Passed over summit of Saugeen & Beaver rivers.

Saturday, 26th: Stopped at Wrights tavern 28 miles from Owen Sound. 7/6. Dinner at California House. 2/6. Started this morning for Owen Sound. Snowed about 6 inches during the night. Country a good deal broken from this place to the Sound. Arrived about 5 oclock. Called on Mr Rankin, had tea, saw plans if the various townships. Saw Mr Brown & Mr Kyle. Made arrangements with latter to go to Southampton. (Saugeen tomorrow.)

Sunday, 27th: Started with Mr Kyle for Saugeen (horses left to rest), fine rising ground round the Sound. Country gently rolling and fine timber (beech, maple, rock elm) nearly all the way to Saugeen. Road very rough and beginning to be broken up. Stopped at Mr MacNabb. Saw Reid & Peter Brown. Land in vicinity sandy. Hemlock & cedar but fine country up the river and settling up very fast.

Monday, 28th: Went round the village with the principal inhabitants. Examined river & coast & started for the Sound about 11 oclock. Dinner at Hamiltons. Saw Morton & Pinter, Irish & English gentlemen settlers. Arrived about 8 oclock. Went down to Browns postmaster. Spent the evening. Exp 30/.

Tuesday, 29th: Exps at Sound, horses & self £1/8/6. Left for Barrie by lakeshore road. Dinner at Meaford Temperance house 2/6. Section of ancient beaches & terraces at right angles to shore between 4 & 5 con. These ancient beach marks are concentric & continue east & west. Passed over Beaver river and stopped at Walters log shanty in center of Collingwood township.

Wednesday, 30th: Left Walters 7/6. Passed over high land of Collingwood from which had a magnificent view. Some parts of Collingwood must be 10 or 1,200 ft above lake. Miserable dinner at MacNabbs tavern and went on to Crows in Sunnidale.

Thursday, 31st: Left Crows for Barrie, 10/, and arrived about 3. Rain & sleighing going fast. Saw Leland &c at Barrie.

April 1853

Friday, 1st: Left for Cookstown. Breakfast 2/6. Exchanged for buggy. Arrived at Bradford in time for Toronto stage. Samson, Emerson passengers. Arrival at Toronto ½ past nine. Went down to Fathers and up to Parliament Buildings to see about Conversazione. No one there. In pocket £2.

Saturday, 2nd: Saw Cumberland. Newspaper war been going on. Sent Stewart £1. Engaged most of the day preparing for the Conversazione tonight. Went off not so successful as last time. Capt Lefroy presented with silver vase as a testimonial on his leaving the country.

Sunday, 3rd: At St Andrews church forenoon.

Monday, 4th: Making plan of country west of Nottawasaga & Saugeen. Reporting on d[itt]o.

Tuesday, 5th: Called at Mr L. At Mechanics Institute after.

Wednesday, 6th: Taking home some things from Conversazione room. At Dr Stratfords.

Friday, 8th: Peter Cameron in the evening.

Saturday, 9th: In a great way all this week about note at Commercial Bank. Went to call on Mr Ridout once but had not the courage to go into his room. Last meeting of Canadian Institute this session. At theatre.

Sunday, 10th: Took medicine. At home all day.

Monday, 11th: At office as usual. Meeting of shareholders called by opposition with the view of thwarting the decision of Directors with regard to Northern terminus. A failure. Confidence vote. Invited to dine at Mr Hancocks. Did not go in the evening. Saw Mr Paterson of Orillia. Logic.

Queen's Wharf at the foot of Bathurst Street was a busy place on the Toronto waterfront. From Landmarks, Volume 1 *(1894) by J.R. Robertson.*

Tuesday, 12th: At Osgoode Hall making affidavit about terminus lots. At Royal Engineers office. Plans returned from Montreal — give great satisfaction. Called on Mr Ridout cashier B[ank of] U[pper] Canada. Very readily discounted note with nominal endorsement for £50. Recd £49/14/7. Settled note at Commercial Bank exp 7/1. Paid £50/7/1. Copying plans Queen's Wharf terminal. At Grand Terminal plans evening.

Wednesday, 13th: At large plan of company land at Queen's Wharf. Cumberland goes to Quebec tomorrow. Preparing plans. Took them down about 9 oclock evening. Called on Mr Paterson at Leasks afterwards.

Thursday, 14th: Cumberland left for Quebec with Sladden [Northern Railway Director]. Instructed to form party for inland survey of line to Owen Sound. At MacNabbs (John) to tea. Canadian Institute council afterwards. Wrote to Gibson of Ospry.

Friday, 15th: Wrote to John Boland.

Saturday, 16th: Finished plot of Co[mpany] land east side of Queen's Wharf.

Sunday, 17th: At Knox church twice. Walk afterwards.

Monday, 18th: Out with Wilkinson & Walker planting boundary stones at west end of Garrison Reserve. 1/10/3. Dr Burns and Lublin! Dr Willis does not believe Dr Burns. Logic. Passmore present.

Tuesday, 19th: In office making large plan of Company's land at Queen's Wharf. Called at Sprys.

Wednesday, 20th: Out today with Lieut Wilkinson & Walker planting boundary stones round faces & curves. Wrote this morning to Millar the surveyor. Engaged Mr Bay. Bought watch from Millar £8. Old one £3, to pay £5. Writing letter. "Grand Terminus plan" evening.

Thursday, 21st: Notifying owners of property round Ordnance lands about planting boundary stones. Staking out corner to Market block terminus. Goods locomotive being taken down to track. Writing letter "Grand T plan."

Friday, 22nd: Staking out curves & finishing plan of Co's land Queen's Wharf. Saw Smith, surveyor. Directors decided on not commencing survey of extension to Owen Sound for a week. Wrote to Millar.

Saturday, 23rd: BMO. Placing stones round commissariat office and Victoria Square. Borrowed from Stewart £5. At Council meeting Canadian Institute.

Sunday, 24th: At home forenoon. Passmore evening.

Monday, 25th: BMO. At R.E. office examining plans & documents and rectifying finished plan. Called on Mr Howard who refuses to sign plan without going over survey. Evening Logic & Cameron.

Tuesday, 26th: Went out with Mr Cheney at ½ past 7 this morning to his place at the Humber measuring &c. He gave me £1. Went out to Thornhill to examine country for proposed branch. Exp 12/. Returned about 8 P.M. BM poorly.

Wednesday, 27th: BMO. Placing boundary stones commissariat stores & preparing at foot of Bathurst st. Making survey for laying track on plan & setting out curve of new track. Paid Mrs Buchan for last month £3. At home evening.

Thursday, 28th: BMO. At Queen's Wharf with Mr Bay making rock soundings &c, also planting boundary stones as follows, at Bathurst st continued, Adelaide st., N.E. cor Asylum & near Dr Gwynnes. Exp. 5/. All placed except two at Queen's Wharf. Goods engine, first made in Toronto, perhaps Canada, commenced running on track this afternoon. Anna leaves with Father for Dundas tomorrow, gave her £1/5.

Friday, 29th: Rains heavy this morning. Plotting soundings & in office. Afternoon went round to examine all the boundary stones with Lieut Wilkinson. Got home about 7 oclock. In the evening Cameron & Logic.

Saturday, 30th: Preparing to make further soundings but blows too hard. At Council meeting C.I. evening. Steamer *Ocean Wave* burnt on Lake Ontario this morning. A good many passengers lost.

May 1853

Sunday, 1st: At church forenoon. Writing paper on Nottawasaga valley afternoon & evening.

Monday, 2nd: Too rough for sounding this morning. Setting out foundations of Terminus building, market block. Engaged in office. Getting map of Nottawasaga valley lithographed. Peter Cameron came in! Went down to office. Making sketch of iron bridge for General Terminus plan. Directors decided that survey of extension should be suspended at present. To go up line tomorrow. Sent portion of paper on N.V. to editor of *Canadian Journal*.

Tuesday, 3rd: Received order on Bank Upper Canada for £17/4/3. being expenses to Owen Sound & Saugeen of which I have to pay back £10 to

Cumberland. Left with Bingham for Bradford. Expenses 4/. Saw Read got appt to estimate of work to be done from Bradford to Barrie.

Wednesday, 4th: Paid Merrick horses to Owen Sound £8/11/6. and expenses today. Started to go over road to estimate how much is required force employed & time before opening. Got engine at Matchells, met handcar from city to meet me. Arrived in Toronto about ½ past 5. Exps 5/.

Thursday, 5th: Making report of condition of line. To Brunel. Passmore & Cameron evening.

Friday, 6th: Making soundings at Queen's Wharf in the afternoon.

Saturday, 7th: Paid Johnston for Canadian Institute testimonial fund &c £2/10/0 Recd from him exps of conversazione. Finished plotting soundings at Queen's Wharf. Went up to Dundas st. Bridge to make measurements for law suit. At Canadian Institute evening.

Sunday, 8th: At home all day. Writing letter about improvements of water for *Canadian Journal*. Finishing paper on Nottawasaga.

Monday, 9th: Making plan of Dundas St Bridge for law suit. Cameron! Logic! evening.

Tuesday, 10th: Attending court case, decided in favour of Company. Cameron over in evening. Reading proof of paper on Nottawasaga.

Wednesday, 11th: Rain this morning. Making out description of land required for Thornhill station. Paid Millar watchmaker £4. Still owe him £2. Watch cost £8. Exchd old one $12. At Mr Hinds in the evening.

Thursday, 12th: Cumberland arrived from Quebec this morning. Getting plan of city put on press for transfer. Making calculations for Brunel. Succeeded in making transfer of part of the city. Paid [brother] Johns school fees £1/10. At office in the evening.

Friday, 13th: Recd quarters salary £87/10. Paid bill at Bank U. Canada £50. Paid John MacNabb for ½ lst instalment on Park Lot 10 in the tenth concession of £10/10, Sydenham, to be taken up in the name of his father. MacNabb & I to go shares in purchase & profits. Making description of land required for gravel pits. Walked to Yorkville with Cameron evening. New hat £1/50.

Saturday, 14th: Wrote to Mr Walker R.E. Making timetable for Brunel. Received order from Cumberland to make survey of Harbour, Saugeen, Fishing Island & Owen Sound. Recd proof of letter to *Canadian Journal*. At council Canadian Institute. Correcting proof evening until late.

Sunday, 15th: At Knox church forenoon. Correcting proof of letter about Railway terminus & mastodon giganteus. Wrote to A. MacNabb, Saugeen.

Monday, 16th: Gave MacNabb £6 to buy up Robinson right to park lots near Owen Sound. Go shares for them both. Left corrected proofs at Scobies. Left with train for Matchells station. Cumberland, Brunel — Bay & Rodgers to set out siding on King st. Got Mr Downs horse & buggy to Bradford. Met Dr Beattie & Judge Orton. Got steamboat to Barrie. Steamboat 5/. Saw Boland & other men. Made arrangements to start next morning at 5 oclock.

Tuesday, 17th: Paid off acct Mr Downs £3/5. Paid off Jas Young £4/10. Went with steamboat to mouth of bay. J. Boland & men row me down to examine grassy point. Paid steamboat exps of men & meals 12/6. Finished at grassy pt and caught boat to Bradford. Paid exps of men back to Barrie 10/. Very cold. Letter from poor B. Gave John Boland yesterday £7.

Thursday, 19th: Received from Sladden order on extension survey cost £50. Reporting on Innisfil station. Correcting proof *Canadian Journal*. Got proof of plan of terminus. Answering B. Letter. See copy.

Friday, 20th: Paid board Mrs Buchan £3. Returned Cumberland £10. Ordering provisions for survey. Pd John Boland £7 on the 18th, makes

£16 to be divided equally among the 4 men. Pd Mr Bay to acct £5. Mr Rodgers £4 & exps of trip to Barrie £2/0/7½ — £6. Correcting proofs of *Cdn Journal* — at Frasers concert evening (failure).

Saturday, 21st: Preparing for start on Monday. Pd Ridout Brothers — tradesmen £2/7/11, J & W MacDonald tent blankets etc £5/7/11, John McGee tins etc £1/9/1, John Nasmith £2, £10 to pay Liddell yet. Answer from poor B. At Canadian Institute. Cash balances.

Sunday, 22nd: Late getting up. At Knox church morning. Rains heavy evening. At Mr Walkers afternoon.

Monday, 23rd: Propeller has not arrived from Kingston. Johns articles signed to me today. Saw B. Saw Lieut Wilkins & Walker. I signed plans. Received from Tuckman additional £50. Pd John £4. Groceries Leask £3/19/12 — £7/19/11½. 1 brl Biscuit £1. Medicines 19/4. Sundries 10/ — £2/9/4. Bought oil coat £1/17/6 hat 5/ [miscellaneous] 6/. Paid instalment Canada Life Assurance £9/2/6. Next due January 1854.

Tuesday, 24th: No Boat yet! Cash in pocket £36/2/6. Saw John MacNabb this morning, he is to take up land near Saugeen & Owen Sound in his name & equally there with me, I paying half exps. Already taken up No.9 11th half Part 1. I have paid him up to date on acct of this partnership £16.10.0. Gave Mother for cheese £2/10. Pipes etc 2/10. Queens Birthday. Excursion train. Walked up to Yorkville with B.

Wednesday, 25th: No Boat yet! Attending to *Canadian Journal* &c, making corrections of Lithographs. Bought socks &c at Leasks 13/1. Newspaper from Peterboro! Called at Mr Ls evening. Gave parting gift to B. At Passmores office & MacDonalds.

Thursday, 26th: Boat arrived about noon today — to leave tomorrow. *Canadian Journal* out in the afternoon. My paper on Nottawasaga & letter on Termini &c in it. Rain all day. "The Casse" in the evening with Passmore.

Friday, 27th: Packing up clothes for start. Left umbrella at the Casse last night. Paid board of men £3, 8½ days each. Pd Mr Edwards case for tripod & leather bag. Sundries at Patersons hardware 1/6. Pd tailor making coat 17/. Drinks & sundries between this & Tuesday 10/. Left Toronto in propeller "Ranger." Cash in pocket £20. With Mr Bay, Rodger, John, J. Boland, S. Boland, W. Ransom & Moreau — from Penetanguishene & Coldwater. Notice of *Journal* in *Colonist* today. Scobie by mistake gives me as author of letter on termini in it.

Saturday, 28th: Passed through a great many locks. Got up at 5 A.M. Arrived at Thorold — about 27 locks in the Welland Canal — summit I think not more than 60 feet above Lake Erie. Very pleasant passage, beautiful in some parts towards Lake Erie, not so good heavy rock cut south end of canal. Sand thrown up along beach of Lake Erie about 30 or 35 feet for miles.

Sunday, 29th: A most beautiful morning. Lake quite calm. Steamer had gone inside of Long Point by mistake — lost about 20 miles — arrived at Port Stanley afternoon. Fine valley with high clay table land on each side about 70 feet high [rough line-sketch of terrain entered in diary]. Goods not allowed to be landed on Sunday, had to stay all night, commenced unloading after 12. Six or eight acres of gravel & sand washed up on west side of piers apparently since they were erected.

Monday, 30th: Blows hard this morning. Left Port Stanley about 9 oclock. Came on a fearful gale from N.W. of shore, vessels head to wind — blew so hard that engine stopped several times. Nearly all on board sick. Turned out fine afternoon with fresh breeze got up sail, passed "rond—eau" [now Rondeau Provincial Park]. Young Rodgers great fun. Point Pelee lighthouse in sight at sundown.

Tuesday, 31st: Up until two — in the morning fine fresh breeze. Arrived at Amherstburg about 5 oclock — went with Rodgers to his fathers. Capt R an old Waterloo man. Breakfast & lunch with him. He has two fine sons. Went round the town with him. Arrived at Windsor opp[osite] Detroit. Detroit not a very fine town. Ry Depot large, convenient & plain. No fine architectural buildings in Detroit. Terminus of Gt W[ester]n at Windsor. Started for Lake St Clair [indecipherable] 6/3.

June 1853

Wednesday, 1st: Anchored for 5 or 6 hours at head of Lake St Clair on account of shoals. Arrived at Port Sarnia after dinner, after stopping to take in wood about 10 miles below when we had a short trip. P Sarnia a small place. Mr Vidals house pointed out — no one else. St Clair beautiful river — bought oars. A little poetical feeling still hangs over P. Sarnia. Left for Goderich. Lake beautifully calm, banks of St Clair not more at any place probably than 20 feet high. Great laughing with Rodgers. Aurora.

Thursday, 2nd: Woke up about 6. Reckoning lost. Steamer — turned back — head wind — arrived about 11 oclock. Maitland River runs between banks said to be 150 feet high. Goderich well laid out. Saw Mr Percival, Sheriff Macdonald. Great thunderstorm evening. Had difficulty in persuading Capt to take us to Saugeen [Southampton]. Several acres of shingle & sand. Walked up with him to Goderich harbour. End of piers destroyed by ice & storms.

Friday, 3rd: Steamer left Goderich about 3 oc[lock] this morning. Thick fog. Could not attempt to enter Saugeen, continue on to Cape Hare. Steamer put in for the night at Tobermory Harbour — a very singular place near N.W. corner of Canada — very rocky shore and deep water close in side — paid person for passage of self & party £10/2/6. Stewart £1. Cabin boy 2/ — £11/5. Propose to leave luggage here and go on to Manitoulin with the view of getting Boats.

Saturday, 4th: Gave Mr Bay £2/10. Started about 5 oclock with steamer, course over to Manitoulin Island with the men — got into two Indian Boats about 8 miles from Equessicum village — 5/ — got to village about 10 oc but could not induce Indians to sell or lend us two boats. Called on Jesuit priest. At last got boat at 7 P.M. for £6/10. Old beach marks seen distinctly here, gradually rising up to 60 or 70 feet where water must have stood for a long time.

Sunday, 5th: All the points of law. Have this appearance meeting. Paid for sugar, fish & potatoes yesterday 5/. Left in small boat at 4 this morning.

Breakfast at mouth of Bay. Calm & gentle breezes occasionally. Went into another Indian village (*E-quien-i-con-si*) about 23 miles this side to get a canoe or Boat but did not succeed. Had a fair wind a little while chopped round and blew strong in our teeth with heavy swells from Prince William to Rabbit, sail about 3 hours to pull 5 miles. Very hard but landed safe.

Monday, 6th: Cash in pocket (believe right) £5/3/9. Wind blew strong all night but slept sound. Island very rocky, immense blocks with inclined strata. Appears as if a softer rock had been washed from underneath and caved in. Pure shingle spit N.E. corner of Island. Towards night rain & fog clears away and wind falls a little. Trace distinct pure round pebble beaches at north end of island to a height (roughly measured) 50 ft above lake, above this surface rough & broken.

Tuesday, 7th: Rain heavy during the night — strong Northwester, very heavy swells. Our provisions getting very low. Put on two meals a day. Very huge waves breaking with great violence on shingle beach. Wind commenced to fall a little about sundown. Provisions done except 1 piece of dried beef. Ransom sat up the night and tried to shoot rabbits, succeeded in killing one.

Wednesday, 8th: Fine morning with slight breeze from S.West. Started about 4 oclock without breakfast and rowed over to Tobermory Harbour. Found the three that were left there waiting patiently. Had breakfast. Packed up traps — left 1½ biscuits at fishermans hut. Started for Fishing Islands with head wind. Dinner at Cape Hurd. Wind fell … Row along shore [west side of Bruce Peninsula] a great distance until sundown. Camped at a small bay which we thought was near Segal Island. Very calm all afternoon. Wind rising from S.E.

Thursday, 9th: Strong winds from S.West — started after breakfast to go inside of Lyal island — from that the inlet was only a long bay. Attempted to go out by the main Lake, found breakers too heavy, obliged to go back. Walked along the coast 1 or perhaps two miles, could see no indications of Lyal island except a great way off. Shore very barren — low & stony — breakers long way out. One of the men sick — took medicine & made camp until wind falls. Picked up some pretty …

Friday, 10th: Fine morning. Gentle wind from N.W. Started out about 5 A.M. round to Lyal island about 5 miles, breakfasted. Put up sail and went rattling through between Fishing Islands to Chiefs Point — bad landing & camping ground. Found a suitable place on edge of sandy beach. Commenced exploring round mainland. Took observations of North Star and set of bearing of line 1 &c &c.

Saturday, 11th: Started Mr Bay to traverse beach. With J. Boland & Moreau went off to Saugeen. Fair wind. Arrived about 2 oclock (3 hours sail). Mr MacNabb & Saugeen people glad to see us. The blacksmith had arrived two days previous by way of Owen Sound. Inhabitants of Saugeen [Southampton] had subscribed and chartered a schooner to go in search of us. Very thoughtful. It returned this morning. Wrote to Cumberland. Stopped at MacNabbs. Got sundry provisions &c at Reids.

Sunday, 12th: Excellent night rest. Fair wind home in the morning. Made ready to start about ½ past 11. Wind completely died away & lake calm. Had to row the whole way to Chiefs Point. Very hot. Received letter from Mr Stevenson of Eldon. No newspapers from anyone. Rice pudding to tea. Went to bed. Musquitoes, black flies & sand flies exceedingly troublesome. Slept very little.

Monday, 13th: Continued traversing mainland shore — very swampy — placing stations on the islands & exploring. Long day — commenced about 5 A.M. & got home by 7. Flies very troublesome. Anchored the Boat out in the Bay. John & I slept in one and Rodgers & G. Boland in other. Slept pretty well. Not so many flies. Blanket wet with dew in the morning.

Tuesday, 14th: Out as yesterday. Very hot. Pease to dinner. Mr Bay measuring angles. Moved camp over to small island. Commenced to lay down part of survey. Forgot to bring parallel rules — cant get on well without. Island small & rocky, not so many Musquitoes. Slept very well.

Wednesday, 15th: Fine sunshine with slight breeze. Plot survey on small scale. Mr Bay measuring bearings & calculating triangles. Sounding after dinner. An Indian called with his boat, squaw & papoose. Allowed watch to run down last night. Moon half full — water gently rippled, constant sound the whole time. Very few Musquitoes. Slept long. Pleasant day.

Thursday, 16th: Out sounding nearly all day. Gentle breeze from south. After tea a white squall passed over a little to the north of us, we also had a good deal of wind. Saw a fire on Whitefish Island which turned out to be Mr Reid & Godfrey.

Friday, 17th: Thick fog this morning. About 8 oclock a Boat made its appearance. Mr Reid & Godfrey, had been on Whitefish Island all night. Fog cleared away. Went over and traversed Bare Island. Wind blows strong from S.E. Quite a gale in the afternoon.

Saturday, 18th: Still blows very hard this morning. Mr Reid cant get away. Mr Bay measuring angles & commenced traversing south from Station No.1. Protracting survey 12 ells to an inch and calculating distances. Wind very strong all day! Anniversary Battle of Waterloo! Gave Mr Bay £1/5.

Sunday, 19th: Up at ½ past three. Had an early breakfast and started for Saugeen. Reid & Godfrey in my boat. The two frenchmen who brought them up went up about 1 mile — disinterred the son of the old man who had drowned 4 years ago. He wants to put the remains in consecrated ground at Goderich. At Saugeen. No letters. Newspaper from B.

Monday, 20th: Stopped at Mr MacNabbs — had nightmare from drinking a glass raspberry vinegar before going to bed. Wrote to Cumberland. Got some more supplies. Left for Fishing Islands about three P.M. Calm & high wind. Accompanied by Messrs Gardiner & Valentine. Arrived — had been stormy today. Moreau cut his leg very bad with axe. Thunder & lightning!!!

Tuesday, 21st: Thunder, lightning & stormy nearly all night. Mr Bay traversing Chimney Island. In camp plotting. Calm afternoon — out exploring Island and sounding. Messrs Valentine & Gardiner left with Indians for Saugeen. Most beautiful sunset! Thunder clouds over the sun, also fine moon rise. Gorgeous!

Wednesday, 22nd: Blows hard again from South this morning. Too rough for sounding. Poor Moreau very lonely in camp with leg cut by axe. Protracting survey. Mr Bay traversing South shore towards Chiefs Point. Heavy swell! The night looks very wild.

Thursday, 23rd: Wind blows a perfect gale from S.W. Rain! Bracken washing over a great portion of our Island, not yet reached the camp. Impossible to go out. Repairing boats.

Friday, 24th: Very stormy all day. Traversing islands.

Saturday, 25th: Still stormy. Traversing Main Station Islands. Lake very rough in the morning.

Sunday, 26th: Fine calm morning. After breakfast went off in boat to Riviere au Sauble north and went up as far as the Falls about 2 miles from the mouth. They are abrupt rapids — steps of about 8 ft altogether say 15 ft. Flies very bad. Sand dunes at mouth of river, lake side scooped out by wind, the other covered with grass. Returned home. Biscuit pudding to dinner.

Monday, 27th: Calm until noon. Recd packet of papers & letter from Melville by schooner from Saugeen. Mr Bay measuring bearings round island. Sketching Islands near Fishing Islands. Sand flies very bad in camp during the night, which with boil on neck slept very badly.

Tuesday, 28th: Could not sleep for sand flies — up at three oclock — walked — had breakfast. Lake calm. Commenced sounding at 5 oclock in open lake near Chiefs Point. Measuring bearings. Mr Bay some errors. Wind got up afternoon. Protracting soundings. Calculating distances.

Wednesday, 29th: Off to Main Station Island. Sounding. Blows too hard, had to give up. Mr Bay traversing mainland. Took salts. Boil on neck very bad. Calculating distances & protracting. Rice pudding to tea. Plotting survey evening. Wind blows!

Thursday, 30th: Stormy. Mr Bay off to traverse some of the Islands. Plotting & protracting in camp. Mr Bay left for Saugeen. Anxious to have letter from home.

July 1853

Friday, 1st: Out sounding all day near Main Island. Wind too strong to do much outside. Having hoisted red blanket on flag pole were surprised on return to find it gone. Thought someone had been robbing the camp — found it in the water. Protracting & inking survey until about 10.

Saturday, 2nd: Packed up & started for Saugeen, little wind & calm. Pitched our camp on Chantry Island, got a very fine spot. Returned to village. Mr Bay chaining along shore. Got provisions & returned to camp. Letter from Mr Stevenson of Eldon & a few newspapers from someone in Toronto unknown, one from Peterboro.

Sunday, 3rd: Strong wind this morning. Started for Chantry Island — Rodgers, John, Moreau & George — quite a gale. At church — to collection ½ Eagle £1 — chiefly on acct Saugeen people sending up schooner for us, it cost them £5. Dinner at Mr MacNabbs. At Indian village. Afternoon sail up rapids. Tea at Mr Reids. Church evening. Wind blows, sky dark, looks bad - didnt go over, stayed at Mr MacNabbs.

Monday, 4th: Wind very strong, cant go exploring south along the beach. At Mr MacNabbs to dinner. Met Rev Mr Bale. Wind fell down during afternoon. Mr Bay measuring angles. Mail came in. One letter, newspapers, *Colonist* from Scobie 28th May about letter in *Canadian Journal*. Camp at night.

Tuesday, 5th: Commenced sounding but wind rather heavy — traversed shore a long way to the south. Mr Valentine came over for us to spend the evening at his house — went over. Wind from the W., swells from N.W.

"Mountain high." Got into the river with some difficulty. The other boat had to run ashore. At Mr Valentines evening.

Wednesday, 6th: Still a heavy swell but wind falling. Breakfast at Mr MacNabbs. Went over to camp. Mr Bay calculated triangles. Set him to traverse the Island. Protracting survey. Mr MacNabbs little boy came over in the morning with us, took him over afternoon and did some little work.

Thursday, 7th: Fine sounding this morning. Mr MacNabb & McIntosh forenoon. Mr MacNabb & child over to dinner. Blows a little going over. Protracting survey. Pd Mr Bay £1. Pd Mr Rodgers. At Mr P.I. Hamilton spending the evening. Stayed at Mr MacNabbs.

Friday, 8th: Fine morning. Mr Bay chaining N side of river. After dinner went down to McLean Bay. Mr Bay to traverse. Started off ... inland to the river with the view of ... coming round by Bridge... returned same way as we came. Walked home to Saugeen. *Canadian Journal* & newspapers. No news from Cumberland.

Saturday, 9th: Very much troubled with boil in the back of neck. Wind blows too much for sounding. Mr Bay traversing north of River. At Mr MacNabbs all day. Mrs MacN very kind bathing neck, poulticing &c, also <u>Dr</u> McIntosh. Smoking at Mr Hamiltons evening. Agnes cutting tobacco.

Sunday, 10th: Saugeen. Boil troublesome during the night, took salts. Not at church. Wrote to Cumberland, Brunel, Passmore & Stewart. At church evening. Mr Bale preaching a very good sermon. At Mr Hamiltons afternoon.

Monday, 11th: Wind — lake unfit for sounding. Walked up to Bridge over Saugeen with Mr MacNabb & McIntosh. Back to village, dinner about 7 oclock. Mail came in, letter from Peter Cameron, *Canadian Journal* & newspapers.

Tuesday, 12th: Sounding a little this morning, did not get much done. At Mr Reids to tea. At MacNabbs plotting survey until nearly 3 in the morning.

Wednesday, 13th: Good sounding today. Rev Mr Bale out with us in the forenoon. Continued sounding until after sundown. Supper at camp by light of fire. Paid for rudder to Boat 7/. Indians for fish &c at Island 5/. In pocket 1/. Mr Bay, Rodgers & church £4/10. Cash balance June 6 £5/3/9. Cash in pocket 1/3.

Thursday, 14th: Plotting & protracting. Wind & rain. Out sounding a little after rain. Plotting & inking survey until about eleven oclock at night. Rodgers very bad with bowel complaint.

Friday, 15th: Very stormy all night, wind from south. Too much for sounding this morning. Sky very cloudy. Sounding in river, calmed down about noon. Sounding from Island to McLeans Bay. Finished about seven. Went to village as mail comes in. Boat to Island. Sky looks very stormy. Laying down soundings.

Saturday, 16th: Northwest storm this morning, heavy swell all day. Went down with Mr MacNabb to his farm to trace boundary. Preparing to start on Monday. At Mr Jardins to tea. Mrs Jardin beautiful player on pianoforte, sings well. Mr Fisher from Montreal also sings well. Went home to Mr MacNabbs about eleven. Plotting and arranging about securing Lots.

Sunday, 17th: Boil bad. No service forenoon. At Reids to dinner. Fire apparently out in Lake afternoon, it turned out to be mainland at Lyal Island. Wrote to David.

Monday, 18th: Made draft on Tiechures Ry — £50. Left in MacNabbs hands £20. Fury for Beef 16/8 — J. Belcher £1/18 [total] £2/14/8, Mr Reid £2/13/10 — MacNabb £7/6/3 — [total] £10/0/1 groceries &c — Bay £4 — Rodgers £1/5 — John £1 — Girl at MacNabbs 5/ — [total] £39/4/9. In pocket £10/15/3. Left with Rev Mr Bale & Neil McIntosh from Montreal for Owen Sound. Camped on small island near Main Station Fishing Island.

Tuesday, 19th: Up by daylight. Finished sounding from Main Station channel. Had breakfast and left camping ground about 9 oclock. Fair wind portion of the way & fresh head wind. Camped at place marked Boat on chart. Pease soup at night.

Wednesday, 20th: Started very early — head wind this side of Cape Hurd. Had dinner on shore. Rowed round Cape Hurd, then fair wind rather too strong to Cabots Head. Went ashore about ½ way, singular gravel beach to steps of an amphitheatre across a gully. Swells as much as boat could stand but arrived at Cabots Head safe. Musquitoes bad. Slept on gravel beach with blanket round us.

Thursday, 21st: Up early & had breakfast. Fine fair wind to start but soon calmed down. After touching at Cape Ching, struck across to Cape Croker. Biscuit & lager to dinner on board. Men had a long hot pull — continued to Cape Cornadise where steamer *Kalloola* made up to us. Before sundown got a tow down. McIntosh paid 10/. Mr Bale & McIntosh went off with steamer to Toronto. Saw Rodgers & as they had lost the path coming across from Saugeen slept out all night — nearly starved.

Friday, 22nd: Mr Bay traversing. Exploring coast & preparing for Sunday. Letters from David & Stewart. Ogilvie & Johnson & Macdonald gone off to New York. Letter from Mr MacNabb, Saugeen. Wrote to Cumberland & Sladden. Paid plan of Sydenham 5/, cotton 3/9, axe head 10/ [total] 18/9.

Saturday, 23rd: Fine working day. Got a good deal of sounding done. Breakfast before going out. Lunch at noon & dinner on our return to Tavern about sun down. Walked down to wharf but steamer very late before she came in.

Sunday, 24th: Taking it easy.

Monday, 25th: Paid the four men each £1 — £4/0. Thunder shower. Mr Bay out part of the day. Protracting remainder of Fishing Islands soundings. Making calculations for Owen Sound. Protracting evening. Mr Lyons from Saugeen called.

Tuesday, 26th: Mr Bay out traversing. Rode down to Falls on River Sydenham. about 3 miles forenoon & exploring country S North East in the afternoon. Making out time & expense bills in the evening.

Wednesday, 27th: Out sounding — wind blows rather hard. Got traverse & sounding partially complete. Returned late. Evening calculating & protracting. Boils very troublesome.

Thursday, 28th: Commenced Mr Bay to make cross section in Town plot. Plotting survey & soundings. Getting time Bills signed and preparing to start for Toronto. James Rodgers £1, John £1. Taking luggage to wharf & lunches &c 7/6. Reach terms. £2.17.6. Left about 12 by steamer *Kalloola* for Sturgeon Bay. Beautiful morning sailing through Christian Islands, touched at Penetanguishene and arrived at Sturgeon Bay early in forenoon, took stage to Orillia. Very rough road & steamer *Morning* to Barrie. *Kalloola* 12/6, stage & meal 7/6 — £1. Arrived at Barrie about 9 oclock.

Saturday, 30th: Steamer *Morning* started from Barrie about 3 oclock in time for morning train at Bradford. Arrive at Toronto between 9 & 10 oclock A.M. All well. Steamer *Morning* 11/10½. Boil under right eye very bad and looks disreputable, I wearing long beard & mustaches they scarcely knew me.

Sunday, 31st: Saw Dr Primrose yesterday — taking medicine to purify my blood. Did not go to church. Got advice and medicine from Dr Primrose yesterday.

August 1853

Monday, 1st: Cash in pocket 16/3. Deficit about 9/. At office getting tracings made of surveys. Saw Cumberland about Esplanade. He has adopted & recommended my plan in Report to Directors. City papers taking notice of Report calling it Cumberlands plan. My name not known in the matter. At concert Canadian Institute evening.

Tuesday, 2nd: Making up time & expense. Bits of surveys amount altogether up to 26 July £221. Not to go to Owen Sound this trip of

Kalloola, to go to Port Hope to make soundings of Harbour for Cumberland. Met B — walked round by Yorkville. Explanations &c &c these months.

Wednesday, 3rd: Cumberland certified Bill of expenses. Preparing to go to Port Hope. Ordered seal at Wheelers. Finishing tracings of surveys. Making out acct of Ordnance Surveys in Toronto. Passmore took them up to Lieut Wilkinson. Wrote to MacNabb, Saugeen, & Brown, Owen Sound.

Thursday, 4th: Reporting to Cumberland on surveys. Got check from Sladden for £71, having received £150 previously, in all £221 up to July 26. Left for Port Hope, took man, David. Expenses of self & man to Port Hope 16/10½. Borrow from B.W. Carruthers £1. In pocket this evening 15/. Saw Messrs Benson & P. Smith at Port Hope. Walked down to Harbour, made arrangements to commence survey.

Friday, 5th: Making preparations for sounding & boring. Telegraphed to Toronto for level of water. Pocket knife 3/9, square 2/6, chain 2/6, water scale 3/9, cotton & twine 3/, telegraph 1/7, auger & nails &c 3/6. [Total] £1/5/7. Got check cashed at bank £71. Finished soundings outside. Tea at McLeods.

Saturday, 6th: Commenced boring. Two fishermen... forenoon. Paid David to acct 7/6. Started at ¼ to five for Peterboro. Met James Hall near Rice Lake. Tea at Grahams [Tavern, Baillieboro]. Thunderstorm. Stayed all night. Tally 4d. Cash balance right. In pocket tonight £70/1/10½.

Sunday, 7th: After breakfast left Grahams for Peterboro. Arrived at Peterboro about 12 oclock. Had a good wash & dinner. Afternoon called on Dr McNabb & Mr Hall. Stopped afternoon & tea. Drove Miss Hall down to cemetery — some little improvement.

Monday, 8th: Up about 7 oclock. Called on some friends afternoon. Saw Mr Conger & Judge Hall. Pd Bill at Tavern including bridle 6/3. Report on exploration Toronto to publish. £1. Left for Port Hope about 4 oclock. Grahams &c 2/, paid horse him £1/5.

Tuesday, 9th: Boring in marsh this morning & all day. Got teeth cleaner 2/6. Finished boring, left in steamer *Passport* for Cobourg. Tea &c 5/. Returned by *Arabian* & proceeded to Toronto. Paid Lesperence Bill £2. Boat fare for self & Daniel 15/. Cab wharfage & Boots 2/6.

Wednesday, 10th: Cash in pocket this morning £69/18/9. Deficit 3/. Arrived in Toronto about ½ past 6 oclock A.M. Plantagenet water! Port Hope expenses altogether £8/0/4½. Plotting survey of Port Hope Harbour. Cumberland left this morning for Hen & Chickens. Telegraphed him. Lent Moberly £10. Also lent Passmore £10. Flannel shirt 15/. Shoemaker £4. Daniel £1/2/6. Brown of Owen Sound watch 7/6. Balfour tailor £1/17/6. Total £28/2/6. Called at Lieuts, no one in. At Camerons.

Thursday, 11th: Wrote to Ross C.E. Grand Trunk & Conger. Preparing to start. Passmore at home. Telegraph from Cumberland to meet him at Collingwood. Received quarters salary. Check from D. Beatty. £87/10. Directors acted very handsomely. Sent letter of thanks & £25 to Saugeen for their kindness in sending schooner to us at Fishing Islands.

Friday, 12th: Left on table for Mrs Buchan £5. Baggage 2/6. Passengers for Newmarket, Orillia & *Kalloola*. Mr Leask & boy & Miss Murdoch going. Steamboat & stage to Sturgeon Bay. *Kalloola* not arrived. Stopped at Mr Patersons all night. Out sailing on Lake Couchiching.

Saturday, 13th: Out rowing on Lake again. Miss Ogilvie & Miss Murdoch. Passengers hanging about town, very tired waiting. Stage from *Kalloola* arrived in the evening. To start next morning. Stopped this night at Garnetts.

Sunday, 14th: Left in stage this morning about 5 oclock for Coldwater. Meals &c 2/. John Boland came on from Coldwater. Got *Kalloola* at Sturgeon Bay. Changed clothes & felt comfortable. Fare & porter for self 15/, John Boland 7/6. Mr Worthington of Picton on board, Capt Anderson, Mr Ruttan & Dewey &c. Arrived at Owen Sound about 4 Monday morning.

Monday, 15th: Cash paid on 10th £28/2/6, 10th to 14th £5/12/6, £1/10/— (total) £35/10. Cash in pocket on 9th £64., Salary £87/10. In pocket this morning £115/10. Deficient 10/. Cross sections not finished. Writing Editors Shartz for *Anglo American*.

Tuesday, 16th: Out exploring, partly levelling. Paid Moreau £1/5, G.Boland £1/5, paid Rodgers £5. At Mr Stevens to tea. MacNabb agent & MacNabb lawyer arrived from Saugeen. Long chat. Letter of thanks from Directors. £25 to go to commence of a Library.

Wednesday, 17th: Commence traversing at head of bay. John at home, sore foot. Visited Council meeting Indian village. Capt Anderson & MacNabb. Plotting lands afternoon. Wrote to Mr Hay. His son James to come up.

Thursday, 18th: Very stormy today. Called on Mr Rankin. Paid Mr Bay £12/10, Rodgers 5/10, J. Fleming 2/10, J. Boland 5/0, Rankin, 10, Moreau 2/10, G. Boland. Paid £40. Paid £1/10 expenses of men from Barrie to Toronto. Total £41/10. In pocket £74/ £115/10 cash on hand. Mr MacNabb went off to Saugeen today. Had to get a fire kindled today.

Friday, 19th: Last night gave John MacNabb £50 which along with £16/10 to go towards purchase of Lots in Sydenham, profits to be shared equally by both, in all £66/10. On horseback today exploring for proposed survey of line to Collingwood. Horse & feed 10/. Rawson left this morning, 3/4 of a month due him since July 26.

Saturday, 20th: Preparing to start in the beginning of next week. Ordered biscuit. John making section paper. Chalking out lines on map for survey &c &c.

Sunday, 21st: Taking it easy. At Mr Browns post office to tea. Letter by mail tonight from Stewart with instructions from Cumberland to complete exploration, discharge men and return to Toronto. Stephenson dinner on the 26th.

Monday, 22nd: Wrote to Howard, Hay regretting that survey not going on. Wrote to MacNabb, Saugeen, also to Leland Hen & Chickens. Finishing levels and preparing to start. Received from Mr Brown for watch purchased at Toronto 7/6. Borrowed from Rodgers £1 — lent him 5/, 15/ owed him 2/ formerly. Wharfage & postage 2/6. Exp Mr Bay & Mr Sawyer 8/1½ — 10/7½. Pd exp of 3 men to Penetanguishene 20/. Paid Corbet board of party & sundries £17/7/9. Cash in pocket £6. Balance £74. Started for Toronto by land. Stage fare to Guelph £3/15, dinner &c 5/. Put up at Smiths.

Wednesday, 24th: Supper & beds 15/, dinner 5/. At Fergus & Guelph. Boil or something coming on finger.

Thursday, 25th: Hotel at Guelph 15/. Stage to Hamilton £1.9.0. John stopped at Dundas.

Friday, 26th: Hotel at Hamilton £1, Steamboat £1. Received from Mr Rogers £1/13. Bay £2/10, John £2. At dinner to R. Stephenson in Parliament Buildings. Grand affair.

Saturday, 27th: Up about 11 or 12 oclock today after Stephensons dinner. Down at office. Up at Barracks office. Got check on Commissariat for Military Reserve being balance £100/4/5. At Canadian Institute Council meeting. Evening came home with Brunel.

Sunday, 28th: Hand still sore. Arm in sling.

Monday, 29th: Pd James Liddell grocery acct £10/15/7, Mr Bay £27/10/1½, Rogers £22/10, Wheeler for ring & repairing £1/15. Total £62/10/8½.

Tuesday, 30th: Up line examining Station Buildings. Buggy & exp at Newmarket 7/. Received letter from Saugeen enclosing receipts. On location. Ticket for four lots on lake shore range next summer in Charles & John Pollocks name.

Wednesday, 31st: Up to Thornhill & back by train … at Nettings &c &c. Reporting to Cumberland & writing letter with left hand. Pd for doz ale at Smith & Mitchells 16/. Borrowed from Rodgers £10.

September 1853

Thursday, 1st: Left by train for Orillia. Steamer & cigars 8/9. At Mr Patersons.

Friday, 2nd: At Orillia. Met Mr Docherty when boat arrived. Informed that Cumberland & Brunel came up today to Lelands funeral. Stricken with sorrow & surprise. Shot himself accidentally near Nottawasaga River — poor fellow!!! Met Rev Mr Gray & Mr Hind, also Mr Godfrey & Archy MacNabb here for Lake Huron about establishing lighthouse. Capt McGregor.

Saturday, 3rd: Exps at Garretts 11/3. Left by stage for Coldwater 8/9. Pd Rawson £3/15/. J. Boland £10 plus £1 on return. G. Boland £12/10. Champagne on steamer *Kalloola* £1/15/1. Total £30.

Called at Hen & Chickens but did not stop. Tossed up with McGregor & went on board again. Champagne spree. Messrs Boilleau on board. D Haynes.

Sunday, 4th: Landed on Griffith Island with Godfrey &c about lighthouse. Evening at Manitouaning. Fine weather. Terrace on Griffith Island 43 ft above lake.

Monday, 5th: Going through North Channel. Arrived at Bruce Mines. Steamer lay all night. Saw the various works and collected specimens. Islands generally show marks of Lake Huron having been at a high level.

Tuesday, 6th: Arrived at Sault Ste Marie in the forenoon. Dined on American side 7/4. Examine works on canal now forming. Walked up to top of rapids. Left the Sault about 5 oclock. Appearance of terraces on distant high ground north shore. Various heights, appeared upwards of 100 feet... Stopped all night at Garden river... Passengers Allan MacDonald & others. A little rough on North Channel. American surveyor on Lake St George. Taking in wood at Petit Cormant. Indians by torchlight, fine sight. Called at Manitouaning during the night.

Thursday, 8th: Bottle of sweets 5/. Woke up at Cheboganing. Indian fishing village. Rocky ridges rising east & west. Rocks scored north & south. Godfrey, McGregor & MacNabb left in small sailboat at Horse Isld, westerly wind. At Owen Sound met Mrs MacNabb (Saugeen) & girls on way to Toronto. Champagne in Ladies cabin.

Friday, 9th: Champagne &c Stewarts £2/10. Arrived at Sturgeon Bay. Took stage. Great fun with Mrs Carson. Stage &c12/6. At Orillia called at Mrs Paterson. Ladies out. Steamer for Barrie. Rough on Lake Simcoe. Ladies all sick. Ale, M Watt 3/12.

Saturday, 10th: To Bradford & Toronto 1/30. Saw Mrs Carson off to Montreal. Pd for likeness daguerreotype 12/6. Saw Cumberland. To take charge of section Barrie to Bradford & Buildings on line from Bradford to Toronto. At Canadian Institute.

Sunday, 11th: [Many figures entered here] In pocket £7/16/3.

Monday, 12th: Recd from Cumberland & Storm exp at Port Hope £8. Exps Owen Sound survey last month £81/17/5. [total] £97/14. Pd draft sent to Moreau £12/11/3. Pd John in full £15/10. Pd Rodgers owed formerly after deducting 12/6 paid for his likeness £9/7. Total] £60/5/6. At Mr McLeans evening with Roger to see Mrs MacNabb & children. Bowes examined at Chancery Court today on £10,000 affair. Tea at Laidlaws.

Tuesday, 13th: Went up the line to Bradford & Scanlons bridge. Returned per afternoon train. Ordered trousers & vest. Called on J. MacNabb. Wrote to Mr Stevenson & to Dawson of Quebec.

Wednesday, 14th: Went up the line this morning with Brunel. Engine & baggage car to within ¼ mile of Barrie. Walked over the Grassie Point branch. Heavy rain. After leaving engine walked on to Barrie. Put up at Mr Bysgels 3/9. Met Mr Dennis & brother at works. Slept on board steamer. Dr Burns on board.

Thursday, 15th: Down to Toronto this morning. Saw Cumberland. No word from Capt Whetheral. Letter from Bessie. Letter from Prentice,

Hen & Chickens. Pd Miller for sextant £5, watch glass £5/1. Balfour for trousers & vest 15/. Ps Mr Carruthers board at Port Hope £1. In pocket 10th £60/5/6. In pocket today £53/5/6.

Friday, 16th: Started for Barrie. Staked out siding for McConkey at Bradford. Took engine "Josephine" went up line to end of track 4 miles from Barrie. McGaffy having telegraphed for buggy went on with him. Dined at McGaffys. Saw Reid. Tea at McGaffys. Rain. Went down to steamboat. Saw Bessie. Sat on dock pretty late. Slept on sofa. Rain very heavy.

Saturday, 17th: Steamer left as usual at 3 A.M. Got up about six. Morning train to Toronto arrived at ½ past nine. Paid Petrie washing blankets &c. Reducing soundings and inking Saugeen chart. At Canadian Institute evening.

Sunday, 18th: Up at 10 oclock. Not at church forenoon. Reading *Bacons Advancement of Learning. Novum unganum.* At church evening. Long walk.

The Josephine *was one of the first passenger cars on the Ontario, Simcoe and Lake Huron (later the Northern) Railway. From* Sandford Fleming: Empire Builder *by L.J. Burpee.*

Monday, 19th: Started in handcar to examine line. Estimate ballasting fencing &c. Got up to King St. Returned by train — exps 2/6. Recd from Moberly lent to him formerly £10.

Tuesday, 20th: Morning train to King St. Handcar to Barrie. Dinners (two men) at Bradford 3/9. Arrived at Barrie. Exps 2/6. Slept on board steamer.

Wednesday, 21st: Very little sleep ½ sofa. Arrive Toronto ½ past nine. Cleaning & oiling transit to send up to Barrie. Pd accts Riddell & McLean £7/13/9, Scott & Laidlaw £2/10/9½, Armour £4/12/5, J & W MacDonald £6/15/2. Total £21/12/1½. In pocket today £40/15. Reporting on line. At chart Fishing Islands. Recd letter from MacNabb, Saugeen.

Friday, 23rd: Left this morning by train for the north. Steamer to Orillia, drinks &c 2/6. Tea at Mr Patersons. Stage over portage & tea at Mrs Burns 6/3. Waited there until moonrise and started off over rough roads on stage. Sheriff Smith, Mr & Mrs Kingston, English travellers. Arrived at *Kalloola* 12 P.M. — 2/3.

Saturday, 24th: Woke up at Penetanguishene. Went on shore. Saw no Moreau, left. Wind from Northwest, heavy sea between Giants Tomb and Christian Island. Too rough to go out on Georgian Bay. Cast anchor at Christian Island. Went ashore to small Indian village. Got canoes, went to old Jesuit fort. Indians in costume danced on board evening. I joined dressed in wolf skin.

[Tiny illegible accounts list here]

Sunday, 25th: Steamer lay all night, calmed down towards morning. Exps for dinner Indians. Went into bay Hen & Chickens [Collingwood], 2nd time for steamer only. Found considerable change, evidence of improvement although quiet Sunday morning. Found Moreau here & little brother — went up [to] Hurontario with Melville and he came across my Lot. Slept at Macdonalds.

Monday, 26th: Started this morning with Moreau. Picked out North East boundary of lot, it comes out about 1609 on Railway. Agreed with Moreau to chop & clear, exclusive of fencing 6 dollars per acre and 2/6 per cord wood, he to leave 14 ft cedar pickets for fence. Started about 12 oclock for Barrie with Sheriff Smith & Miss Cathy. Arrived at Creemore Mills after dark. Exps 5/.

Tuesday, 27th: Exps at Creemore Mills 7/6. Started about 5 for Barrie. Fed horses at Shantz Creek, horses tired out. Left waggon at Nottawasaga river, walked to Roots tavern. Rain, wet through. Ox team to Barrie. Pitch dark, rain heavy, arrive about 9. Changed clothes at Marks 3/9. Saw Reid. Went down to steamboat. Slept on sofa.

Wednesday, 28th: Steamer as usual left at 3 this morning. Breakfast on board. Train Bradford to Toronto. Making design & estimate for Harbour Hen & Chickens. To commence approximate estimate of Buildings. Putting up by Netting. Sent fish to some of Directors (from H & C). At L[eas]ks evening. Cost (fish box) ½.

Thursday, 29th: At office as yesterday. Cumberland confined to home. Presented plan of Harbour. He promises to go up line tomorrow.

Friday, 30th: Left this morning on train. Mrs MacNabb on way to Saugeen. Mr McLean accompanied me in handcar to near Barrie — bread & pork 1/3 — men 1/3, Total 2/6. Bridge at Thompsons Creek to be ready for train on Monday, track may be laid to Barrie Monday week. Played cards first time for money tonight at Caseys with McLean & others, gained upwards of $7. Left all on table or in house on steamboat — right! To bed about 1 oclock.

October 1853

Saturday, 1st: Slept on steamboat. Up about 6 to breakfast. Left by train. Stopped at King exps pipes & reservoir at King 7½. Came down by freight train. Got spark in eye. At office. Legs bad, went to bed at 7 oclock. Exps 23rd 10/, 24th 10/, 26th 5/, 27th 11/3, 28th 1/3, 30th 4/12, [total] 2/8/9. In pocket today £38/10.

Sunday, 2nd: Up about ½ past 9. Eye & cold good deal better. At home all day. Passmore called afternoon. At home evening. Made up mind about sunset on 2nd Nov.

Monday, 3rd: Up as far as Bradford about pipes, stations &c. Wrote B. To meet on Wednesday evening.

Wednesday, 5th: Returned by afternoon train Met B. Walked up to Yorkville. Mentioned decision come to about sunset this night four weeks. Appeared astonished mingled with disappointment somewhat, but after explanations quite reconciled. Thus left to fate or to the decision controlled by no human power so far as the event is concerned. I mean the sun. Train to Bradford. Walked [part way]. Handcar to end of track.

Friday, 7th: Came from Barrie this morning. Boat & train. Seeing about supplies. Pd for cigars, tobacco &c at Browns 10/. Pd Mrs Buchan up to 15th £6. Gave Mother £2/10 and for James £1/5.

Saturday, 8th: Up as far as Bradford. Returned afternoon train.

Sunday, 9th: At home forenoon. Mrs Hutchisons afternoon. James tea with me. Went down to Mrs Hollands evening. Wrote to Cumberland.

Monday, 10th: Up at 4 this morning. Off to Queen's Wharf. Lead pipe too small, did not go with iron train. Back to breakfast. Plumber got larger pipe. Off with 8 oclock train. Cumberland & Brunel along. Through to Barrie over Thompsons Bridge (2nd time of engine). Instructed to finish Barrie Station, spare no expense, get it done. "Carte blanche."

Tuesday, 11th: Commenced laying pipes. Plumber fixing syphon air vessel. Passenger train first arrival today. Tried to get horse & cart & then got promises for tomorrow. Very difficult to get. Savigny & Reed laying out ground. Wrote to Melville to employ Allan Cook 18 dollars per acre.

Wednesday, 12th: As yesterday. Living at Marks. Engaged "Jonas" to "boss" men & go down King & city for grubbing tools. Iron truck wheel went over left foot, very painful. No bones broken.

Thursday, 13th: Over on horseback, foot in poultice. "Lee" commenced clearing today. At agricultural dinner evening ...

Friday, 14th: Foot a great deal better. Got on but left letter with young Reid to get hand bills printed. Syphon likely to be a failure. To town afternoon train. Report had it "my leg was smashed." Mr Hall & daughter in town ar Mrs Hutchisons. After at Mrs. L.

Saturday, 15th: At office. Owen Sound plans & mill stones. Saw Hind afternoon. Moberly at tea. Mrs Hutchisons evening. Miss Hall. In Pocket £26/10.

Sunday, 16th: Home afternoon. Mr Hollands evening.

Monday, 17th: Up line to Bradford & Barrie. Freights engine went off track today near gravel pit at King. Negligence of switchman leaving switch open. Upset down embankment. No one killed, 3 jumped, 2 safe under tender. Damage say £500. Spark in eyes.

Tuesday, 18th: At Barrie. Down to town afternoon. Cumberland proposes going on Friday. To finish Owen Sound plans. Eyes getting better.

Wednesday, 19th: In town today. Paid Fowle for scales & iron [indecipherable] from London, steel straight edge say 25/. Saw old smith. Got some instruments from Miller watchmaker.

Thursday, 20th: Up to Barrie. Looking after things. No water in tank yet.

Friday, 21st: As yesterday. Brunel up. Got License of Occupation of Lot 41 in 8th Con from land agent today.

Saturday, 22nd: Paid Marks to this date £2/0/6. Sundries to be charged to company as per note book 8/9. Return to town. Saw Brunel

& Cumberland. At meeting Canadian Institute Council. John Shaw from Woodstock.

Sunday, 23rd: Cash in pocket £21/15. At St Andrews Church evening. At Mrs Hutchisons after.

Monday, 24th: Up as far as Innisfil Station. Went over branch to Cedar Point. Dinner at contractors shanty. At Mrs Hollands to Mrs Hutchisons, acted rather silly. Called at Hollands store. Bought $54 of bronze figures, paid $30.

Tuesday, 25th: Up line to Barrie examining works. To return and go over line tomorrow with Cumberland. At Mrs Leasks. BM alone.

Wednesday, 26th: Up line with Cumberland, A. Morrison & Mitchell, directors. Over Cedar Point branch. Lunch at shanty. Up to Barrie by freight train. Marks on ground where carriages went over works. Dinner at Marks, 4 bottles champagne (McGaffeys), cigars, cards. To bed ½ past 1.

Thursday, 27th: Up at six to breakfast over at Station. Cumberland & Morrison off by 7 oclock train. Up to see stones at Lallys wharf with Reid. Paid Marks for Cumberland present & former bill £3/14/6. Returned to town with estimates for fencing &c. Borrowed from Dawson £2/10. At Mrs Hutchisons.

Friday, 28th: In town today attending to stores for tankhouses &c, millstones, turntable &c &c. Cumberland in office. Walk with B. College Avenue.

Saturday, 29th: Up to Barrie. Examining works. Returned to town. Long letter from the Chief with instructions addressed to me as Resident Engineer. Brunel resigned as Chief assistant. At Canadian Institute meeting.

Sunday, 30th: At Knox [church] forenoon. Saw John Ferguson brother first time, arrived last night.

Monday, 31st: In town attending to various matters connected with the office. Made contract with James Currie for boiler, stoves. Telegraphed young Reid about mens time. He came down. Sent back list for correction. At Mrs Williamsons after nine to spend evening.

November 1853

Tuesday, 1st: In town as yesterday getting drawing of stones ready. Walked up to Queen's Wharf with Stewart. Short walk with B[essie] evening, probably the last one. Cloudy & gloomy. At office a short time afterwards, then at Mrs Hutchisons.

Wednesday, 2nd: Very dull cloudy morning. Went up to Barrie. Orders concerning turntable &c. Rain. Returned to town, examining progress of Station Buildings. Cloudy all day, drizzly rain, sun never appeared. Poor Bessie!!! Decided — keeping in a disagreeable state of suspension terminated. I had fully made up my mind for either way. Hope she has. Indeed it may all be for the best for both parties — we must hope so! We cannot peep a single hour into the future — cannot recall what is past.

Thursday, 3rd: At office as usual. Pushing Currie about stoves. Making up monthly estimates with Board for the first time. Some little difficulty at first, soon get into it. Paid Dawson borrowed on 26th Oct £2/10. At office with estimates &c.

Friday, 4th: Up line today. Poor B going to Miss O. Talked to her, appeared very dull, as if she lost sleep. Felt very very sorry for her poor girl, an orphan. Will always breath feelings of kind remembrance of her — natural, dull, not lively. Saw her on board the steamer. Staked out tanker at Bradford. Walked with A to Holland Landing. Staked out fencing of Stn grounds. Walked to Newmarket. Train to Toronto. Peter Cameron up in the evening.

Saturday, 5th: At office seeing about furnace &c. Making out with Brunel estimates for the month. Evening down to office. Secretary received a letter to Directors from Saugeen ... receipt of £25 from them on account of settlers sending schooner for our relief last summer. Saugeen people decided to found a library with it, to be called "the Fleming Library" — a great mark of respect to me surely! A great honour — can it be true?

Sunday, 6th: A poor boy aged 18 came to this country 8½ years ago with his brother — his only friend on the continent excepting Dr Hutchison, now dead poor man. After several years of doubt & discouragement now to get on so well. It seems that fortune now smiles on him — honours are poured on his hearth! Has many friends and (I hope) no enemies. Must not be too vain! Too sanguine! An evil day may come. Act honorably — push — persevere — do not relax — carry a thing through. An important week to others. How will it end?

Monday, 7th: Up to Barrie attending to various matters. Made 1st weekly progress report. Messrs Leask & Michi on train. Informed Mr L of discontinuance of intimacy with Miss M. To make necessary explanations on his return. At Mr Hollands evening. At shop. Bought another bronze figure, paid £6/5.

Tuesday, 8th: Up to Barrie, as yesterday. Return to Bradford. Mr L, Michi, Mr & Mrs Grey on the train, gone on their marriage trip. Alexr Murray, assistant geologist, returned from six months exploration. Immense beard. Crowd over & back from Lake Huron to Ottawa. Smoking.

Wednesday, 9th: To town. Cumberland gone to Quebec. Called at Mr Leasks. Explained all. Mrs apparently satisfied, he not quite.

Thursday, 10th: Up morning train to Newmarket. Staked out fence. Returned by freight train. At Hollands evening. At election of officers St Andrews Society. Returned to Hollands. Walk Miss H[all]. Paid subscription St.A. 10/. Lent James Hutchison £1/5.

Friday, 11th: In town. Copy of letter relative to "Fleming Library" at Saugeen handed to me by Mr Sladden (advised by Cameron & Passmore) requesting him to thank them cordially and respectfully declining the honour. Donation of the Directors & the gratitude of the parties should be manifested to them, not to me.

Saturday, 12th: Up to Barrie. General examination for weekly progress report. Miss M from Bradford to Toronto. Mr Leask at terminus on arrival.

Sunday, 13th: Not at church. At Farm, tea at Fathers. Annie returned from Dundas yesterday. At home evening.

Monday, 14th: At office seeing about various affairs. Brunel paid Stephenson entertainment, share of for me £10. Seeing about station deeds &c. Gave Dr Beatty estimates for Austin £2. To pay him only at present £100. Weekly progress report.

Tuesday, 15th: At office as yesterday. Preparing contract for fencing. Met Mr McLean. Miss M wants to see me. Apparently much disappointed and mortified. Returned book & letters. Could scarcely get away. Last time to meet. Informed me that we would have to be perfect strangers. (Prayed for her.)

Wednesday, 16th: Up line to Barrie. Turntable getting on. Instructed young Reid to let construction of road. Mr Bay getting on with measurement of line. Log pipes not deep enough. After returning wrote to Austin. Also wrote Harper regarding defective timber for roof. Evening at home.

Thursday, 17th: Seeing about stoves &c for Tank houses. Sladden asked me to withdraw letter related to Saugeen affair, did not do it. Saw Angus Morrison about it. At Professor [Henry] Crofts home evening. Professors of the universities & Canadian Institute, me — quite a grand affair. Felt a little out of water. Reunion. Supper after great men left. Pipes & drink! Mr Holland returned from Buffalo.

Friday, 18th: At office. Getting copies of description at Scobies for Station plans. Getting cases of car springs passed through Customs house & transferred to McLean & Wright. Commenced Buckridge to go over calculations of quantities Queen's Wharf. At Queen's Wharf getting lamp fired & to Garrison — plank walk &c.&c.

Saturday, 19th: Cash in pocket £1/5. Letter from Secretary Reilly. Directors approve of the decision of Saugeen people. At Barrie. At Canadian Institute C[council] M[eeting]. Saw Mr Hall. At Mr Hollands afterwards.

Sunday, 20th: At church forenoon. Raining. At Fathers afternoon. At home evening.

Monday, 21st: At office. Writing progress report for Cumberland & Brunel. Evening at office with Cumberland. Late, writing letters etc. Left part of Toronto Harbour paper at Scobies for Hind [editor of the *Journal*].

Tuesday, 22nd: At Barrie. Turntable finished. At office Cumberland short time. At Mr H. Hollands after nine.

Wednesday, 23rd: At office Queen's Wharf &c. Mr Hollands to tea. Spent evening Miss H[all]. Mrs Holland toothache.

Thursday, 24th: Received from Dr Beatty quarter salary — £87/10. Gave John MacNabb on acct land at Owen Sound £50. At office with Cumberland. Wrote letter to Saugeen people (date yesterday). Late at office. Board long meeting.

Friday, 25th: Up line to King. Man putting up stove. Returned to town. Greatcoat, Walker & Hutchison £2/15. Up to King afternoon & returned. At Mr Hollands. Miss H[all] at Tullys.

Saturday, 26th: Up to Barrie & returned to town. Canadian Institute council mtg evening. Cash in pocket £1/5. Salary £87/10. Total £88/15/. Pd MacNabb £50, coat £2/15. cigars &c 5/. In Pocket £35/10.

Sunday, 27th: Not out. Wrote to Saugeen.

Monday, 28th: At office. At Cumberlands. Preparing data for estimates. Met Miss H, walked to Tullys. Apology about Wednesday night last. Cameron evening.

Tuesday, 29th: At office as yesterday. Tea at Mr Hollands. Paid subscription to Mechanics Institute £5.

Wednesday, 30th: At office. Mr Buckridge left for Hamilton, paid him on acct of payroll for November £17/10. Ticket for St Andrews Ball, gloves &c £1/5. At St Andrews Ball. Took little Ralph Holland in costume. Home about 5 morning — 4 or 500 there.

December 1853

Thursday, 1st: Up at ½ past nine — a little seedy. Busy at office morning. At McLean & Wright about cars ready for delivery. Preparing monthly estimates &c for Board meeting. Pd Mr Bay on acct of Pay roll £2/0. Lend 1/3. Mr Hollands to tea. Estimates evening.

Friday, 2nd: Up line to Barrie & returned. Not very well. Boiler stoves erected in some tank houses. Saw King about Chopping from Collingwood. Cameron evening. In pocket tonight £8/10.

Saturday, 3rd: At office & attending to various matters. At Canadian Institute evening. Cameron & Passmore smoke afterwards. Wine &c 5/.

Sunday, 4th: Took medicine. At home. Scobie died this morning. King from Collingwood called about bedtime & borrowed £2.

Monday, 5th: Recd from Dr Beatty on acct of Pay roll £68/10. Paid John £6/10, pd Holmes £6/10, pd [indecipherable] £2/5, pd [indecipherable] £2/10. Total £34/5. Making out estimates &c.

Tuesday, 6th: Making out estimates.

Wednesday, 7th: Left on table for Mrs Buchan being for Board up to 15 Dec £6. Poor Scobie buried today. McConkeys 5/.

Thursday, 8th: Making out estimates.

Friday, 9th: At Barrie with Mr Cumberland. At Mrs Hutchisons with M.M. Passmore & Cameron. Moonlight walk. Passmore & Cameron.

Saturday, 10th: Pd Mr Bay on acct Pay roll £13/10. *Old Countryman* newspaper 15/. Brandy, wine &c 10/. Canadian Institute nomination of officers. Paper by Prendergast on preparation of food.

Sunday, 11th: Medicine. At home. Proof of Toronto Harbour. Passmore called. Lent him £12/10. He gave note for £20.

Monday, 12th: At office morning. Making soundings at Queen's Wharf shoal afternoon. OBrien, Stewart & Walker.

Tuesday, 13th: At office arranging papers &c [accounts details — paid out £77]. In pocket £7/5.

Wednesday 14th: Preparing statements for Cumberland. Report on expenditure of Company.

Thursday, 15th: As yesterday. Board meeting. Mrs Hollands afterwards.

Friday, 16th: At Barrie. Paid Marks. Cameron Logic. Lent Downie say 1/.

Saturday, 17th: At office, also Queen's Wharf works. Canadian Institute general meeting evening. Election of officers. Self Librarian.

Sunday, 18th: At home reading Paley's *Moral Philosophy.* At Mrs Hutchisons after nine.

Monday, 19th: At Queen's Wharf with Stewart staking out track &c. To Machine Shop. Up to Barrie afternoon with Grant surveyor. At Mr Watts evening & at Caisses afterward drinking. To bed about 3 A.M.

Tuesday, 20th: Up at 6 A.M. Cold. Down with morning train. At office &c Cottons estimates. Mrs Hutchisons after 8 oclock — Annie & David.

Wednesday, 21st: Preparing Cottons estimates & estimate for [indecipherable] Austin water logs. Cameron called. Went to office evening.

Thursday, 22nd: At Cumberlands office nearly all day to meet Cotton about estimate. Paid James Hall train pass to Cobourg & telegraph 16/3. Board meeting evening. Paid David for transfer of Lots at Saugeen, Pollock to him & Alexr £1. Mr Hollands after Board meeting & to Mrs Hutchisons. Hat.

Friday, 23rd: Walked down with tail stuck in hat to office unknown to me. At office certifying accts &c. Afternoon do usual work. At Queen's Wharf. In pocket £6/6. In pocket 13th £7.5. Pd 22nd £1/16/3. Marks 16th say 7/6, Downie 10/. In pocket tonight £4. Cameron evening Logic & sent acct Peterboro survey to Mr Conger.

Saturday, 24th: Up to Barrie. Pd Marks /5. Got venison from Johnston at Innisfil. Returned to Toronto. Philippines &c Christmas. Gifts at Scobies. Venison to Mother. Mrs Holland & Mrs Hutchisons — Santa Claus. Mrs Hollands children 12/6. Cab &c 3/9. At Mrs Hutchisons, Hollands & Passmore.

Sunday, 25th: At Cathedral with Miss Hall. Mrs Hollands Christmas dinner. Mr Holland at Kingston. Spent day at Mrs Hollands. Evening Mrs Hutchisons. Church 1/3. Cigars 1/3.

Monday, 26th: In town Holiday. Saw Mr & Mrs Leather. At office, not much doing. At MacNabbs & Mr H. Hollands party evening.

Tuesday, 27th: At office as usual. Mrs Hutchison & family & Miss H at our house evening dining.

Wednesday, 28th: At office. Borrowed from Father £10. Gave David (on acct Saugeen) £10. At Mrs Hutchisons venison supper evening.

Thursday, 29th: Up to Barrie. David & Alex along. Saw them started for Saugeen. Gave David my plaid & carpet box. Dinner at Reids, exp. 1/6. At Mrs Holland evening.

Friday 30th: At office in deep snow. In pocket 25th £6/6. In pocket £3/2/6. Cameron Logic.

Saturday, 31st: Snow deep & stormy. At office as usual. Commenced making out estimates for the month. Reid to tea with me. At Mrs Hollands to supper. Ned Hawk & Mrs Hutchisons boy, Stewart there. Left about 1. Called at MacDonald on the way home. Similar reflections to those which presented themselves on the 1st of this year may now be repeated. I have been honorably & profitably engaged throughout the year, probably now a much or slightly better man. On the 15th Nov for the first time for many years bowed down my head before the Almighty before retiring to rest & repeated the same every evening since. Sometimes in a proper frame of mind and sometimes not. Felt much the better for it.

An intimacy growing up with Miss Hall of Peterboro. How it may terminate I don't know. An amiable well bred woman with her own peculiarities. Poor Miss Mitchell but it cannot be helped — have done everything for the best. Much dispirited from my early expectations for my own part.

Now promoted in R.R. Company service owing to differences between Brunel & Cumberland. I now act as Chief Assistant Engineer —"Fleming Library at Saugeen" — Librarian Canadian Institute. [Brothers] David & Alexr gone to Saugeen to farm with the hopes of a fine speculation of a R.R. terminus there, 400 acres at the edge of the probable harbour.

AFTERWORD

The holiday celebrations over, Sandford Fleming escorted Jeanie Hall back to Peterborough, setting off on January 6, 1854, travelling by train from Toronto to Newmarket, where they engaged a horse and cutter to proceed overland to Lindsay. Along the way a fortuitous accident interrupted their journey. The sleigh hit a bump and overturned, throwing the driver out against a stump, knocking him unconscious. When he came to, an anxious Jeanie was hovering over him. The two managed to make their way to the nearest farmhouse for help. A doctor was called who took them to his home, where they remained for several days while Sandford regained his strength.

On January 9 they were driven over to Lindsay to board the regular stagecoach to Jeanie's home in Peterborough. The adventure further strengthened their friendship and a week of recuperation with the Hall family brought them still closer together. The young man returned to Toronto knowing that this was a relationship that

Courtesy Queen's University Archives.

Sandford Fleming drew this sketch of Ann Jean Hall about the time of their marriage, January 3, 1855.

was meant to last. Within weeks they were engaged to be married and planning their wedding to take place on January 3 of the following year.

Fleming maintained his office in Toronto and he and Jeanie spent their early married years in the city, while much of his time was spent in the north, continuing the survey of the O.S. & H. Railway. He had become particularly attracted to the Collingwood area, where he had invested in some pieces of land, and encouraged his father to do the same. In 1854, Andrew Greig Fleming decided to sell the farm in Etobicoke and move to Craigleith, where he remained until his death thirty years later. His youngest son, John Arnot, then nineteen, accompanied the family and helped his father in their early years there, but in 1857 he became Henry Youle Hind's assistant on his exploration of the Red River area and the following year accompanied Hind to the Assiniboine and the Saskatchewan Rivers, no doubt introduced by his brother Sandford, who knew Hind through their connections with the Canadian Institute. John qualified as a provincial land surveyor in 1861 and he worked for his brother on all three of his major railway projects, the Northern, the Intercolonial, and the Canadian Pacific. It was on his Red River explorations with Hind that he produced a collection of fifty-four remarkable sketches, 25 in watercolour, (now in Special Collections at the Toronto Reference Library) which demonstrate the talent he shared with his brother.

Sandford Fleming's later career is well documented. In July 1855 he succeeded Cumberland as chief engineer of the O.S. & H., at the same time keeping his office in Toronto in partnership with Thomas Ridout Jr. and Collingwood Schreiber (from 1858). The partnership continued until 1863 when Fleming became chief engineer of the Intercolonial Railway designing the route from Quebec to the Maritimes. He moved to Halifax the following year with Jeanie and their growing family.

Fleming had long advocated a coast to coast Canadian rail route and when he was appointed chief engineer of the Canadian Pacific Railway in 1871 he was in a position to see his hopes materialize. The following year he set off with a small party, including his friend George Munro Grant and his eldest son Frank, on his first westward exploration trip, a journey chronicled by Grant in his bestselling book *Ocean to Ocean*. Jeanie and the children had moved to Ottawa, but they purchased a summer home in Halifax which was to become a favourite family haven for years to come. The Dingle Park, a popular Halifax gathering place, was Fleming's gift to the city. He died in Halifax July 22, 1915, at age eighty-eight.

Sandford Fleming was often a controversial figure and his firm views did not always find agreement among the politicians and others in power. He won his battle over iron bridges rather than wooden on the Intercolonial route, which proved to be a wise decision. He was less successful in his disagreements with Charles Brydges over the Canadian Pacific and in 1880 he was removed from the job, to be replaced by his former partner Collingwood Schreiber. This did not diminish his influence. An investor in the Hudson's Bay Company, he was, in 1881, appointed its first resident Canadian Director, and in 1884 he became a Director of the CPR. He had many other interests, among them his continuing campaign for a Pacific Cable.

In 1879 Fleming made his first speech to the Canadian Institute proposing a system of Standard Time dividing the twenty-four-hour day into time zones. Relieved of his CPR duties he travelled the world giving speeches on the subject. In 1882 he was at an International Conference in Rome chaired by the Czar of Russia, when Canada and the United States both decided to adopt a Standard Time. Two years later he spoke at the International Prime Meridian Conference held in Washington that resulted in establishing the Greenwich Observatory in London, England, as the meridian the world over.

Courtesy Hutchison House Museum.

Fleming's long connection with Queen's University, Kingston, and its principal

Sandford Fleming was Chancellor of Queen's University for thirty-five years, from 1880 until his death in Halifax in 1915.

George M. Grant, was another important preoccupation. He served as Chancellor of Queen's from 1880 until his death. Jeanie had died at only fifty-seven in 1888, and he had kept close touch with his children and grandchildren by planning holiday gatherings both in Ottawa and in Halifax in all the intervening years. On his 80th birthday in 1907 the family presented him with an illuminated scroll commemorating his many achievements, signed by all his descendants. He was survived by three sons and two daughters.

Many honours came his way. He was made a Companion of the Order of St. Michael and St. George in 1877 and knighted by Queen Victoria in 1897, her Diamond Jubilee year. The "Freedom of Kirkcaldy" was presented to him by his native town in 1882. Four universities conferred honorary degrees: St. Andrews University, Scotland (1884); Columbia University, New York (1887); University of Toronto (1907); and Queen's University, Kingston (1908). He was active in many national and international organizations, among them the Royal Society of Canada, of which he was a charter member. His was a rich and satisfying life. The thoughtfulness, imagination, energy, and enthusiasm so vividly demonstrated in the early days depicted in these diaries offer a clear forecast of the accomplishments of his later years.

Courtesy Hutchison House Museum.

Sir Sandford Fleming in 1903, age seventy-six.

APPENDIX
Who's Who in the Diaries

Albro, Samuel (1801–1851), Peterborough. Father-in-law of Sheriff James Hall, MPP. Father of Jane Albro Hall and grandfather of Jean Hall (Fleming).

Allan, William. Canada Company co-commissioner with Thomas Mercer Jones, who replaced John Galt *circa* 1829. Later supervised the Toronto headquarters while Jones ran the Goderich business. He retired from the Company in the 1840s, shortly after Frederick Widder arrived from England to take over the Toronto office.

Allanson, John (1813–1853). Wood engraver. Born in England, apprenticed with well-known Newcastle engraver Thomas Bewick and produced engravings for journals in London and Paris before immigrating to New York in the mid 1830s. About 1843 he returned to Europe and worked for a time for a prominent Leipzig publisher, before coming to Upper Canada in 1848. Allanson and Fleming had shared interests and were fellow members of the Mechanics' Institute and the Canadian Institute.

Balfour, John. Partner with Hugh Scobie in Scobie and Balfour Printing Company until the partnership dissolved in 1850.

Benson, Thomas (1804–1857), born in Ireland, immigrated to New York in 1816, and moved to Kingston, Upper Canada, in 1819. Benson moved to Peterborough in 1845, became mayor in 1850. In 1853 he moved to Port Hope where he became secretary-treasurer of the Peterborough-Port Hope Railway Company, later the Midland Railway. Benson was killed along with fifty-seven other passengers on March 12, 1857, when the railway bridge collapsed over the Desjardins Canal, near Hamilton, Canada West.

Berczy, Charles (1794–1858). Toronto postmaster. Son of the Montreal artist William von Moll Berczy, was born in Newark (Niagara) and served in the commissariat in the War of 1812. Charles Berczy was the founding president of the Ontario (Toronto), Simcoe, and Lake Huron Railway.

Birdsall, Richard (1799–1852). Born in Yorkshire, came to Canada in 1817, first to York (Toronto), then moved to the Newcastle District in 1820 where he did surveying work in the Cobourg area. In 1821 he married Elizabeth, daughter of Zacheus Burnham, of Cobourg, and purchased a tract of land on the north shore of Rice Lake where he built a substantial house in 1827 that is still home to his descendants. In 1825 Birdsall produced the first town plan of Peterborough, and later surveyed several of the townships in Peterborough County. In the 1830s he was a land agent for the Canada Company, and he was Captain of the Asphodel militia unit that was called out in the Rebellion of 1837. In the 1840s he supervised survey parties on the Kingston–Ottawa road. Fleming worked for him for a short time after his arrival in Canada in 1845.

Boulton, W.H. (1812–1874). MPP 1844–1853. Mayor of Toronto 1846–1849. Son of D'Arcy Boulton Jr. Involved with Toronto, Simcoe & Lake Huron Railway.

Brown Judge, Ogdensburg, New York., official of the St Lawrence & Lake Huron Railway committee.

Browne, J.O., F.S.A. Civil engineer and deputy provincial Surveyor. Hired Fleming to survey the Don–Danforth plank road and the Toronto-Kingston railroad route in 1851. Published his map of the Township of York in 1850. Was second vice-president of the first council of the Canadian Institute and active in the founding of the *Canadian Journal*.

Brunel, Alfred (1818–1887). Civil engineer, born in England. Involved in various public works projects in Canada from 1844. For a time during Fleming's tenure was also an assistant engineer with the Ontario Simcoe and Huron Railway (renamed the Northern Railway in 1858). After an active military career he became the inspector of customs, excise, and canals in 1863, and later headed the Department of Inland Revenue. Elected a member of Council of the Canadian Institute in 1851 and was a key figure in the creation of the *Canadian Journal*.

Buchan, John. One of Scobie and Balfour's engravers. Fleming boarded with Mr. and Mrs. Buchan before moving in with his family after they came to Toronto in 1847, and again after they moved to Etobicoke.

Burns, Dr. Robert. Came to Canada from Paisley, Scotland *circa* 1843. Noted preacher, minister of Knox Presbyterian Church.

Cameron, Peter. Toronto friend of Fleming and Passmore, met often in evenings to play "Logic."

Cayley, William (1807–1890). Born in Russia, educated at Oxford University, came to Canada in 1836, called to the Bar in 1838. MPP 1846–1851 and 1855–1861, member of the Executive Council. Married a daughter of D'Arcy Boulton Jr., sister of W.H. Boulton.

Conger, Wilson S. (1804–1865). Born in Canada, successful merchant in Cobourg until he was appointed the first Sheriff of the Colborne District in 1842 and moved to Peterborough. Fleming's first contact with the St. Lawrence and Lake Huron Railway. Member of Peterborough's first town council, elected mayor in 1856, warden of the county in 1859, MPP 1863–1865. Conger was an active promoter of the development of the Trent-Severn Waterway, and was mayor of Peterborough when the town provided funding to assist in building the Midland Railway branch line linking Port Hope and Lindsay to Peterborough. Conger was Fleming's first contact with the St. Lawrence & Huron Railway group.

Cowan, Alex. Father-in-law of George B. Holland, Martha Hutchison's brother.

Croft, Henry H. (1820–1883). Born London, England. Professor of chemistry and proctor, King's College, became vice-chancellor, University of Toronto. Member of the first Council of the Canadian Institute.

Crookshank, George. Dean of Arts, University of Toronto, supporter of Trinity College.

Cull, Edward L. Clerk with the Canada Company, member of the first Council of the Canadian Institute.

Cumberland, Frederic (1821–1881). Born London, England, architect. Married Wilmot Bramley, whose sister was the wife of Thomas Gibbs Ridout, of Toronto, and with their encouragement in 1847 came to Canada where the Cumberlands soon became established members of Toronto society. One of Cumberland's first major projects was the rebuilding of St. James Cathedral after the disastrous fire destroyed a stretch of King Street in April 1849. The Ridout's son, Thomas Jr., was in partnership with Cumberland 1850–1852. William G. Storm joined the firm in 1852 and it became Cumberland and Storm. Their business expanded in the ensuing years to include such projects as University College, the centre portion of Osgoode Hall, the Mechanics' Institute (now demolished) and the Magnetic Observatory on the university grounds (also now gone), a number of courthouses throughout the province, and many imposing homes for Toronto's elite. Both Cumberland and Storm, with Fleming, were founding members of the Canadian Institute.

Daly, Charles. The clerk of the Toronto City Council, resided on King Street West near the Garrison Common.

De Moleyers, Captain. Royal Engineers. Fleming's chief contact on his survey of the New Garrison and Military Reserve.

Dennis, J. Stoughton (1820–1885). Architect, commissioned in 1842 as surveyor of public lands. Employed Fleming in his Weston office in 1849 and started him on the large Map of Toronto project.

Duggan, George, MPP. George Jr. and John D. Father and sons were Toronto barristers.

Ellice, Edward. Balbirnie, Scotland. Influential member of the committee of the Hudson's Bay Company and deputy governor in London of the Canada Company land developers. Provided Sandford Fleming with a letter of reference to Canada Company officials in Toronto in 1845.

Fleming, John Arnot (1835–1876). Artist and surveyor. Youngest brother of Sandford Fleming.

Gibson, David (1804–1864). MLA, 1834–1835. Provincial land surveyor and prosperous farmer north of Toronto. Avid reformer and supporter of W.L. Mackenzie who worked in New York on the Lockport Canal for ten years after the 1837 rebellion. Returned to Canada to survey the Durham Road in 1848–1849. In 1853 he was appointed commissioner of Crown Lands Agencies and superintended the colonization roads for Canada West.

Gzowski, Casimir (1813–1898). Born in Russia. Came to Canada in 1841 after eight years in the United States. Civil engineer and railway builder. Board of Works superintendent of roads and waterways in Toronto in the late 1840s. In 1853 Gzowski and Company got the contract to build the Grand Trunk Railway from Toronto to Sarnia. Highly successful in later diversified business interests. K.C.M.G. 1890.

Hall, George Barker. Peterborough MPP, 1844. Judge of the Colborne District 1848–1850, Judge of Peterborough and Victoria Counties 1851–1858.

Hall, James (1806–1882). Peterborough MPP, 1847–1851; mayor of Peterborough, 1852 and 1856; reeve, 1857; sheriff, 1856–1872. The Hall family was neighbours of Dr. John Hutchison and his family. Their daughter Jean became Sandford Fleming's wife in January 1855. (James Hall's son James Albro Hall was sheriff of Peterborough, 1872–1923.)

Hind, Henry Youle (1823–1908). Geologist and explorer, born in England and immigrated to Canada in 1846. Taught chemistry and mathematics at the provincial normal school in Toronto 1848 to 1853, when he became professor of chemistry at Trinity College. Later, Hind conducted scientific expeditions in western Canada with John Arnot Fleming, Sandford's youngest brother, as his assistant. Active in the Canadian Institute and edited the *Canadian Journal* 1852 to 1855.

Holland, George B. Martha Hutchison's brother, born in Montreal 1816, educated in Peterborough, moved to Toronto in 1837. From 1841 he was with the Royal Mail Steamship Lines, secretary from 1843; later had successful mercantile career.

Howard, John G. (1803–1890). Architect and surveyor. Born near London, England, he came to Canada in 1832 and settled in York (Toronto). Appointed city surveyor in 1843. Encouraged Fleming in getting established in Toronto. In 1836, Howard purchased 165 acres on the east bank of the Humber River where he built his house, Colborne Lodge, the following year. Later in life he donated the house (now a museum) and lands to the city of Toronto to become High Park.

Hutchison, David. Toronto, brother of Dr. John Hutchison.

Hutchison, Dr. John (1797–1847), Peterborough. From Kirkcaldy, Scotland, came to Canada in 1818 after a year practicing medicine in New York. Hutchison, who was a cousin of Andrew Fleming, welcomed Sandford and his brother David to his home in Peterborough (Ontario) when they first arrived in Canada and assisted them in finding work in their chosen fields. The Hutchison House in Peterborough is now a living history museum which commemorates both the doctor and Sandford Fleming.

Hutchison, Martha (1806–1871). Wife of Dr. John Hutchison, she lived in Peterborough for several years after his death in 1847, then moved to Toronto in 1851 to be near relatives and friends there.

Jones, Thomas Mercer (1795–1868). Born in England, came to Canada in 1829, a protégé of Edward Ellice, deputy-governor in London of the land development Canada Company. Jones was made co-commissioner of the Canada Company with William Allan, replacing John Galt, and assumed direction of the one-million-acre Huron Tract bordering on Lake Huron. In 1832 Jones married Elizabeth Mary, daughter of Archdeacon John Strachan (later Bishop) and soon after moved to Goderich, where he built an imposing house and became involved in local affairs. When Frederick Widder was sent out from London in 1839 to replace the aging William Allan, Jones remained in charge at Goderich while Widder ran the Company's business from the head office in Toronto. On the death of his wife in 1857, Jones retired to Toronto where he remained until his death in 1868.

Keefer, Samuel (1811–1890). Brother of Thomas Keefer. Appointed deputy-commissioner Department of Public Works in 1853, after more then ten years as engineer on the Trent Severn Waterway. Later involved in planning the building of the new parliament buildings in Ottawa.

Keefer, Thomas (1821–1915). Hydraulic engineer, he and his brother Samuel were both prominent in the building of the Welland Canal.

Leask, James. General merchant, corner of Yonge and Queen streets, Toronto.

Leather, William Beaumont. Architect, in partnership with Fleming, with an office on Yonge Street in Toronto, for a year after his arrival from England in 1849.

Lefroy, Captain J.H. Director of the Royal Magnetic Observatory of Canada on the university grounds. In 1850 he was elected vice-president of the first board of the Canadian Institute. He returned to in England to live in 1853.

Liddell, James. Toronto merchant who provided supplies for Fleming's northern survey crews.

MacDonald, James. Toronto friend of Fleming whose family lived in Markham.

Macdonald, John. Sturgeon Bay, acquired land with Fleming in the Collingwood area. Sometime member of Fleming's survey crew.

MacFarlane, Walter. Toronto dry goods merchant, King Street East at corner of Market Square.

McGaffey. A.A. Contractor in the Collingwood area.

McGlashen, James. Friend of the Flemings from Kirkcaldy who provided introductions in Toronto.

MacNab, Sir Allan Napier (1798–1862). Hamilton. Born in Niagara, called to the Bar in 1826. Influential Tory. MLA for Wentworth, 1830; Speaker of the House, 1837–1840; United Canada MPP, 1841–1857; leader of the Tory opposition, 1841–1844 and 1848–1854; Speaker of the House of Assembly, 1844–1848; prime minister of the province, 1854–1856. Created a Baronet in 1838.

MacNabb, A. Keeper of a small hotel and tavern in Saugeen (Southampton) where Fleming and the survey crew often stopped when in the district.

MacNabb, John. Son of A. MacNabb, who purchased land in the Sydenham area with Fleming.

MacPhail, Alexander. Peterborough pharmacist, friend of Dr. John Hutchison.

Melville, Dr. Henry. Toronto, one of the founders of the Upper Canada School of Medicine, which in 1851 became the medical faculty of the University of Trinity College. Member of the first Council of the Canadian Institute and assisted in organizing the *Canadian Journal.*

Merrilees, James. Scottish friend of Andrew Fleming who introduced Sandford to potential employers in the Hamilton area. Merrilees visited Scotland in 1847, the year the Fleming parents came to Canada.

Moberly, Clarence. Worked with Fleming in 1853 as an assistant engineer on the Ontario, Simcoe & Huron Railway.

Moberly, George. Mayor of Collingwood and local merchant who provided supplies for survey crews. Enthusiastic promoter of the Northern Railway. Father of Clarence and Walter Moberly.

Moberly, Walter (1832–1915). Surveyor and engineer. Worked for a time for Frederic Cumberland but went west in 1859 and pursued a successful career in British Columbia.

Passmore, Frederick F. Prominent Toronto architect and land surveyor. Friend of Fleming and fellow founder of the Canadian Institute. Named its curator in 1850.

Paterson, P. and Son. Hardware merchants, King Street West, Toronto.

Primrose, Dr. Francis. Practised medicine on Richmond Street, near Church Street, Toronto.

Radenhurst, John. Deputy clerk, land office.

Riddell, William. Tailor with Riddell & McLean, merchant tailors, King Street West.

Ridout, Thomas Gibbs (1792–1861). Third son of surveyor-general Thomas Ridout. Influential Toronto businessman and Family Compact associate. Thomas G. Ridout was for many years clerk (manager) of the Bank of Upper Canada and was heavily involved with the building of the Grand Trunk Railway. By his first wife he was a brother-in-law of Robert Baldwin. His second wife, Matilda Ann Bramley, and Frederic Cumberland's wife, Wilmot Bramley, were sisters.

Ridout, Thomas Jr. Son of Thomas Gibbs Ridout; partner in Cumberland & Ridout, 1850–1852. In Fleming's Toronto office in partnership with Fleming and Collingwood Schreiber, 1858–1863.

Ross, John (1818–1871). Toronto lawyer; solicitor-general of Upper Canada, 1851–1853; attorney-general, 1853–1854; speaker of the Legislative Council, 1854–1856. Director of the Northern Railway, 1862–1869 and 1852–1857; director of the Grand Trunk Railway and later became president. Named a senator in 1867.

Rowsell, Henry and William. Booksellers and stationers, Rowsell & Thompson Printers, King Street East, Toronto.

Ruttan, Henry J. (1792–1871). Born Adolphustown, Upper Canada. After military service in the War of 1812 he went into business in Cobourg in 1815 where he was elected MLA for Northumberland from 1820 to1824. In 1827 he was appointed sheriff of the Newcastle District (from 1849 United Counties of Durham and Northumberland) and served for thirty years.

Ryerson, Egerton (1803–1882). Superintendent of Education, 1841–1876. Gave lectures at Mechanics' Institute and Canadian Institute.

Sang, John. Prominent surveyor in Fifeshire, Scotland. Fleming apprenticed with Sang in Kirkcaldy for four years before coming to Canada. They continued to correspond regularly.

Scadding, Reverend Henry (1813–1901). Rector of Trinity Church, Toronto, 1847–1875; Classics master, Upper Canada College; active in the Canadian Institute. Author of *Toronto of Old* (1873).

Schlatter, Charles L., Ogdensburg, New York. Chief engineer of the St. Lawrence and Huron Railway. Engaged Fleming to survey Gloucester Bay at Nottawasaga. Associate of Wilson S. Conger.

Schreiber, Collingwood (1831–1918). Shared Fleming's office in partnership with Thomas Ridout Jr. *circa* 1858–1863. Succeeded Fleming at CPR in 1880. Later became chief engineer of the Department of Railways and Canals. K.C.M.G in 1916.

Scobie, Hugh (1811–1853). Journalist, born in Scotland and studied law before coming to Canada in 1832; editor of the *British Colonist* from1838 until his death in 1853. In the late 1840s he employed Fleming at his printing and lithographing company, Scobie & Balfour, publishers of *The Canadian Almanac*.

Shanly, Walter. Surveyor who partnered with Casimir Gzowski in Grand Trunk Railway.

Sheridan, Walter. Peterborough County Clerk 1851–1866.

Stewart, Frances (1794–1872). Born in Ireland and came to Canada in 1822 with her husband Thomas A. Stewart and settled on a 1,200-acre tract of land a short distance north of Peterborough. Her letters home to Great Britain were edited by a daughter after her death and published in 1889 as *Our Forest Home*.

Stewart, George. Son of Frances and Thomas A. Stewart of Peterborough. Joined Fleming's survey crew and assisted Fleming and Leather in their office from 1849.

Storm, William G. (1826–1892). Architect, in partnership with Frederic Cumberland from 1852. Active in the Canadian Institute.

Thomas, William (1799–1860). Born in England, where he had a career in building and architecture before coming to Canada with his wife and eight children in 1842. He became a prominent Toronto architect, designer of numerous churches (including St. Michael's Cathedral), banks, and public buildings (St. Lawrence Hall). A member of the first Council of the Canadian Institute.

Timson, Thomas R. Mathematical instrument maker, Adelaide near Yonge Street, Toronto.

Tully, Kivas (1820–1905). Architect, born in Ireland, came to Toronto in 1844, where his brother John, also an architect, was in the office of John G. Howard. Tully set up on his own and in his first year was commissioned to design the Bank of Montreal and the Customs House at Front and Yonge streets. He designed numerous public buildings, including the new Trinity College on Queen Street in 1851, the County Court House in Welland, and Victoria College, Cobourg, as well as numerous churches in smaller communities in Upper Canada. He had a long association with provincial public works projects. One of the founding members of the Canadian Institute. Married Marie Elizabeth, daughter of Samuel Strickland of Lakefield, Ontario, brother of Catharine Parr Traill and Susanna Moodie.

Webster, C.H. Hamilton pharmacist. Introduced Fleming in Hamilton. Employed James and John Hutchison, sons of Dr. John Hutchison.

Widder, Frederick (1801–1865). Sent to Canada from London by the Canada Company in 1839, he soon replaced commissioner William Allan in the Toronto office, where he took over direction of the Company's affairs. Involvement in railway projects caused a rift between Widder and Thomas Mercer Jones, resulting in Jones's dismissal from the Company in 1852. Ill health brought on Widder's resignation in 1864 and both he and his wife died within months of setting off for retirement in England.

Workman, Dr. Joseph (1805–1894). Born in Ireland, came to Canada with his parents in 1829. Medical diploma from McGill University in 1835, to Toronto in 1947, on staff of Dr. John Rolph's School of Medicine. In 1854, appointed superintendent of the Toronto Lunatic Asylum.

*NOTE: The children of Andrew Greig and Elizabeth Arnot Fleming: David (1823–1887), Anne (1825–1905), **Sandford (1827–1905)**, Andrew (1830–1872), Henry (1831–1917), Alexander (1833–1926), John Arnot (1837–1876), Jane (1839–1931).

EDITOR'S NOTE AND ACKNOWLEDGEMENTS

These diaries have been transcribed faithfully with minimal changes for clarification, mostly in punctuation such as periods where Fleming frequently used dashes, especially at the end of a sentence or paragraph. In cases where it took several references to arrive at the correct spelling of a word or a name (e.g. J.O. Browne rather than Brown, to distinguish him from other Browns in the text) I have used Fleming's final version throughout. With words unfamiliar to him such as "mosquito," I have left his several interesting variations. A few indecipherable words, brief passages or lists of figures have been omitted. The diaries, now in the collection of the Library and Archives, Ottawa, are pocket-sized, with a week's entries spread over two small facing pages, the handwriting often condensed in an attempt to fit the space. To avoid numerous footnotes, I have provided brief biographies of many of the characters referred to (often just by surname) in the diaries, in the Appendix: Who's Who in the Diaries, while identifying them with their first names in square brackets in the text.

I am grateful for the assistance of the staff of the Library and Archives of Canada, Ottawa; the Archives of Ontario, Toronto; Toronto Public Library, Special Collections; Queen's University Archives, Kingston; the Peterborough Museum and Archives and the Trent Valley Archives, and especially to Bernadine Dodge and Jodi Aoki of Trent University Archives, Bata Library, Peterborough, and to Gale Fewings of Hutchison House Museum, who went far beyond the call of duty to help further this project.

I would also like to thank my fellow members of the Peterborough Historical Society Publications Committee for their support and advice throughout the development of this publication, particularly Michael Peterman, chairman, for his editorial skills; Elwood Jones for his technical assistance; and Dale Standen for formatting and processing the illustrations.

SUGGESTED READING

Blaise, Clark. *Time Lord: The Remarkable Canadian Who Missed His Train and Changed the World*. Toronto: Alfred A Knopf, 2000.

Burpee, Lawrence J. *Sandford Fleming: Empire Builder*. Milford, NY: Oxford University Press, 1915.

Cole, Jean Murray. *Sandford Fleming: No Better Inheritance*. Peterborough, ON: Peterborough Historical Society, 1990.

Grant, George M. *Ocean to Ocean: Sandford Fleming's Expedition Through Canada in 1872*. Toronto: James Campbell & Son, 1873; Cole's Reprint 1979.

Green, Lorne Edmond. *Sandford Fleming*. Don Mills, ON: Fitzhenry & Whiteside, 1980.

Simmins, Geoffrey. *Fred Cumberland: Building the Victorian Dream*. Toronto: University of Toronto Press, 1997.

INDEX

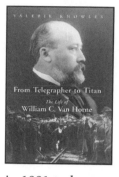